THE COMPLETE
BOOK OF
UNITED STATES
COIN
COLLECTING

THE COMPLETE
BOOK OF
UNITED STATES
COIN
COLLECTING

Norman M. Davis

REVISED EDITION

MACMILLAN PUBLISHING CO., INC.
NEW YORK

COLLIER MACMILLAN PUBLISHERS
LONDON

TO EVERYONE

WHO HAS LOOKED

AT A COIN AND FELT

A SENSE OF WONDER

Macmillan Publishing Co., Inc.
866 Third Avenue, New York, N.Y. 10022
Collier Macmillan Canada, Ltd.

Library of Congress Catalog Card Number: 70–117963
Revised Edition 1976
Printed in the United States of America

CONTENTS

PART THREE
Twenty Cents to Trade Dollars

PREFACE

A *complete* book of collecting, to be honest, is impossible. There's just too much information to get into one volume. But this book *is* as complete as it *should* be—basic information to get you started in almost any phase of coin collecting and supplementary information to help you keep going. There are no price or mintage lists because (1) I'm giving you the most important mintages and prices as guides, plus general ranges of cost where possible, (2) the price-mintage area already is well covered, and (3) I'm more interested in *collecting*.

This is a living hobby, and those who enjoy it most are people who are alive with enthusiasm. Enrico Caruso is a good example of a man who was extremely *alive*—and a numismatist.

This is for you, if you're

—*just starting*: you'll find a basic introduction to the hobby, and plenty of guides to more detailed information.

—*already collecting*: you'll gain added enjoyment as your numismatic horizons expand.

—*on the verge of specializing*: you'll be able to consider each denomination and type, and make your decision an informed one.

—*a veteran collector*: you'll be surprised by some items which appear for the first time in a general collecting book.

—*an investor with an eye to profit*: you'll be able to choose coins with profit potential by following Star-Line, the investment plan I've developed for my own use.

—*a noncollector who wants to get an idea of what coin collecting is all about*: you'll get it, with all the flavor of one of the world's top hobbies.

—just someone looking for a book to enjoy: you've found it.

Collectors have a patron saint in St. Eligius (b. 588 A.D.), an engraver who later was master of the Limoges Mint. My own preference is for the ancient Greek goddess Athena, whose connection with coinage is far stronger, longer lived, and more meaningful.

Since there's a point when you must stop researching and get a book down in type, I've had to omit some areas and miss some references. Specialists have covered most of these.

Much of the information here is based on my syndicated newspaper column, "The Coin Box." Most mintage figures are based on those in *A Guide Book of United States Coins;* my thanks to Richard S. Yeoman for his permission to quote from this and other Whitman references. Also thanks to editor Ed Rochette for permission to quote from ANA's *Selections from The Numismatist* books and the magazine itself. Also, thanks to Krause Publications, Inc., in whose *Coins Magazine* "Double Puzzle of the Double Eagle" and "Interview with Miss Liberty" appeared, for transferring copyright. Gratitude also goes to Dr. and Mrs. Vladimir Clain-Stefanelli, curator and assistant curator of the Numismatics Division of the Smithsonian Institution, who helped with facts and opinions and who let me photograph rare coins in the National Collection.

Who else helped? The Secret Service and Bureau of the Mint people who patiently answered my questions; editors of papers in which my column appears; collectors *and* noncollectors who read it; Kirk Polking, whose editorship of *Writer's Digest* has brought priceless practical aid and encouragement; Helen Bottel, who inspired me to start my coin column; and Helen A. Cummings, who when I was in high school taught me to type and to care about it.

I've been collecting coins since the 1940's. The sense of wonder has never left me. May it be yours, and never leave you, either.

Chevy Chase, Maryland
March 1975

Part One

This Fascinating Hobby

So You Want to Collect Coins

"This is a thrilling hobby, the finest and most wholesome."—
Mrs. Mary Brooks, Director of the Mint, quoted
in *COINage*

GETTING STARTED

For every person who enjoys coin collecting, probably a hundred
try it and quit. But even these "temporary collectors" *are* collectors.

What starts your interest? Maybe it's a coin you find (I once
found a cent embedded in a new highway's still-warm asphalt).
Maybe it's a bus token from a trip you took. You or a friend
might go abroad and bring back coins.

One test for "collector potential" is your reaction to a coin. If to
you it's just metal with designs and letters, money you can use to
buy something, you're not a collector. But

—if you see a coin as a symbol of great men's achievements, a
work of art and proof that man someday will reach the stars;

—if you find yourself asking how well the coin gets its message
across to those who see it;

—if you recognize that there *is* a message here, more than a
statement of commercial value, and find yourself determined to
know as much of this message as possible—

then the chances are that you're either collecting already or the
right kind of person to collect someday.

COME IN, THE COLLECTING'S FINE

What does it take to become a coin collector? The coins in your pocket. Period. You need no study course, expensive equipment, or license.

Some people start with a clear idea of what they want to collect, but most just start accumulating coins. Beginners without a clear plan should stick to coins available from circulation. You can try out "specializing" on a small scale by seeing how many different dates and mint marks you can find in one or more denominations.

What Presidents—or others—appear on U.S. coins, and why? Where do our coin mottoes and designs come from? Which metals has the U.S. used. What happens when coins are in short supply?

Many coins are increasing in value. If you collect sensibly, your coins will be worth more as years pass. Also—and no other hobby shares this advantage—your coins provide available cash in case of emergency.

You should invest in coin envelopes, which cost about 50¢ to 75¢ per hundred; these give relatively good protection to coins. Regular low-sulphur cardboard coin files hold about 700 to 900 coins (the ones advertised as holding 1,000 coins), and cost around $5 up.

Another item worth buying is a magnifying glass. This helps you inspect design details, and it's valuable to those interested in varieties and errors. A good one costs from about $4 to $8.

Every collector should be familiar with Richard S. Yeoman's annual, *A Guide Book of United States Coins*, called the "Red Book."

SHOULD YOU JOIN A COIN CLUB?

Have you considered joining a club? It's an excellent way to expand your numismatic horizons.

My local club has an excellent educational program during the first half of its meeting, then an intermission, then the club auction. There are door prizes, a "current materials" table where we can buy various items at low prices, and several exhibits by club members.

In addition to belonging to a neighborhood, city, county, state, or regional club, you might look into the American Numismatic Association. This 25,000-plus membership group is the largest "coin club" in the world. Its goals are to encourage and promote numismatics; spread information, especially to young people; aid good relations among other groups in the hobby; maintain a large numismatic library; and do whatever it can, as a national organization, to benefit those who follow the hobby. Membership is open to anyone aged eleven or more.

2

Basic Information and Tips You'll Want

A little history and some practical hints.

THIS IS HOW IT WAS—SOME BACKGROUND

Alexander Hamilton's January 28, 1791, "Report on the Coinage," states,

> The inequal values allowed in different parts of the Union to coins of the same intrinsic worth, the defective species of them . . . , and the dissimilarity in the several moneys on account, are inconveniences which, if not to be ascribed to the want of a national coinage, will at least be most effectually remedied by the establishment of one. . . .

Our coins would show the President's portrait if the Senate version of the Act of April 2, 1792, had become law. The House of Representatives voted against this because it would be too much like showing a king's portrait. In the end, the House convinced the Senate. Section 10 of the Act says,

> And be it further enacted, That upon the said coins respectively, there shall be the following devices and legends, namely: Upon one side of each of the said coins there shall be an impression emblematic of Liberty and the year of coinage; and upon the reverse of each of the gold and silver coins, there shall be the figure or representation of an eagle with this inscription: "United States of America," and upon the reverse of each of the copper coins there shall be an inscription which shall express the denomination of the piece. . . .

Later this was amended (Act of January 18, 1837) by adding that gold and silver coins should show the value on the reverse, "but on the reverse of the dime, half-dime, cent and half cent, the figure of the eagle shall be omitted."

The Coinage Act of 1965 supersedes the 1792 and 1837 laws. In addition to providing for clad coins, it says,

> Upon one side of all coins of the United States there shall be an impression emblematic of liberty, with an inscription of the word "Liberty," and upon the reverse side shall be the figure or representation of an eagle, with the inscriptions "United States of America" and "E Pluribus Unum" and a designation of the value of the coin; but on the dime, 5-, and 1-cent piece, the figure of the eagle shall be omitted. The motto "In God We Trust" shall be inscribed on all coins.

Because the U.S. was formed of former British colonies, English coins were familiar. Prices were quoted in shillings and pence for many years, a usage that declined slowly after 1800. For instance, New Jersey merchants Jas. and Jno. P. Jackson advertised in the July 8, 1829, *Paterson Intelligencer*, "400 sacks Liverpool Fine Salt, discharging from Schooner Hetty Jackson, for Sale at nineteen shillings per Sack."

Use of the comma to separate dollars and cents lasted well into the 1860's (for instance, an 1835 stagecoach fare of "$3,00").

At various times, coins were scarce. From 1810 to 1860, little gold circulated. From around 1862 to 1875, few silver *or* gold coins were available. But another coin shortage, a century later, had a greater impact.

In the 1960's, silver got too valuable for coinage use. The silver shortage paralleled the coin shortage. The result was today's clad cupronickel coinage. Wholesale melting of silver coins, by private interests and by the government, has taken place since the 1960's.

TAKE CARE OF YOUR COINS

To best safeguard your coins, keep them sealed in inert plastic in steel cabinets locked in bank vaults. But this is too expensive, impractical, and troublesome for most collectors. I cherish my coins—but I want to be close to them.

Clear plastic holders, one of the best ways to preserve coins, have three drawbacks: they seal the coins off from you, they take up lots of space, and they're expensive. There are slightly less protective, but far less expensive, ways to care for your coins.

Handle coins with clean, dry hands; always hold a coin by its edge. These practices protect the luster and reduce the amount of oil and perspiration transferred to the coin.

Coins in Very Fine or better condition should *not* be cleaned. I'm against cleaning or chemically treating any coin other than one made of zinc or another material doomed to crumble away unless given protective coating. If you're determined to clean coins, start with common ones from pocket change: this way, an error won't damage a valued coin. Talk to a dealer or experienced collector first—he'll probably be able to give you helpful advice and tips. Make a note of cleaning or processing on the coin's envelope, when treating coins from your collection.

ENVELOPES OF ALL KINDS

One of our goals is the protection of coins against sulphur, oxygen, and other damaging substances. The question is, what's the safest way?

Dr. and Mrs. V. Clain-Stefanelli, the Smithsonian Institution's

Numismatics Division curators, showed me their black cardboard trays mounted on cardboard bases. Mrs. C-Stefanelli said these work well, and Dr. C-Stefanelli added that they're "supposed to be sulphur-free." However, such trays would take more space (and, probably, money) than most of us have.

Vinyl envelopes? Some collectors praise them, others (including me) avoid them. Mrs. C-Stefanelli showed me greasy deposits she said formed within months on vinyl envelopes.

"Penny board" albums are strictly for circulated coins. Window albums are "the most popular type," a dealer told me. The best known are the "Whitman Bookshelf" and the Coin & Currency Institute's "Library of Coins." But coins in albums have their edges against cardboard.

Dr. C-Stefanelli joins others in urging that coin holders be made of inert material—something which won't form chemical compounds with the metal in coins.

In the May 1958 *Numismatist*, Dr. F. S. Epps listed ethyl cellulose, polystyrene, and polyethylene among safe, inert materials. Space-age technology has added Mylar, Lexam, and others. These should be safe as windows, linings of mounts, or coin envelopes.

Popular 2 × 2 paper coin envelopes draw surprising dealer comments. "Not for Uncirculated coins!" insists one. Kraft paper ones are "exceptionally high [in] sulphur," charges another. A third dealer cautions against putting top-condition coins in *any* paper container without special protection. But other dealers defend coin envelopes as relatively low in corrosive substances. Dr. and Mrs. C-Stefanelli say they often leave incoming coins in paper envelopes until coins are prepared for display.

What's the safest, simplest and lowest-priced system?

First, put your coin in an inert transparent envelope of some safe material.

Second, with this protection, put the coin into a regular paper coin envelope.

Now your coin has the best protection available at reasonable cost, you have access to it, you can see details without touching the coin's surface, and there's space to write identifying information.

A locked cabinet is enough protection for most collections, but the safest way is to rent a safety-deposit box and, for a few dollars a year, keep your most valuable and expensive coins in the bank's vault. If you store part of your collection, keep a list of the coins—note denominations, dates, mints, conditions, and values.

THIS IS "THE RED BOOK"

Each year brings a new edition of Richard S. Yeoman's *A Guide Book of United States Coins* (Western Publishing Co., Racine, Wis., $3). Like long-named dictionaries we call "the Webster's," this rarely gets its full title. Because of its red cover and because it is so universally highly regarded, collectors call it simply "the Red Book."

In each new edition Yeoman and his staff, aided by a nation-wide panel of experts, estimate average retail prices of coins in various conditions. Grading comments are based on Brown and Dunn (see Chapter 3). A measure of the book's stature is that many dealers and collectors quote prices and offers in terms of Red Book value.

There always are new items of information, additional facts inserted in the text, and more information in less space. No matter what you collect, you should own this standard reference.

YOU CAN HELP THE HOBBY

If you spot an error in a coin book, or have a coin the catalogs and references appear to have missed, let the publisher know. You'll help the hobby by reporting your find. But don't just say, "I've got a coin your book left out." Know which book is involved. Write to the author or editor, in care of the publisher. If the person you write to has a title, use it in the address.

Can you send a photograph? It may help immensely. The best way I've found to get good coin photos is to set the camera on a tripod, attach a closeup lens and point the lens straight down, using the smallest possible aperture (highest f-stop number). The coin should be on white paper or dark cloth, depending on where it shows up best. Strong light coming at a sharp angle often helps.

If you can't photograph your coin, the next best thing is a rubbing. Hold damp onionskin tissue paper over the coin and press down to mold the paper to the coin's features. Apply ink gently until the coin's design appears clearly. A good ink applicator is a cotton ball wrapped in silk. You can make rubbings in aluminum foil by pressing foil over the coin and going over the surface with a fingernail or pencil point. It takes only a little practice to make good rubbings. Make your first ones on common items from pocket change, for safety's sake.

If you can't furnish a rubbing, tell the author, editor, or publisher where the coin is (in your possession, in a museum, described in a certain book or article) and write as detailed a description as possible. Remember—*you* can see the coin but *he* can't.

Clubs 'n' Pubs

This is an arbitrary selection of the many clubs and coin publications collectors can enjoy. Addresses, dues, or other matters may change; publications may cease and new ones may enter the field. Use this list as a starting point.

Clubs

American Numismatic Association. $11 for first year, including admittance fee, $6/year afterward. Contact: Executive Director, ANA, P.O. Box 2366, Colorado Springs, Colorado 80901.

American Vecturist Association. Contact: Donald Mazeau, Secretary, AVA, P.O. Box 31, Clinton, Connecticut 06413.

Civil War Token Society. $5/year. Contact: Gail Levine, Secretary, CWTS, 6222 Little River Turnpike, Alexandria, Virginia 22312.

Token and Medal Society, Inc., 611 Oakwood Way, El Cajon, California 92021.

Publications

Coin World, P.O. Box 150, Sidney, Ohio 45365. Weekly; 35¢/copy, $6/year. Mostly news, shows, clubs, etc., with some features.

COINage, 16250 Ventura Boulevard, Encino, California 91316. Monthly; 75¢/copy, $8/year. General numismatic publication.

Coins Magazine, Krause Publications, Inc., Iola, Wisconsin 54945. Monthly; 75¢/copy, $6/year. General numismatic publication.

Error Trends Coin Magazine, P.O. Box 158, Oceanside, New York 11572. Arnold Margolis, publisher. Monthly; 50¢/copy, $5/year. Deals with errors, varieties, oddities of various kinds.

The Fare Box. Published monthly by American Vecturist Association.

Numismatic News Weekly, Krause Publications, Inc., Iola, Wisconsin 54945. Weekly; 35¢/copy, $6/year. Mostly news, shows, clubs, etc., with some features and columns.

The Numismatic Scrapbook Magazine, P.O. Box 150, Sidney, Ohio 45365. Monthly; 60¢/copy, $5/year. General numismatic publication with some tendency toward scholarly features.

The Numismatist. Monthly; $7.50/year to nonmembers. Published by ANA. General numismatic publication with much scholarly work, some more popular features.

3

Grade It Right

Why "Good" *isn't* and "Fine" *is*.

CONDITION CONTROVERSY

A good grading system is important because a coin's condition (grade) has a major effect on its price. But different systems use different language to describe conditions. Ask three collectors for their ideas of "slight wear on highest spots," "faint evidence of wear," and "less desirable than Uncirculated." You'll get nine definitions covering plenty of territory—yet these all are for "Extremely Fine."

Some years ago, I said in "The Coin Box" that we needed a standard set of descriptive phrases. There *is* such a standardized grading system. The key is the phrase:

"STRICT B & D GRADING"

How often have you seen that line in coin dealers' ads? It refers to Martin R. Brown and John W. Dunn's *A Guide to the Grading of United States Coins* (Western, $3).

Brown and Dunn uses sketches of each coin by Arthur Mueller, showing the various conditions. Each series of conditions begins with clear sketches of the coin and a brief description. Coins covered are regular issues only, half-cents through double-eagles, though the authors list incorrect starting dates for Flying Eagle cents, Liberty Seated dollars, and Coronet double-eagles. In higher grades, B & D use small circles, ellipses, and arrows to locate the key wear points. There also are written descriptions of the various grades. Many "Special Notations" add information on specific dates, how to avoid altered coins, and similar helpful facts.

B & D list six basic conditions: Good, Very Good, Fine, Very Fine, Extremely Fine, and About Uncirculated. For scarce and some early coins, they add Fair and About Good.

They also use a system of code letters and numbers to describe varying shades of difference within grades—for example, VG-A for a coin that's almost Fine, but not quite, Code 9 for a rim nick, and Roman numerals I to XII to represent the position of a specific feature as if the coin were a clock face. This can be complicated—but a collector who learns the system will find it a handy kind of shorthand.

The only serious defect is the "Not collectable" listing for certain low-conditions, and B & D have taken a step toward dropping this by grading Roosevelt dimes and Franklin half-dollars as low as Good. There are no price or mintage figures in B & D (for the same reasons I don't have them).

The intelligent, accurate, and easy-to-use B & D system helps collectors grade their coins and gain a knowledge of commonly used numismatic abbreviations.

NUMISMATIC SHORTHAND

Condition descriptions represent steps along the way between perfect, never-used coins, and barely identifiable, worn-out ones.

I think the most misunderstood numismatic term must be "Good." In everyday life, we're attracted to good things; we want good reputations; we hope to "live the good life." But capitalizing that first letter turns the meaning completely around! A Good coin is in one of the *lowest* conditions.

Here's a list of conditions and their abbreviations:

Condition	*Abbreviation*
Poor	None
Fair	Fr. (usually *with* period)
Good	G
Very Good	VG
Fine	F
Very Fine	VF
Extremely (or Extra) Fine	XF or EF (I prefer XF)
Uncirculated	Unc (sometimes U)
Proof	Prf (sometimes Pr)

A "subcondition" more and more popular recently is Brilliant (or Bright) Uncirculated. A BU coin is Unc with full mint luster and no flaws. Two other terms coming into wider use are "MS" (Mint State) and "Condition Census," meaning one of the six best-condition specimens known; both are from Dr. William H. Sheldon's book on large cents, *Penny Whimsy.*

What if a coin is between grades? The most common way to show this is the use of A (for "about" or "almost"), to indicate a coin that's just short of qualifying for a certain grade: a coin that's almost VF, but not quite, is AVF.

Another way is the use of both conditions, connected with a dash: a quarter that's better than VG, but not quite Fine, is VG–F.

Because conditions are words with different meanings to non-collectors, I feel strongly that they should be capitalized. A coin in "good condition" may mean, to a noncollector, one that's mint-new, without any wear. But a coin that's Good is badly worn. I wouldn't offer anything for a coin that's extremely fine, because I haven't the faintest idea of how worn it is—but a coin that's Extremely Fine is one I might want to buy.

See the difference?

Since Proofs usually aren't meant for circulation, those that were used as coins need special grading. The simplest way would be to say "circulated Proof" (we could abbreviate it cP) plus a regular grade based on the amount of wear. A Proof worn down to Very Fine would be graded "cP–VF."

4

But Where *Are* Those Coins?

Everyone has heard of someone else who found a rarity in his pocket. Want to join those who really *have* found such coins?

RARITIES IN CIRCULATION

Rare coins *are* circulating, and you can find them in your change if your luck is good and your eyes are open. Disregard people who gloomily tell you there's nothing worth collecting from circulation anymore. A surprising number of coins you might buy for investment *are* around, and you should be on the lookout for these in all conditions.

LINCOLN CENTS—Most that you see date from 1930 or later. The rare 1931–S catalogs at approximately $25 in Fine. It's worthwhile watching for 1931–D, too, whose low mintage of about 4.5 million makes it hard to find.

JEFFERSON NICKELS—The famed 1950–D is the only rare date. Several others have low mintages: 1931–D had just over 3.5 million made; 1951–S had over 7.75 million struck, but that's low in contrast to Philadelphia's 28.5 million-plus and Denver's more than 20 million.

ROOSEVELT DIMES—No rarities; scarce dates are silver, unlikely to circulate.

WASHINGTON QUARTERS—1936–D is scarce and 1937–S is rare, with mintage totals of 5.3 and 1.6 million, respectively. And 1939–S (just over 2.5 million) and 1940–D (under 3 million) also are rare.

FRANKLIN HALVES—Rare dates are 1953 and 1955, both under three million; however, these and the scarce 1948, 1949, and 1949–S are 90 percent silver and had a short issue period, so they're particularly hard to find in circulation now.

KENNEDY HALVES—The only rare date worth watching for is 1970–D (2.1 million).

EISENHOWER DOLLARS—Cupronickel-clad ones with low mintages are 1973 and 1973–D (2 million).

Remember to cultivate what I call "the habit of open eyes"— alertness that brings you rarities others miss. One man told me he had just taken a glass bank full of coins to the bank and deposited them. When I informed him that he may have overlooked collectable items, he moaned, "You're breaking my heart!" and vowed to watch his change more carefully.

WHAT'S YOUR BID?

If you want more than coins in circulation, but want to avoid paying dealers' prices, you might explore another phase of numismatics—auctions. One way to get acquainted with auctions is to join a coin club that holds them. At my club meetings, we can inspect auction items at intermission, before the auction itself. And we sometimes *do* get bargains. However, most of your dealings will be with mail-bid auctions.

Mail-bid auction catalogs range from a few mimeographed sheets to beautifully printed small books; most are free; a few cost $1 or $2. Coins are listed by lots, with one lot consisting of possibly one coin or more than a hundred. You bid on each lot as if it were a single item.

Bid requirements vary widely. Some catalogs list minimum bids for certain lots; many list approximate values to guide you; a few leave you on your own. Many auctions offer a list of "Prices Realized" for a dollar or less, which can help you decide how high to bid on similar lots in the future.

At the beginning of most catalogs is a section labeled "Conditions of Sale" or "Auction Rules." One standard rule is, "In case of Tie Bids, first one received will be awarded the Lot." Most auctioneers refuse ridiculously low bids, to protect consignors, but honor "bargain price" bids on a reasonable level.

A few auctioneers let you bid "buy." This means, "I will pay *any price* to get this lot." If two "buy" bids arrive, the auctioneer contacts bidders to request limits. However, many auctioneers refuse "buy" bids.

After the "closing date," when bids must be received, the auctioneer picks the highest for each lot. Let's say you made five successful bids. Anywhere from two days to about two weeks after closing date, you'll receive the coins and a bill (if the auctioneer knows you) or simply a bill; when you pay for your lots, you get the coins. A few auctioneers pay postage and insurance, but most don't.

When you receive coins, check immediately to be sure they're the ones you bid on. If a coin is different, and represents an auction error, you can return it for a refund. I've rarely had to do this. But it works both ways: if you mean to write lot 1219 but mark the bid sheet 1218, you're stuck. *You* are responsible for errors in bidding.

Pay for auction purchases promptly, by either check or money order. *Never send cash through the mails.*

Auctions offer a pleasant and sometimes exciting way to add to your collection. And learning the art of skillful bidding sharpens your wits!

COIN SHOW REPORT

I hadn't attended an auction until my first coin show. Every collector should visit at least one coin show. My first was in 1967, at the third annual convention of the Metropolitan Washington Numismatic Association, in Washingtron, D.C.

It was like an Oriental marketplace: dealers' booths lined the hotel exhibit hall, each with hundreds of coins spread out for visitors' inspection. Here were rows of BU silver dollars, piles of $5 gold pieces, coins in all metals from all countries. Most dealers were from Washington, Maryland, or Virginia, but several had come from other states and one had traveled all the way from Seattle.

Exhibits included such themes as flight, British monarchs, ancient coins, Adolph Hitler on medals, paper money, animals on coins and stamps, and other subjects.

At the auction I had the pleasure of bidding successfully on several lots. This was pure impulse buying—absolutely the worst way to bid—but I wanted a souvenir of my first auction. (By chance, almost nobody else wanted these lots, and I paid about one-third of catalog value.)

There were free identification tables, where collectors could bring coins for attribution by experts. Nearby were stacks of free samples of various hobby publications. Door prizes were drawn hourly, with winning ticket numbers announced on the public-address system. Every few minutes the p.a. system called someone to the registration desk for a message or to help a visitor. The atmosphere was one of enjoyable hustle-and-bustle.

All in all, an enjoyable experience. Noncollectors, too, would enjoy it. They can't share our knowledge and intimacy with numismatic lore—but when standing before a pile of $10 gold pieces, they can marvel as well as any of us!

5

Star-Line Coins—Your (and My) Best Investments for Profit

New collectors, tomorrow, will want
the coins we buy today.

STAR-LINE

With so many "systems" touted as sure-fire ways to get rich fast,
you'll be asking some questions right now. What is "Star-Line"?
Why are these coins good investments? What profit can you make
—and over how long? What must you invest?

Star-Line is the investment plan I've developed for my own
use. I chose this name because it's a good label for something
special, you'll find it easy to remember, and I like its quick, clean,
and dramatic sound.

My investments take two to twenty years to mature. But when
I wait that long, I'll do all I can to make the profit good. The least
I want to make is 100 percent—and I aim for 500 percent. That's
what I said—*five hundred percent.*

Your investment depends on your financial situation. There are
many coins in these lists, so choose with care. *Invest only what
you can afford without going out on a financial limb.*

To make these profits, you must put your coins out of the
way—you can look at, study, and enjoy them, but you cannot sell
or spend them. So be careful. It's better to aim for 5 percent
profit and make it than go for 200 percent and overreach.

Why are Star-Line coins good investments? The quickest way
to answer is to give you the guidelines and show you the system
in action.

*Star-Line coins must be rare now, or likely to become rare.
Mintage should be as low as possible.*

If lots of investors buy the same coins, won't this depress prices?

No—because more important than mintage, in setting coin price, is the balance of supply and demand. In 1949 there were only about half a million collectors in this country. Today there are, including all kinds, close to 15 million. Tomorrow there'll be more. And collectors in other countries are interested in U.S. coins.

We can only guess how many really dedicated collectors there are. Let's be cautious and say a total of eight million. Probably at least half collect U.S. coins in general. By 1980, I estimate we'll have around 15 million collectors, with at least 7 million interested in U.S. issues. By 1985, we should have 19 or 20 million numismatists, with at least 12 million hungry for U.S. coins. And among those who don't collect *all* U.S. coins are many who collect one or two, and swell demand for those.

New collectors, tomorrow, will want coins you and I buy today. We'll pay $5, $25, or $100 for a single coin—but if we hold it long enough, someone will want it enough to pay $20, $100, or $500 for it. Nobody can guarantee when or how much a specific price will increase. The market can go two ways. But the general trend is UP.

Coins should sell at or below prices of others of the same or higher mintage in the same series.

These are the "underpriced" coins, the ones likely to show the biggest price increases. A recent coin usually has a lower catalog value than earlier ones of the same mintage. This is to our advantage—with passing time, the lower value will soar.

Star-Line coins' mintage, high or low, must be lower than that of most other coins in the series.

Many early coins were minted in low amounts. A rare coin doesn't stand out in a series in which *all* dates are rare.

Star-Line is restricted to regular-issue and Proof coins, with regular issues in Fine or better condition.

Always buy coins Uncirculated when you can. *Never buy coins below Fine for long-term investment unless they are so rare that they're almost impossible to get in Fine.*

Avoid buying U.S. coins overseas—and especially avoid buying U.S. gold coins in any other country: *they probably are counterfeit.*

Star-Line coins must have performed well over the past 20 years, posting minimum 100 percent increases each ten years.

Some coins perform well, but have higher mintage than Star-Line permits; others haven't done well, but are far underpriced. Some excellent investment coins violate one or more of Star-Line's rules. These are listed *with* Star-Line, but in a second column; they're the Marginals—coins on the borderline.

You'll notice that Star-Line includes only certain coins, while there are Marginals for more denominations and types.

If this were a game, I could relax the rules and include one of everything. But Star-Line requirements are high, and not every coin type qualifies. Since every denomination and type has some devotees, and since Marginal requirements are lower, the Marginals include representatives of almost every value and design. And while Marginals aren't as good as Star-Line coins, they're still pick-of-the-lot.

STAR-LINE IN ACTION

Let's see what some Star-Line coins have done. If in 1950 you had bought all Star-Line half-dimes Unc, your investment would have been:

1800	$50.00
1866	4.00
1867	4.00
Proof 1862	4.00
Investment	$62.00

If you had held these until 1971, their book value would have been:

1800	$1,150.00
1866	85.00
1867	90.00
Proof 1862	90.00
	$1,415.00

Now, suppose you had to sell and the only offer were half of book value. You'd receive $707.50. After subtracting your original investment, you'd be left with a profit of $645.50—*which is better than 1,000 percent.*

Let's check Marginals, too:

Coin	1950	1971
1801	$100.00	$1,250.00
1829	3.00	92.50
1830	2.50	82.50
1831	2.50	82.50
1832	2.50	82.50
1847	3.00	40.00
1859	1.75	45.00
1865	7.00	100.00
1868	3.00	45.00
1870	1.65	40.00
Proof 1865	12.50	200.00
Proof 1871	5.25	77.50
Proof 1872	5.25	80.00
Proof 1873	6.00	135.00
	$155.90	$2,352.50

This edition's Star-Line calculations involved the 1964–65 "boom" and reflect shifting interest from some rare issues to certain "type coins." As collecting tastes change, these lists will reflect those changes. Remember that these are predictions, not guarantees. There's no 100 percent perfect coin investment list—but I think these are the best choices now.

Half of 1971 book value was $1,176.25; minus the original $155.90 investment, we have $1,020.35—a profit percentage of over 650 percent.

How many businessmen do you know who could be forced to sell an investment at half book value and still make 650 percent? How many would even dare dream of it?

The wider you spread your buying, the safer your investment is. Coins have styles, just like clothing, and it's good to be able to sell during such a fad—but you have to have some of the popular coins. It's safer to own 10 half-dimes, 10 dimes, and 10 quarters than to have 30 of any one denomination.

I suggest you give your investment program a multiple goal. Remember that we, as numismatists, are more than investors. Coins we buy for investment should improve our collections, bring us new knowledge and help us grow as collectors and human beings.

I'm leaving you plenty of leeway to make decisions. Your skill, judgment, and maturity will determine how well you do as a coin investor. You'll make your own choices, as I'll make mine.

But we'll both be far ahead of the random buyer and impulse investor. For these coins have passed through such a rigorous analysis that each and every one has proved to my complete satisfaction its right to be called "Star-Line."

Part Two

From Old Colonials to New Dimes

6

We Call Them "Colonials"

Some were official, some were
private issues and a few came from
a tiny independent nation.

OUR MANY COLONIAL MINTS

With her own civil war on, England had no time for such frills as
coins for colonies. Foreign coins, musket balls, and wampum
weren't meeting the need for coinage, so the Massachusetts General Court bought silver, and in 1652 John Hull began making
NE coins in or near Boston. Joseph Jenks is believed to have
made the dies for these; he apparently also designed the Pine
Tree coins that followed them.

Hull struck the coins by hammer blows on the dies. His pay
was a shilling or a bit more for each 20 shillings made.

Most of NE coins' surface is *blank*. The obverse has a small NE
("New England"); the reverse has a Roman numeral showing the
value in pence—III for 3 pence, VI for 6 pence, and XII for a
shilling. The coins are about 91.6 percent silver.

"Tree" coins appeared after widespread counterfeiting and
shaving of precious metal (clipping) from the edges of NE coins.
The new series showed a willow (1653–60), oak (about
1657–67), and pine tree (1667–83) on the obverse, in a circle of
tiny dots or "beads." Around the rim is MASATHVSETS IN. Reverses
have NEW ENGLAND at the rim, sometimes with AN DOM ("Anno

FIG. 6–1. Massachusetts Pine Tree threepence. This was struck some-time between 1667 and 1682, but it's dated 1652. Coin is in the National Collection, Smithsonian Institution.

FIG. 6–2. Reverses of four "Colonials." Massachusetts cent, 1788, upper left; Connecticut cent, 1787, lower left; New Jersey cent, 1787, lower right; and the British-issued Virginia halfpenny, 1773, upper right.

Domini"); in a beaded circle is the date above a Roman numeral showing the value in pence.

But there's a catch. In 1652, England had ordered her American colonists to stay out of the coin-making business. So *all* tree coins except a 1662-dated twopence are dated 1652. This way, nobody could prove the coins were made after having been declared illegal!

Shillings, sixpences, and threepences were made for all three trees; the twopence shows an oak.

COINS OF THE CONFEDERATION

Under the Articles of Confederation, the states shared the right of coining money with the nation as a whole.

Massachusetts established a mint in Boston and issued cents and half-cents in 1787 and 1788. These show an Indian with bow and arrow on one side, and an eagle with the date and MASSA-CHUSETTS on the other.

Connecticut cents were minted by a private firm at Morris Cove and Westville. The coins usually show a stylized laureate bust facing right on the obverse and a seated figure on the reverse. There are about 340 different varieties for 1785–88.

New Jersey's 1786 and later coppers feature a right-facing horse's head above a plow, with NOVA CAESAREA (Latin for "New Jersey") around the upper rim. Reverses have an eagle and, at the rim, E PLURIBUS UNUM. The date may be on either side. These are the earliest North American coins with "E Pluribus Unum."

Coinages planned for Maryland, New Hampshire, and Virginia never reached the circulation stage. Patterns were struck, though, and may have served as money in all three coin-short states.

PRIVATE COLONIAL MINTS

Many "Colonial coins" are actually tokens. Permission to mint coins was rarely granted by either England or Colonial governments, but blacksmiths, goldsmiths, and others operated mints anyway.

Among the best known tokens are those of Dr. Samuel Higley and John Higley, of Granby, Conn. The obverse shows a crude deer facing left, with a Roman numeral III below. The most common reverse shows three crowned hammers; another has a large axe.

At first the obverse rim legend was THE VALUE OF THREE PENCE. The reverse has the date at bottom, CONNECTICVT at the rim, and I AM GOOD COPPER (hammers) or J CUT MY WAY THROUGH (axe). J and I were used interchangeably until J established itself as a separate letter.

Local supply outran demand, and merchants refused to accept what we call "Granby coppers" or "Higley tokens" for threepence. Higley changed the inscription to VALUE ME AS YOU PLEASE—but left the III below the deer. These tokens are dated 1737 and 1739.

Annapolis goldsmith John Chalmers minted silver shillings, six-pences, and threepences that were used locally. The nickel-sized shilling's most common variety has clasped hands on the obverse, in a wreath, and I. CHALMERS, ANNAPOLIS around the rim. On the reverse are two doves pulling at a worm, with ONE SHILLING and the date 1783 at the rim.

New York silversmith and jeweler Ephraim Brasher made one of our most famous early coins, the gold "Brasher's Doubloon," in 1787. This features part of New York's coat-of-arms, a rising sun over some mountains. The rim has NOVA EBORAC COLUMBIA EX-CELSIOR ("New York and America, Ever Upward"). The reverse has an eagle with a U.S. shield on its chest and arrows and an olive branch in its talons. Outside a wreath are E PLURIBUS UNUM and the date.

EAST COAST REPUBLIC

New Hampshire's Governor Benning Wentworth sold 108 land grants to settlers in 1761. New York simultaneously granted the same land to its own settlers. When Colonial authorities asked England to settle the dispute, the British supported New York and commanded New Hampshire settlers to buy their land again.

Three men led those who said they'd keep their land—without paying twice. Their names were Seth Warner, Remember Baker, and Ethan Allen. It was the start of the Green Mountain Boys.

The settlers founded a tiny nation, called it New Connecticut and on January 15, 1777, adopted a Declaration of Independence. New Connecticut sent representatives to the Continental Congress at Philadelphia, where Dr. Thomas Young advised them to rename their country "Vermont" to memorialize its mountains and evergreens. New Connecticut became the Republic of Vermont.

George Washington wasn't sure what to make of it. Should he send troops north, capture the republic, and force it into the new U.S.A.? He wisely decided against it—very soon he'd need every available man.

One of the privileges of sovereign nations is coining money. In June 1785, the Republic of Vermont granted Reuben Harmon, Jr., exclusive permission to make copper coins. Goldsmith Col. William Cooley of New York made the dies, and in 1785–88 Harmon produced the Vermont cents.

There are 38 or more varieties, from crude and ugly to well struck, craftsmanlike, and artistic. Most obverses have a laureate bust facing right. The usual rim inscription is AUCTORI VERMONTIS (Latin for "By the Authority of Vermont") or an abbreviation of it. Reverses usually show a left-facing seated figure probably symbolizing the spirit of Vermont, holding an olive branch in her outstretched right hand and a pole or spear in her left. The usual rim legend is INDE ET LIB ("Independence and Liberty"); the date is below the ground line. The coins cost about $25 in Good condition.

An earlier design, which lasted 1785–86, shows mountains covered with evergreens and a plow in a field. Around the rim is VERMONTIS RES PUBLICA, 1785 ("Republic of Vermont"). On the reverse is the Eye of Providence surrounded by rays whose ends are separated by 13 stars.

Thirteen stars? The symbol of the United States?

That's only half of it. The rim has QUARTA DECIMA STELLA— Latin for "The *Fourteenth* Star."

It's clear that the settlers meant from the first to join the Union. The U.S. never recognized the little country, but on March 4, 1791, it accepted the Republic of Vermont as the first state to join the original 13.

Vermont's days as a republic were ended, but her coins' prediction had come true.

MIND YOUR BUSINESS

Under the Articles of Confederation, adopted July 9, 1778, Congress could regulate alloy and value of U.S. coins, whether issued by the central government or the states. The first copper coin issued by the U.S. itself was an outgrowth of the pattern Continental Dollar. This is the Fugio Cent.

It's not 100 percent certain that Ben Franklin designed this coin, but many people credit him with it, and with the saying, "Time flies, so mind [take care of] your business."

FIG. 6–3. The Fugio cent, 1787. This is the "States United" variety, so named because of the position of the national identification. Coin is in the National Collection, Smithsonian Institution.

On Friday, July 6, 1787, Congress passed a resolution

that the board of treasury direct the contractor for the copper coinage to stamp on one side of each piece the following device, viz: thirteen circles linked together, a small circle in the middle, with the words "United States," round it; and in the centre, the words "We are one"; on the other side of the same piece the following device, viz: a dial with the hours expressed on the face of it; a meridian sun above on one side of which is the word "Fugio," (The meaning is, "time flies") and on the other the year in figures "1787" below the dial, the words "Mind Your Business."

It's interesting to note that "Fugio" actually means "I fly." The correct form would be "Fugit" or "Tempus Fugit." However, since "Fugio" is on all varieties of these cents, the error must have been in the resolution.

Contractor James Jarvis got a 20-year government obligation, and must have subcontracted the job, for we think these coins were struck at New Haven, Conn., New York City, Rupert, Vt., and probably elsewhere. There are many varieties; at least 27 obverse and 24 reverse dies were used.

In 1858, fourteen-year-old C. Wyllys Betts found some Fugio cent dies in New Haven; since then restrikes have been made in brass, copper, silver, and even gold.

Prices for originals vary widely. Since some of them are as low as $20, every collector can enjoy owning one of these historic coins.

NOTE—Copies, replicas, counterfeits—whatever we call them, there must be millions of fake Colonials around. Unless you're an expert on these coins, get a guarantee of genuineness. As with all rare coins, you're safest when you *know your dealer*.

7

Something of Very Slight Value

The "un-spendables."

The lowest denomination coin the U.S. issued was the half-cent. Although you'll read in some books that half-cents weren't legal tender, they were included in the Act of April 2, 1792, which authorized our coinage. They were to be made of pure copper, weigh 132 grains, and be valued at $.005. Before minting started, the Act of January 14, 1793, cut the weight to 104 grains (about as much as a modern nickel and dime together).

Alexander Hamilton was one of the half-cent's few enthusiastic supporters. He believed it would help the poor by letting merchants price some items at a half-cent level instead of at the next higher cent. But the coin became one of our least liked and least wanted ones. Very few people were willing to "admit to being poor" by *using* half-cents.

Many half-cents were restruck or overstruck because so many were held out of circulation for so long. Mintage varied widely, increasing one year and plummeting the next. Thousands of half-cents held in government vaults were melted to provide copper for alloying with gold and silver in higher-denomination coins or sold to private firms to fill industry's needs for copper.

The first type issued was the Liberty Cap design of 1793–97. On the obverse is Liberty facing left in 1793 and facing right from 1794 on. A liberty cap is close behind the portrait. LIBERTY is at the obverse top and the date is at bottom. On the reverse is HALF

FIG. 7–1. Half-cent, 1793, obverse. Coin is in the National Collection, Smithsonian Institution.

CENT in a wreath, with UNITED STATES OF AMERICA around the rim and ½₀₀ at bottom. The wreath is made of two olive branches tied with a ribbon.

At first, these coins were struck by hand, on an old screw press; starting in 1794, the machinery was powered by horses. Most "horsepower half-cents" have a better obverse than reverse; few are well-struck on both sides.

These coins' edges were lettered TWO HUNDRED FOR A DOLLAR until 1796. A Presidential proclamation on January 26 cut the coin's weight to 84 grains, and the thinner coin had no room for edge lettering. Edges were plain after that; however, some 1797 coins have a lettered edge.

The Draped Bust type appeared in 1800. Liberty's portrait is larger and heavier, showing her to below shoulder level; the liberty cap is gone. As with earlier half-cents, varieties are plentiful.

While few users liked half-cents, the coins did have a place in the economy. Nathaniel Dearborn had a circulating library in Newport, R.I., in 1808, and advertised his catalog for 12½¢.

FIG. 7–2. Half-cent, 1804, obverse.

FIG. 7–3. Half-cent, 1804, reverse. Note this coin's similarity to the 1798 cent's reverse. For the most part, half-cents and cents used the same design.

FIG. 7-4. Half-cent, 1833, obverse.

FIG. 7-5 Half-cent, 1833, reverse.

John Reich's new design, the Turban Head, appeared in 1809. It has been more and more called the Classic Head, a more accurate name. The portrait is heavier, and turns back to face left. Liberty wears a coronet with LIBERTY on it; her hair arrangement has some resemblance to a low turban. Around the rim are 13 stars arranged seven at left and six at right. The fraction is off the reverse at last, an improvement since the value already was indicated clearly. The wreath becomes a single branch of laurel whose ends are tied with a short ribbon.

Some half-cents were pierced with two holes and used as buttons; others served as teething rings. But the coins *were* spent. They often helped make change for the Spanish real, which was worth 12½¢. However, storekeepers and others sometimes refused them.

Then, in 1811, the banks *all* refused them! The boycott worked: 1811 saw only 63,140 half-cents minted, and then came a break until 1825, when only 63,000 were made.

"Notwithstanding this small emission," wrote Montroville W. Dickeson in 1859, "they are plenty and *well preserved*, showing that, in the fourteen years during which there had been no issue, the people had acquired the habit of disregarding fractions, and felt no disposition to renew them in making change."

But Dickeson added that he remembered "when, in some portions of our country, the half-cent was rigidly exacted, and when many a war of words, and sometimes of fists, grew out of such a controversy."

In 1840 William Kneass and Christian Gobrecht—two men we'll meet often here—produced the Braided Hair type. On these coins a sharper-faced Liberty wears her hair in a coil behind the coronet. The stars are spaced evenly around the obverse and are more pleasing.

In 1840 you could use a half-cent in Clarksville, Tenn., where Kerr & Williams offered shoes at their New Cash Store for 62½¢ up. And in 1841 druggist Edward Bringhurst invited his Wilmington, Delaware, customers to try his cough candy at 12½¢ per box. W. S. Peebles of Cincinnati sold a Souchong tea for 62½¢ per pound in 1844, claiming it was "selected with great care and cannot be excelled as to quality and price west of the mountains."

FIG. 7–6. Half-cent, 1851, obverse.

The rarest regular-issue half-cent *may* be 1831, with 2,200 made; but for some years we don't have mintage totals. Dates of 1840–48 were struck only in Proof. It's "not too clear" when or why these were made, half-cent expert Roger S. Cohen, Jr., told me. "There are many, many unanswered questions" about these coins, he said. Proofs also were made for 1832, 1833, and other dates. The most plentiful half-cent, according to the figures we have, is 1809, with 1,154,572 coins struck. Some dates cost under $10 in Fair condition and less than $25 in Fine. Top prices are in the $3,500 to $4,000 range, for high-grade 1793 and 1796 coins. Some people hoarded and later buried these "un-spendables," and hoards discovered later have helped keep prices relatively low.

Thanks to the coin's unpopularity, many dates list at $10 or less in Good. Some people hoarded these "un-spendables," and eventually buried them. Hoards that have been found have helped keep prices down.

Naturally, you can't expect to find half-cents in your change. But how about this? In the winter of 1968–69, in Washington, D.C., a man about to board a bus glanced down and saw a coin on the ground. Thinking it was a quarter he could use for his fare, he picked it up and was about to drop it in the fare box when he took another look—and saw that it was a half-cent! It was only Good, but that's still quite a find.

Most of us won't be this lucky—we'll get our half-cents from dealers, auctions, and other collectors.

Star-Line dates are 1806, 1826, 1850, and 1854. Marginals are 1803, 1804, 1832, 1833, 1834, 1835, 1851, and 1853.

The year 1857 was the half-cent's last. By then the coin was used only rarely outside large cities. Only 35,180 half-cents were made that January, and most were melted without ever reaching circulation. The reason was the Act of February 21, which halted half-cent coinage for good; and the coin quickly lost what little interest it still had for the general public.

Ironically, it's more popular now than ever during its 65-year life.

8

When Cents Were *Big*

"The public . . . can be supplied with Cents in exchange for gold or silver. . . ."—newspaper advertisement, 1817.

You can see the similarity to Fugio cents in the reverse of the first large cents of 1793—ONE CENT above a tiny $\frac{1}{100}$ within a circle of chain links, with UNITED STATES OF AMERICA around the rim. This is credited usually to Henry Voigt, but sometimes to J. P. Droz. It evidently was taken from the Fugio cent. The obverse has a stringy-haired Liberty facing right, LIBERTY at the top, and the date below. The edge has a leafy vine decoration. These coins were made around February 26 to March 12, when the supply of either dies or planchets (coin blanks) ran out.

Meanwhile, public criticism was rising against the chain, which people took as a symbol of slavery. Adam Eckfeldt redesigned the reverse to show a wreath, and moved the fraction to the bottom. Minting began early in April, with some coins receiving a new edge, lettered ONE HUNDRED FOR A DOLLAR.

FIG. 8–1. One cent, 1793. The Chain type was one of the first American coins to cause a public outcry against a coin design. This specimen is in the National Collection, Smithsonian Institution.

The same year brought a *third* cent design, probably by Joseph Wright. This shows a more lifelike Liberty portrait, with a small liberty cap behind the head.

The cent was to weigh 264 grains according to the Act of April 2, 1792, but the Act of January 14, 1793, changed this to 208 grains. That weight lasted until December 27, 1795, when another law cut the weight to 168 grains. As on half-cents, smaller planchets brought an end to lettered edges.

The 1795 "Jefferson head" cents actually aren't U.S. Coins. John Harper made them as patterns, in an effort to win a contract from the mint. He didn't get the contract.

In 1796 the mint began importing planchets from England; others were made at the mint from melted scrap that was cast into ingots, then flattened between horse-powered rollers into strips from which blanks were punched.

Another new Liberty is on Draped Bust cents of 1796–1807. She wears a low-cut gown; her hair is partly tied up, partly falling loose. Mintage ranged from 348,000 in 1806 to nearly 3.5 million in 1802; some dates cost only $10 to $15 in Good condition. The lowest prices for 1793–95 cents in Good are in the $30 to $45 range. The top price is $3,750 for a 1793 Chain cent in XF.

A pocket full of large cents would be inconvenient, but you only needed a few for that era's low prices. Five of these coins would buy a pound of veal in Frankfort, Ky., late in 1801.

On the short-lived Classic Head type of 1808–14, Liberty turns left, drawn by John Reich. LIBERTY is on the headband tying back her hair; there are seven stars left and six right. On the reverse the single major change is removal of the unneeded fraction.

This type is hard to find in top condition today. A major reason is that the alloy was softer than usual during these years, so the coins wore down quickly. Mintage varied from 218,025 (1811) to 1.4 million (1810); some dates cost only $12 to $15 in Good condition.

But in 1810 you might spend 12 of the coins to buy a pound of eightpenny nails at the Penitentiary Store in Richmond, Va.

Today we view large cents as long-gone, beautiful, and romantic. Those who used them would disagree. The coins were almost half-dollar size, very heavy, and rarely usable in any volume. Mint workers probably didn't much like them, either. Cents were counted by men who poured coins into wooden trays which had cut-out spaces for 500 coins. The worker would shake the extras out, pour out the "counted" 500 and start over. A full tray weighed about 15 pounds—and workers were supposed to move fast and keep moving.

Sometimes the mint sent out barrels of large cents. Many coins were melted for industrial copper needs. Some kegs, lying forgotten in bank vaults, later provided collectors with many Uncirculated specimens.

FIG. 8–2. One cent, 1802, obverse.

FIG. 8–3. One cent, 1798, reverse. Even though the coin's denomination is clearly stated in the wreath, there's a $\frac{1}{100}$ at bottom.

FIG. 8–4. One cent, 1812, obverse. Coins can have historic associations. This cent was minted two years before Francis Scott Key wrote "The Star-Spangled Banner." The author of our national anthem may have used this coin.

FIG. 8–5. One cent, 1812, reverse.

The year 1815 is notable for one reason: it is the only year in the history of the United States which does not appear on a one-cent coin!

After that came the Kneass-Gobrecht Coronet type of 1816. Liberty's portrait is a shade smaller, but more lifelike. Her headband is better detailed and takes the form of a coronet. Some of her hair is tucked into a braid at the back of her head. The stars are evenly spaced around the obverse.

Before the new coins could get into circulation the supply of cents had run low. G. J. Wolfe of Wilmington, Del., obtained some and announced in the *American Watchman* on Wednesday, April 23, 1817, under the heading "Cents!!!," that "The public are informed that by calling at the Shop of the subscriber they can be supplied with Cents in exchange for gold or silver or notes of the Bank of Delaware."

FIG. 8–6. One cent, 1818, obverse. Like many collectors, I was started in our hobby by the gift of a U.S. large cent. This coin catalogs at $9 to $12, but it's the first coin I can recall owning, and to me it's priceless.

But the mint soon got cents out into circulation. In 1828 six of them would buy you a copy of the New York *Morning Courier*.

Mintage was high in several years, and today every collector can own one of these, the most attractive of our large cents. Rarest is 1821, with only 389,000 struck; top mintage is that of 1838, when 6.3 million were made. Prices in Fine go as low as $7 to $9 for some dates.

As with half-cents, many large cents ended up as buried hoards. Somebody buried more than 15,000 in Georgia, apparently just before the Civil War. There were several kegs of coins, most dated 1818; other dates were 1817, 1819, 1820, and 1825.

The merchant who found them, around 1865 or so, found that they were in excellent condition—many were Uncirculated. He sold them to William H. Chapman, a Norwich, N.Y., grocer, for 90¢ per hundred.

Chapman thought the old coins would please his customers, but he got a rude surprise: people thought such old coins in such well-preserved shape must be counterfeit!

Into the picture came coin dealer John Swan Randall. And with the mention of his name, collectors will know at once which coins I'm speaking of. For Randall bought the cents from Chapman for

FIG. 8–7. One cent, 1854, obverse.

90¢ per hundred, and it was the dealer's name that became attached to the coins: today we call them the Randall Hoard, and they've provided many of us with treasured specimens.

During the period around 1834–43, Kneass and/or Gobrecht used a whole series of different Liberty Head portraits—one each in 1834–35, 1835–37, and 1839, another in 1837–39, two that appeared only in 1839, and 1839–43.

At last came 1839 and Kneass's Braided Hair coin, last of the large cents. Liberty is a bit smaller and sharper-faced, and her coronet is larger. Nearly all her hair is in one large braid at the back of her head.

In the 1840's you could use two of these cents in Philadelphia to buy a cup of dried lavender from a woman who sold it on the street. A. J. Foster advertised in the Freeport, Pa., *Columbian* on February 2, 1841, that he had "a most splendid assortment of Toy Books for children, from one cent upwards. . . ."

Almost ten million cents were minted in 1851. With prices for some dates about $6.50 for Good and $8 to $10 for Fine, it's easy to add one of these coins to your collection.

You won't get these in change, of course—again it's a case of dealers, auctions, and other collectors with duplicates to trade.

Star-Line dates are 1795 Lettered Edge, 1796, 1803, 1805, 1807, 1824, 1827, 1829, 1854, and 1855. Marginals are 1793 Chain, 1798, 1819, 1825, 1845, 1846, 1848, 1850, and 1851.

Only 333,456 large cents were made in 1857.

Why so few that year? Because 1857 brought the first issue of Flying Eagle *small* cents. The large cent would continue circulating together with the new size for years, but it never again would be issued. With a massive changeover campaign, the day of the "big coppers" ended forever.

9

The Eagle and the Indian

By changing from large to small size,
the government showed it had good cents!

OPERATION SMALL CENT

Silver, copper, and nickel cent patterns were minted in different
sizes in 1850, seven years before the first issue of small cents.
Some trial pieces have center holes, some have U.S.A., and some
are lettered ONE-TENTH SILVER. A wide range of designs and sizes
appeared in the later 1850's. Some involved regular-issue dies of
other denominations: one 1853 pattern has the obverse of the
quarter-eagle.

Probably the best-known, yet most mysterious of all pattern
cents are the 1856 Flying Eagle ones. How many were made? We
don't know. In the September 1938 *Numismatist*, Wesley R.
Hauptman claimed that 960 Proofs were struck. The Red Book
says 1,000, but lists values as low as Good. Some collectors believe 5,000 were made; others say 10,000 is the correct figure.

It's not settled why the coins were released, either—but it's
certain that some were. Maybe minting was resumed after initial
pattern striking and the not-yet-approved pieces were put into
use to ease the shortage of small change. Just to make the situation worse, these may have been restruck during the 1860's.

The obverse shows Longacre's flying eagle soaring to the left
with wings spread and raised. Around the upper rim, held in
place by the beak at left and tail at right, is UNITED STATES OF
AMERICA. The date is at bottom. On the reverse is ONE above CENT
in an ornate corn-cotton-tobacco-wheat wreath.

In spite of its simplicity, this is one of our most attractive coins.
Mintage was 17.45 million in 1857 and 24.6 million in 1858, and

prices begin at around $7.50 for the 1857 in Good. Proofs were struck in both years and catalog at $2,300 up.

Small cents had two initial tasks: first, to replace U.S. large cents; second, to help get rid of foreign coins still in circulation. The depreciated coinage of several other nations had become a nuisance; the Act of February 21, 1857, gave it a monetary heave-ho.

That May, workers put up a temporary building in the mint yard. Over one window was "Cents for Cents"; over the other was "Cents for Silver." People brought large cents or foreign silver to the correct window and carried away the new small cents in exchange.

The program worked—too well! By 1859, according to Adams and Woodin, the job was almost done but there were so many small cents in circulation that "they became almost as much of a nuisance as had the depreciated silver currency." People had more Flying Eagle cents than they could use, "and had begun to pay bills of $1, $2, and even $3 with the little coins, this practice prevailing to an almost unendurable extent."

So the Flying Eagle cent lived out a two-year life and most of the coins disappeared from circulation. In 1895 the Washington (D.C.) *Evening Star* reported that "The flying eagle on the nickel cent was removed because people insisted that it was a buzzard." The short issue period, which prevents Star-Line from operating, was possible because the law to limit design changes to once every 25 years hadn't yet been passed. Thus the Flying Eagle cent was replaced in 1859 by one of the most popular U.S. coins.

FIG. 9–1. One cent, 1858, obverse. This eagle is a direct descendant of the one on the 1836 silver dollar.

LONGACRE'S INDIAN

Many of us have one or more Indian Head cents, and almost everybody has at least seen one. But *who is on the coin*—an Indian, Miss Liberty, or Sarah Longacre?

The first Indian Head cents were struck in the same cupronickel alloy as Flying Eagle cents, 88 percent copper and 12 percent nickel. The obverse has a left-facing portrait wearing a feathered headdress with LIBERTY on the band; UNITED STATES at left and OF AMERICA at right; and the date at bottom. James B. Longacre used a laurel wreath for the 1859 reverse; in 1860 he changed it to oak and added a small shield at top. ONE CENT is in two lines centered in the wreath.

We're used to calling our 5¢ coin a "nickel," but back in 1859 that coin hadn't appeared yet. Because of their composition, cents of 1859–64 were called nickels! Since the 5¢ piece has taken over this nickname, cupronickel cents are better known today as "white cents" from their whitish color.

FIG. 9–2. One cent, 1901, obverse. It's rare that anyone sees one of these coins in circulation today.

The Civil War made it hard to get nickel for coins. When the government could get this metal, coin blanks were so hard that the dies kept breaking. And when coins were issued, people hoarded them. Once again cents were scarce. At one point in 1863 they brought a 20 percent premium in Philadelphia.

To solve the problem the government switched in 1864 to a bronze alloy, 95 percent copper and 5 percent tin and zinc. The weight was cut by one third, from 72 to 48 grains, and cents became thinner.

A Washington, D.C., newspaper called *The Daily Critic* was sold for one cent in 1879. Six years later, at the closing-out sale of the Chicago Dry Goods Store, in Indianapolis, Ind., you could buy calico at 4¢ per yard.

Longacre's Indian lasted from 1859 to 1909, with all except two dates struck only at Philadelphia; until 1906, the law said that only that mint could make minor coins.

Late in November 1908, San Francisco produced the first branch mint cents. With a mintage of only 1,115,000, 1908-S is popular and consistently sought by collectors; but it's overshadowed by the even better known 1909-S, whose 309,000 mintage makes it one of the favorites in the entire cent series (and also a favorite with counterfeiters). Luckily, these are exceptions: many mintages are in the 30's, 40's, and 50's of millions, with average prices of under $1 in Good and $2.50 or less in Fine (as contrasted to about $25 for 1908-S and about $80 for 1909-S in Fine). The popular 1877 rarity is widely counterfeited and often is altered from 1873, 1874, and 1875 coins.

You still hear of people finding Indian Head cents in circulation, but not often. The best sources are auctions, dealers, and other collectors.

FIG. 9–3. One cent, 1901, reverse.

Star-Line dates are 1870, 1908, and Proof 1881, 1882, 1889, 1895, and 1908. Marginals are 1880, 1883, 1884, 1889, 1895, 1896, 1909, and Proof 1869, 1870, 1871, 1880, 1884, 1890, 1891, and 1892.

The Red Book calls it an Indian Girl. Frank Spadone's *V&O Guide* tells the traditional story of an Indian chief's visit to Longacre's home during which the designer's daughter put on the chief's ceremonial war bonnet. In some versions of the story there are several Indians; sometimes it's one of them who puts the feathered bonnet on Sarah's head; in one version, Longacre immediately sets to work with pad and pencil to make preliminary sketches for a new coin.

It has been called illogical that Longacre could have shown a Greek goddess wearing an American Indian headdress. But if you look at the figure as Miss Liberty, the feathered bonnet is perfectly appropriate. It's sometimes said that the source of the figure was the Venus Acroupi, a Greek statue in the Vatican Museum. It also has been suggested—and this is important—that Sarah posed, but that the portrait *isn't meant to show her*.

Now, how can we tie all these ideas together?

Longacre saw or knew of the Venus Acroupi, and had the statue in mind in planning the coin design. He already planned to show Miss Liberty, and considered the Indian ceremonial bonnet a good symbol of the nation's westward expansion. Whether because of a visit by one or more Indians or simply as part of the design work, he posed Sarah in an Indian headdress and modeled the portrait based on her appearance, then revised it.

You can see that the face has a smoothness and softness that don't fit an Indian, but a maturity and air of confidence that don't fit a young girl—yet these qualities *do* fit Miss Liberty.

One thing's certain: *whoever is* on it, the Indian Head cent is one of our most popular coins!

10

Gentlemen, Mr. Abraham Lincoln

The "gigantic" initials caused a furor.

A MATTER OF WORDS

Most of our country's founders were Englishmen, so they thought in English terms. After saying "penny" all their lives, they kept thinking in terms of it. "Cent," from the Latin *centesimus*, a hundredth part, is in our coinage laws—but "penny," which grates on many collectors' ears, probably is more widely used.

The alloy used for cents is 95 percent copper and 5 percent zinc; until 1962 the composition included some tin. The term "bronze cent" has stayed in use and probably will remain; the "95–5" alloy is called "penny bronze" by some, "gilding metal" by others. "I'd call it a brass," declares one metallurgist, and I agree with him. However, we tend to think of "brass" as equivalent to "low quality," so it's doubtful the alloy ever will be named accurately.

V.D.B.

President Theodore Roosevelt visited the studio of sculptor Victor David Brenner to discuss the Panama Canal medal, and found that Brenner was a fan of Abraham Lincoln and had made several Lincoln portraits. One story says the President asked Brenner to design a cent for the centennial of Lincoln's birth; another says Brenner suggested the coin.

The first design included the sculptor's last name; when the government ordered this changed to just initials, the 1909 cents were struck with a small v.d.b. at the reverse bottom.

But when the coin began circulating on August 2, the public began complaining about the "gigantic" initials. Three days later, Treasury Secretary Franklin MacVeagh ordered the mints to halt production. The v.b.d. was removed from the master die, and new working dies were made. A tiny b was supposed to be on the new coins, but was canceled, probably because this initial already was on dimes, quarters, and half-dollars to represent Charles E. Barber. Brenner's initials weren't restored until 1918, when they were made tinier and incuse (cut into the metal) and moved to the portrait's shoulder.

George A. Beck's grocery store, in Minneapolis, would sell you 25 paper napkins for three of these coins in 1912.

Lincoln cents are common—we use them all the time in paying sales taxes, feeding vending machines, and making change.

Everyone is familiar with the dignified-yet-warm portrait of Lincoln which faces right on this coin. Variety collectors are quick to check the date, in front of Lincoln's coat, and the small LIBERTY behind him, for doubling and partial filling of numbers or letters. IN GOD WE TRUST is around the top rim in tiny letters. The first reverse used for this coin has a large ONE above CENT

FIG. 10–1. One cent, 1909 V.D.B., reverse. The initials look small to us, but they seemed gigantic to those who protested against them in 1909.

FIG. 10–2. One cent, 1968–S, obverse.

with a smaller UNITED STATES OF AMERICA below, two large stylized wheat ears at the side rims and a tiny E PLURIBUS UNUM at top. This was used 1909–58.

Philadelphia has been making Lincoln cents since 1909; so has San Francisco. Denver made its first ones in 1911. The first year when mintage topped one billion was 1941, but it took all three mints to produce that year's 1,108,099,100 cents. Three years later, Philadelphia alone made 1,435,400,000.

If you class the V.D.B. coins as separate issues, the rarest regular-issue Lincoln cent is 1909–S, V.D.B., with only 484,000 struck. However, if you class them as varieties, the rarest date is 1931–S, with mintage of 866,000.

Plenty of early dates still circulate, and I find 1910, 1913, and 1925 every so often; I've even found 1909 V.D.B. in my change. Even scarce and rare dates turn up. There are dangerously accurate counterfeits of 1909–S. V.D.B., so be certain the coin is genuine before you buy it.

Some of these coins, especially 1937 cents, have been given a reeded edge after minting. They are *not* legitimate varieties.

The most famous Lincoln cents probably are the elusive varieties struck on regular bronze planchets but dated 1943.

1943

While 1943 bronze cents have a place in our hobby, nobody *knows* how many there are, how they were made, or what they're worth, and the government steadfastly refuses to admit that there are any genuine ones.

When writing an in-depth report on these, I asked the Bureau of the Mint for comments. Miss Eva Adams, then Director of the Mint, replied that her only comment was that "no bronze cents were struck at the United States mints during 1943, wartime needs for that metal having necessitated a change of alloy to zinc-coated steel."

By the middle of World War II it was obvious that the 95 percent copper cents were using too much of this strategic war material. The government experimented with *plastic*, striking patterns in 1942, but the final decision was in favor of steel planchets coated with a zinc layer five-thousandths of an inch thick.

Philadelphia made 684,628,670 steel cents; Denver minted 217,660,000; and San Francisco struck 191,550,000. Except for their "silvery" appearance and slightly lighter weight, these are the same as other cents. Most have lived out their useful lives and been retired.

How do we get 1943 bronze cents, then?

It has been suggested that they're unauthorized pieces made by mint employees; or that bronze blanks couldn't be retrieved from the machinery at the end of 1942 and were struck when the works were started in 1943. It also has been suggested that these are die trials.

It seems most likely that bronze planchets for 1942 cents were left accidentally in a hopper or cart that later was filled with steel planchets for 1943 cents. When the steel blanks were dumped into the machinery, the bronze ones went along.

Most "1943 bronze" cents are *not* genuine.

Copper-plated steel cents have been popular since 1943; professional magicians used them in tricks. I have one, and its envelope is carefully marked "1943 bronze—copper-plated replica," so that there'll never be any chance of its being mistaken for a real 1943 bronze cent.

Estimates of the genuine pieces range from four to ten for 1943 and two to three each 1943–D and 1943–S. A 1943 was sold for $15,000 several years ago; an AU 1943–S was auctioned for $12,000 in February 1974.

What if you're offered, or find, what appears to be a bronze 1943 cent?

First, *keep quiet*. For one thing, there are cases of seizure by Treasury agents of suspected 1943 bronze cents. For another, the wise collector announces a major find only when he can prove it's genuine.

Second, check the coin with a magnet. A copper-plated steel cent will be attracted unless it has had special treatment.

Third, inspect the coin under at least a 10-power magnifying glass. Compare the date with that of a 1943 steel cent; there should be no difference. Compare it with such frequently altered dates as 1945 and 1948. Machinery adjusted for steel planchets should produce a sharp, clear, and well-detailed strike on the softer bronze. The V.D.B. on Lincoln's shoulder should be perfectly clear; the rim should be well-defined. There should be no blurred details, pitting, or weakness in the strike.

But don't waste your time hunting for 1943 bronze cents. Too few can exist for it to be worthwhile.

ABE, MEET MR. LINCOLN

On January 2, 1959, President Dwight D. Eisenhower approved a new reverse design for that year's cent, featuring the Lincoln Memorial. Cents of 1959 and later show a stylized front view of the building, with UNITED STATES OF AMERICA around top and side rims, E PLURIBUS UNUM below this, the Memorial in the center and ONE CENT at bottom. Lincoln, whose statue is visible inside the Memorial, is the only person shown on both sides of a regular-issue U.S. coin.

It's interesting that designer Frank Gasparro, whose FG is at the Memorial's lower right corner, was born in Philadelphia, site

FIG. 10–3. One cent, 1959, reverse. Memorial reverse cents with sharp strikes, clearly lined columns, and distinct steps are relatively hard to find.

of the main U.S. Mint, in 1909, the Lincoln cent's first year of issue.

In the new reverse's first year Philadelphia made almost 611 million cents. Denver struck over 1.25 *billion!* Top-mintage date is 1974–D, with 4,235,098,000 made. Memorial-reverse cents have been made at Philadelphia, Denver, and San Francisco, and each branch mint has made cents both with and without mint mark.

THE CENT TODAY

Cents don't have much purchasing power, but you can buy a 1¢ stamp with one, or a piece of candy from a "gum-ball machine."

When mint officials demonstrated the new mint at Philadelphia for visitors, they accidentally revealed that 1969 pattern cents were struck. Publisher Chester L. Krause asked a technician to let him see some finished coins from the new coin roller (which the mint later abandoned). The man picked up a handful from the receiving hopper and held them out—until Krause saw that one was a *pattern* with a Liberty portrait much like the one on the "Mercury" dime. Mint officials refused to allow a close inspection of the piece.

There are so many cents, with so many dates, from our three cent-making mints that varieties are plentiful. You can find date, mint mark, motto, portrait, manufacture, and other varieties of all sorts, and there are organizations devoted to just this type of collecting.

Minor die improvements were made in 1974. The rim was widened and the bust relief was lowered slightly, as it had been in several recent years, to provide more metal for the reverse design.

It's difficult to put together a full set of cents from circulation, but it can be done. However, the popular method is to collect all except scarce and rare dates, then buy or trade for these.

Star-Line dates are 1911–D and Proof 1911. Marginals are 1909 V.D.B., 1930–S, 1931–D, 1931–S, 1933–D, and Proof 1909.

I I

In God We Trust

A motto and the coin it made famous.

THE MOTTO

As everyone knows, "In God We Trust" first appeared on the U.S. 2¢ piece in 1864 and has been on all our coins ever since.

But that's not quite true.

Religious mottoes have been on English coins since the time of King Edward III (1327–77). The custom continues in today's "D. G.," for "By the Grace of God." Some French coins have "May God Protect France" (in French), while several German ones have the German for "God With Us" on the edge.

Many people who prayed for the end of the Civil War wrote to Treasury Secretary Salmon P. Chase to ask that our coins be given some reference to the Supreme Being. One writer was Rev. Mark R. Watkinson of Ridleyville, Pa., who in mid-November 1861 suggested the motto "God, Liberty, Law."

Chase liked the idea. He wrote to Mint Director James Pollock to endorse the suggestion that our coins recognize the importance of God, adding, "You will cause a device to be prepared without unnecessary delay with a motto expressing in the fewest and tersest words possible this National recognition."

Pollock had patterns made, and wrote to Chase December 26 that he had thought of "Our Trust Is In God," but had found it too long and had tried "God Our Trust." He expected people would be familiar with this, Pollock added, because of the line in "The Star-Spangled Banner" that proclaims, "And this be our motto: 'In God is our Trust.'" Pollock had the three-word motto put on pattern half-dollars, half-eagles, and eagles.

By mid-June 1862, the impatient Pollock was supposed to be preparing 1863 coinage dies, but Chase hadn't commented on the proposed motto. Pollock repeated the past year's half-dollar and eagle patterns, changing only the date.

He wrote to Chase again December 8, suggesting that a 2¢ coin would be a "great public convenience." He recommended a bronze coin weighing 96 grains (twice the cent's weight). The patterns he enclosed included some by Longacre, with the familiar shield with crossed arrows and an inverted laurel wreath in the background, topped by a banner lettered GOD OUR TRUST and with the date below. The reverse has a large number 2 above CENTS in a wheat wreath, with national identification around top and sides. One variety has a slightly different motto: IN GOD WE TRUST.

The 1863 patterns were struck in bronze, cupronickel, and aluminum, with mintage from 2 or 3 up to 200 and current prices of several hundred dollars. Patterns would continue, but for all practical purposes the motto's testing was finished.

Yet it would be 1938 before it would appear on U.S. regular-issue coins. In most cases the reason was lack of space, or reluctance to change a design established years before. This group includes the "Indian Head" cent, silver and cupronickel 3¢ pieces, half-dime, dime, 20¢ piece, gold dollar, and Coronet type quarter-eagle ($2.50 gold).

The motto is *on* Shield nickels, but was left *off* Liberty Head and Buffalo nickels even though there's enough space for it on these coins' obverse rims.

In the mid-1860's the $3 gold coin had a quarter-century of life remaining; certainly there's room on the reverse, outside the wreath, for "In God We Trust." However, the motto never even appeared on trial pieces for this denomination. As we'll see later, the motto was left off $10 and $20 coins of 1907 and early 1908, but was restored during 1908.

As for commemoratives, most of these do have the motto, but several do not: the 1892 Columbian Exposition half-dollar, 1900 Lafayette dollar, and 1903 Louisiana Purchase Exposition gold dollar all are "no motto" commemoratives.

FIG. 11–1. Two cents, 1863 pattern, obverse. The three-word motto is better balanced, but the four-word one was chosen.

FIG. 11–2. Two cents, 1863 pattern, reverse. Note sharply curved CENTS and absence of ribbon-ends at bottom of wreath.

FIG. 11–3. Two cents, 1865, obverse.

FIG. 11–4. Two cents, 1865, reverse.

THE COIN

Catalogs usually list 2¢ pieces with issue dates of 1864–73, but the last year of issue was 1872. The 1,100 or so struck in 1873 all are Proofs. Some of these did circulate, though; I've seen 1873 offered as VG.

Nearly 20 million 2¢ pieces were coined in 1864. This initial mintage was the largest. Though 1865 brought another 13.6 million, later mintages declined steadily: only 65,000 were struck in 1872. And many 2¢ pieces were returned to Philadelphia later for melting.

One of these coins would buy a copy of the Washington, D.C., *Evening Star* in 1875. And if you had one of the few remaining in use in 1884, you could buy the Baltimore, Md., *Day* with it.

Thanks to high mintage in its first two years, you can own a 2¢ piece for about $5—or less, if you make a lucky auction bid. Several dates cost below $12 in Fine.

Despite the relatively short issue period, varieties are plentiful; 20 or more are known for 1864 and 1865, and over 15 for 1868; there are double dates, rotated reverses, die breaks, overdates, and others.

There's no Star-Line date. Marginals are 1868 and 1869.

Every collector should have a 2¢ coin. It's within the range of the most limited budget, it's tasteful and well-balanced, and it represents an important change in our coinage.

12

The U.S.A.'s Three Cents' Worth

> ". . . Not only very convenient, but
> a safe size."—Dickeson, in 1859.
> Well, that was *his* opinion.

TRIMES

Congress approved the silver 3¢ in 1851 with the same law that cut postage from 5¢ to 3¢. The "trime" was meant to make stamp buying easier—and also help push small foreign coins out of circulation.

Around the obverse top and sides, James B. Longacre put UNITED STATES OF AMERICA; the date is at bottom. A six-pointed star encloses a U. S. shield at the center. On the reverse is a III in an ornamental C, with 13 stars around the rim. The edge is plain.

FIG. 12–1. Trime, 1851, obverse. Although national identification is supposed to be on the reverse of U.S. coins, this side is considered the obverse. This is one of the more than 5.4 million struck by the Philadelphia mint in the trime's first year of issue.

FIG. 12–2. Trime, 1851, reverse. The first reverse used on this unpopular coin.

FIG. 12–3. Trime, 1861, reverse. The Type 3 coin with the modified reverse with olive sprig and arrows.

FIG. 12–4. Trime, 1861, obverse.

The first of these were struck in an alloy 75 percent silver and 25 percent copper, and weigh 12.375 grains. The star on Type 1 coins of 1851–53 has a single outline. In 1877, Joseph Wharton wrote that early trimes were "marked by a yellowish and paltry appearance. . . ."

The law of March 3, 1853, cut the weight to 11.5 grains but raised the fineness to .900. From 1854–58, the star has a triple outline. An additional change on Type 2 coins is the addition of a tiny olive branch above the III and a bundle of arrows below it, to show the changed weight and fineness.

Type 3 coins, starting in 1859, differ from earlier ones by having two outlines instead of three to the star.

Trimes are attractive, especially in VF and better condition. Despite the popular belief that they were universally scorned, there seems to have been some pre-issue demand for them. And they had uses—even if not as coins. Women liked the trime's delicate appearance, and many silver 3¢ coins ended up as ornaments.

Montroville W. Dickeson, in his *American Numismatical Manual* (1859), defended the coin, saying, "As issued, however, it is a very useful coin, and custom has rendered it not only very convenient, but a safe size." Well, that was *his* opinion. But he could have gotten arguments from those who lost trimes through tiny holes in pockets, merchants whose trimes disappeared into cracks in cash drawers and floors, and just about everyone who found our smallest silver piece hard to hold onto and use. Dickeson's claim that the trime "is now a great favorite" may have been true for a while, but not for long. Wide counterfeiting added to the growing dissatisfaction with silver 3¢ coins.

In 1856 you could buy tallow for four of these coins in Lawrence, Kan. William S. Godbe of Salt Lake City advertised in June 1856 that he'd deliver ice to your house for 3¢ per pound; I suppose he'd take pay in trimes for a few pounds. In September 1860 a trime would buy a copy of the 16-page *Household Journal*.

Mintage figures reflect the growing disenchantment. The only high mintage years are 1852 (18.6 million) and 1853 (11.4 million). Half of the mintage figures are below a quarter-million. All were struck at Philadelphia except for 720,000 made in 1851 at New Orleans. Proofs were struck for almost every year; only Proofs were struck for 1873. Most 1863–72 regular-issue trimes were either melted or exported, creating one of those unusual cases in which Unc coins are far rarer than Proofs! A 1974 advertisement offered an 1863 Proof at $295 and a BU coin at $335.

Like other obsolete coins, this isn't something you can expect to find in circulation. But with prices of common dates around $8 in Good an $11 to $17 in Fine, it's possible for every collector to have one of these tiny bits of Americana.

Star-Line dates are 1860, 1862, and Proof 1862. The Marginals are 1859 and Proof 1867, 1868, and 1869.

High mintages in other denominations in 1853 and 1854 swelled the formerly thin supply of silver coins. Addition of 5¢ nickels in 1866 helped destroy the trime's sinking popularity. Too small and thin for convenience, replaced by other coins and out of place in a decimal-based coinage, the trime was abandoned with the Act of February 12, 1873.

THREE-CENT NICKELS

The 3¢ denomination lasted a while longer in the form of 3¢ nickels. Dr. Lewis Feuchtwanger invented a cupronickel-zinc alloy, and in 1837 suggested to Congress that his metal would be good for coins. Congress said no.

But early in the 1860's more and more people were asking why the government didn't substitute something—*anything*—for the trime.

Patterns much like the issued coins were struck in copper, aluminum, and nickel in 1865. The obverse has a left-facing Liberty head wearing a coronet inscribed LIBERTY, with the date at bottom. UNITED STATES is at the left rim, OF AMERICA at right. The reverse has a rim wreath around a large Roman numeral III. The edge is plain. The designer was James P. Longacre.

The alloy of "nickel" 3¢ coins actually is slightly different from Dr. Feuchtwanger's: instead of including zinc, it's three-to-one cupronickel—75 percent copper and 25 percent nickel. The coin weighs 30 grains, about three-fifths as much as today's cent.

FIG. 12–5. Three cents, 1865, obverse. The Liberty portrait on this cupronickel coin is one of the least pleasing. That might be one of the reasons why 3¢ "nickels" were so unpopular.

FIG. 12–6. Three cents, 1865, reverse.

Nickel 3¢ coins were issued 1865–89, except 1877, 1878, and 1886, the Proofs-only years. However, some of the Proofs of all three dates did reach circulation. Top mintage was just under 11.5 million, in 1865. After that, mintage declined until only 21,561 coins were made in 1889 and 3,436 of those were Proofs.

In Philadelphia in 1866 you could have bought a copy of the *Evening Bulletin* with a nickel 3¢ piece, and two 3¢ coins would get you a gallon of blackberries in Morgantown, W. Va., in the summer of 1880. In the last year of issue a 3¢ coin could buy a copy of the Washington *Post*. But the nickel coin, like its older brother, just wasn't well enough liked to be successful.

Prices for common dates are around $4 to $7 for Good condition specimens and $6 to $9 for Fine. Like trimes, the cupronickel 3¢ coin is much more attractive in higher grades.

Star-Line dates are 1883 and 1889. The lone Marginal is 1884.

This isn't our most striking design, but it's well put together and a competent example of numismatic art. It deserves a spot in your collection.

Among varieties are 1865 with date positioned left or right, 1887 with 7 over 6 (7/6), and 1870 with double date.

13

Our *First* Five-Center

Our 5¢ coin hasn't always been a "nickel"—once it was *half of a dime*.

The half-disme (that "s" was dropped after 1793) is accepted as one of our first coins, even though it wasn't struck in the new U.S. Mint at Philadelphia. That mint, in fact, was still being built at the time. The coins evidently were minted in the basement of Mr. John Harper, a saw-maker, at 6th and Cherry Streets (the mint

FIG. 13–1. Half-disme, 1792, obverse. One of our most famous coins. The story of Washington's giving his silver for these coins once was thought to be legend, but it's evidently true. This piece is in the National Collection, Smithsonian Institution.

was at what's now 7th and Filbert). The coin is silver and weighs half as much as a dime. The word "disme," an early form of our modern "dime," was the Americanized form of the French *dixième* ("tenth").

John Dye wrote in 1883 that the imported coin-presses "arrived at the mint on Friday, the 21st day of September, 1792, were put in operation the ninth day of October following, and first used for striking the pattern half-dimes of 1792." Though Dye calls these "patterns" here, he repeats that passage almost word for word later in his *Coin Encyclopedia,* and *omits* "pattern." According to several sources, the 1792 half-dimes were made from silver plate furnished by George Washington. Mintage estimates of 2,000 apparently are the right ones; it's reported that $100 worth of coins were struck.

These half-dismes are a little smaller than today's dime. They show a left-facing portrait which looks as if it ought to be Martha Washington. Some collectors think it was, but Adams and Woodin say it probably was "a crude imitation of Dupre's beautiful 'Libertas Americana' medal." The date is below the portrait. Around the rim is LIB. PAR. OF SCIENCE & INDUSTRY (abbreviations are for "Liberty" and "Parent"). On the reverse is a scrawny eagle with outspread wings. National identification (UNI STATES OF AMERICA) is around the rim, and HALF is above DISME at bottom. A small star is below the value. The coin weighs 20.8 grains, about half as much as a modern cent.

Joseph Wright and Robert Birch are variously credited by some collectors with engraving the dies for this coin. It's sometimes said that Ephraim Brasher designed it; he reportedly made part of the silver service for Martha Washington.

Dye says many 1792 half-dismes "went into general circulation for a time, hence should be considered a regular coinage. . . ." A Harmer, Rooke auction catalog comments, "Washington . . . seems to have regarded them as a regular issue."

Patterns were made and dies evidently were prepared in 1794; but coins with Robert Scot's new design weren't struck until February 1795. It would be natural to use prepared dies when coins at last could be struck. Half-dimes made later in 1795 are dated correctly.

These show Liberty facing right, with LIBERTY above and the date at bottom. Around the rim at left and right are varying numbers of stars, from 13 to 16. The reverse features a moderately realistic eagle standing and spreading its wings. UNITED STATES OF AMERICA is at the rim, outside a wreath.

A third design, the Draped Bust type, was issued 1796–1805. Its right-facing Liberty is no more realistic than the lady on the earlier design. Beginning in 1800 the small eagle on the reverse is replaced by a "heraldic" one with a U.S. shield on its chest, a scroll lettered E PLURIBUS UNUM in its beak and 13 arrows and an olive branch in its talons. Above the eagle are stars and clouds.

Five of these coins would buy a pound of maple sugar in Frankfort, Ky., in October 1801.

After a 24-year pause, half-dimes again were issued in 1829. This Liberty Cap (or Capped Bust) design features a left-facing Liberty wearing a turban-like liberty cap with LIBERTY inscribed

FIG. 13–2. Half-dime, 1800, obverse. This LIBEKTY variety is in the National Collection, Smithsonian Institution. The apparent misspelling was caused by either a broken letter punch or a filled die at the top of the R.

FIG. 13–3. Half-dime, 1829, reverse.

on it. The portrait is larger, but no more lifelike, than the discarded one. The reverse, though, is improved. It still shows a heraldic eagle, but the shield is smaller and the eagle is more realistic; instead of holding the E PLURIBUS UNUM scroll, the eagle stands below it. And for the first time the half-dime shows a denomination—5c is at the reverse bottom.

Half-dimes shared the trimes' problems, and were less than overwhelmingly popular. If you had one in your pocket, it slipped through even a tiny hole. Merchants found half-dimes easy to lose, as coin after coin disappeared through cracks in the wooden cash boxes.

In January 1837 Congress passed an Act cutting the coin's weight to 20.625 grains and boosting the proportion of silver from 89.24 percent to 90 percent.

On the Liberty Seated type of 1837–73 our American goddess holds a shield in her right hand and a pole with a liberty cap on top in her left. Liberty sits facing right, but with her head turned to face left. The date is at bottom and LIBERTY is inscribed on a diagonal band crossing the shield. The reverse has a laurel wreath around HALF DIME, with UNITED STATES OF AMERICA outside the wreath. The obverse rim is plain on 1837 and 1838–O coins; the 1838–59 ones have 13 stars around the rim, and the U.S. shield is closer to vertical.

On January 20, 1849, J. Irving of Alexandria, La., advertised in *The Red River Republican* that his new butcher stall "will always be supplied with a good article of meat, which he will charge but 5 cents a pound for." In 1852, three half-dimes would buy a pound of smoking tobacco at the Fountain City Grocery in Fond Du Lac, Wis. And in 1856, two half-dimes could pay for a pound of codfish or one of bacon in Lawrence, Kans.

Until 1838 only Philadelphia made these coins. New Orleans also made them 1838–60 and San Francisco joined in for 1863–73. You'll find the mint mark on the reverse, usually inside the wreath but just below it on certain coins.

Top mintage belongs to the 1853 Philadelphia "with arrows" variety—over 13 million were made. The "arrows" are small arrowheads put next to the date after the weight was cut to 19.2 grains that February. They remained on the coin through 1855.

FIG. 13–4. Half-dime, 1850, obverse. One reason few collectors are enthusiastic about half-dimes probably is that the little coins have no individuality in design.

FIG. 13–5. Half-dime, 1855, with arrows, reverse. National identification was part of the reverse design when this coin was made.

FIG. 13–6. Half-dime, 1872, obverse. National identification replaced the stars around the rim beginning in 1860.

FIG. 13–7. Half-dime, 1872, reverse. The value-in-wreath design is on many U.S. coins.

From 1860 on, national identification replaces stars around the obverse. During the process of changing the design some half-dimes were struck without UNITED STATES OF AMERICA on *either* side (only 100 were struck in 1860). These are commonly called the "transitional patterns," but numismatist Walter Breen charges that Mint Director J. R. Snowden made them to sell to collectors. Logic supports Breen, for there was no reason to strike patterns lacking national identification. On 1860 and later coins, the wreath, with more space available, becomes a larger and better detailed one of corn, cotton, tobacco, and wheat. You could use one of these later coins in Virginia City, Mont., in 1864, to buy a pound of candles.

Mintage ranged from 8,000 in 1867 to the 1853 figure, but some dates are special cases. For instance, many of the 160,000 "no arrows" 1853–O coins were melted at New Orleans. Proofs were struck at least in 1829–32, 1843–48, and 1855–73. Many later regular-issue dates cost $7.50 or less Good, and under $12 Fine.

There are many varieties in design detail, varying letter and number sizes and overdates. Two famous error coins are the 1796 with Liberty spelled LIKERTY and the 1800 one with LIBEKTY.

Star-Line dates are 1843, 1847, 1848, 1849, 1852, 1861, 1870, and Proof 1862. Marginals are 1841, 1858, 1863, 1865, 1865–S, 1869, 1872, 1873, and Proofs of 1868 and 1869.

14

Shield Nickels

Cupronickel 5¢ pieces date back to
only 1866. Here's the story of
the first one.

Congress passed an Act on May 16, 1866, authorizing our first nickel 5¢ coin, the Shield nickel. Its weight and its 75 percent copper, 25 percent nickel composition are the same as those of today's nickels. It's .75 mm. smaller in diameter than later nickels. Like nickel 3¢ pieces, Shield nickels were supposed to replace fractional currency in denominations under 10¢.

For the obverse James B. Longacre used a large U.S. shield in an inverted laurel wreath similar to the design he'd drawn three years before for the 2¢. IN GOD WE TRUST is above; the date is at bottom. The reverse has a large 5 surrounded by 13 stars symbolizing the original states. UNITED STATES OF AMERICA is around top and side rims, with CENTS at bottom flanked by dots.

In 1866 and early 1867 the stars were separated by lines representing rays of light. Dropping these rays made the design cleaner and created a famous variety. "No rays" coins, made during most of that year, cost much less than "with rays" ones.

Patterns dated 1865, all of which I thought were made in preparation for the coin's issue, include some with stars and rays round the 5, as issued, and some *without* rays. The latter, R. W.

FIG. 14–1. Five cents, 1868, obverse. Note the resemblance this coin bears to the 2¢. James B. Longacre designed both, and evidently wanted to get more use out of this design.

FIG. 14–2. Five cents, 1868, reverse. Early issues had rays between the stars, but the rays made the coin look too crowded.

Julian charged in the January 1975 *Coins,* almost certainly were made in 1867 or 1868. The "1865 no-rays" pattern is, therefore, "an outdated concoction designed for sale to collectors," he said.

In the first year of issue there were 14.7 million Shield nickels issued. You can buy one in Good for $7 to $9—but a Proof lists at $1,200 and is one of our highest-priced nickels.

High mintage came in 1867, with 30.9 million; in Fine, the "with rays" (Type 1) costs about $27 and the "no rays" about $11. Lowest mintage, for 1877, is an *estimated* 500 Proofs that aren't even listed in official mint records!

You could take three Shield nickels to Corning's, in Hartford, Conn., in 1867 and buy a pack of lawyer's envelopes; or pay one for a drink of soda water at the same city's Lambe Apothecary.

Like 3¢ nickels, Shield nickels were struck only at Philadelphia. The last year of issue was 1883, when 1,456,919 were made.

The 18-year issue period was short enough to curtail varieties, but there are several recut dates and mottoes, as well as overdates (1869 over 8, 1882 over 1, and 1883 over 2), double dates (1866, 1868), and others.

Star-Line dates are 1881, 1882, and Proof 1882. Marginals are 1870, 1872, and Proof 1879.

These coins were issued together with half-dimes until the half-dime was abandoned in 1873. From then until the Liberty nickel appeared, Shield nickels represented the 5¢ denomination in our coinage.

15

Nickel With a "V"

*Any idea where our expression
"to josh" comes from?*

The Liberty or "V" nickel replaced the Shield design in 1883. Nickel, bronze, and aluminum patterns had been struck in 1882, and Charles E. Barber's design had been in the works for some time. Some 1882 patterns either entered circulation or were carried as pocket pieces for many years. Liberty's portrait, facing left, is on the obverse. She wears a coronet inscribed LIBERTY, behind which is a wreath of cotton and wheat. Thirteen stars are around the rim and the date is at the bottom.

Now, the *first* reverse used has a large v in a wreath of corn, cotton, tobacco, and wheat. UNITED STATES OF AMERICA is around the rim with E PLURIBUS UNUM at the bottom. But the word "Cents" *doesn't appear anywhere on the coin!*

That's surprising enough by itself, but add this: several patterns have a reverse with FIVE at top and CENTS at the bottom!

Immediately, wide-awake but low-minded persons plated new nickels with gold. Many fakers reeded the coins' edge, probably

FIG. 15–1. Five cents, 1883, obverse.

FIG. 15–2. Five cents, 1883 no-cents type, reverse. Plating these coins with gold produced the famous "racketeer nickels" which today are —illogically—prized by collectors.

FIG. 15–3. Five cents, 1883, with CENTS type, reverse.

with a file. A swindler would walk into a store, choose an article of merchandise and then, *saying nothing*, put the plated nickel down on the counter. The storekeeper assumed the coin was a new type of $5 gold piece.

When his suspicion finally was aroused—maybe when later customers paid with *un*plated nickels, the storekeeper went out looking for the man who'd spent the "gold piece"—and for a policeman. But when the swindler was arrested, he proved he'd never *said* the coin was a half-eagle! And it was no crime to accept the "gift" of extra change.

One of these fakers is supposed to have been a deaf mute named Josh Tatum. It has been speculated that this man was responsible for the addition to the language of "to josh," meaning to joke or fool.

So mint officials got busy to add the needed word. One idea was to put a curved banner with "Cents" across the V. Patterns were minted, but they didn't click. Instead, E PLURIBUS UNUM was shifted above the wreath, which, along with the v, was made smaller, and CENTS was added at the reverse bottom.

Strangely, though the mint made only 5,479,519 "no cents" coins and over 16 million "with cents" ones, the more plentiful coin costs more. In Fine, "no cents" costs about $2.50, while "with cents" costs about $8.

These plated coins, usually called "racketeer nickels" today, were illegal for many years. "The gold plating puts them in a contraband category," a U.S. Secret Service spokesman explained to me several years ago. Some coin dealers plated regular "no cents" nickels with brass to circumvent the ban on this use of gold. Others went ahead and sold gold-plated nickels. Based on an April 23, 1971 amendment to the Gold Regulations, the Office of Domestic Gold and Silver Operations finally ruled that genuine racketeer nickels are legal for us to own.

Top mintage was over 39.5 million for 1911. Common dates cost about $2 to $4 in Fine. The rarest regular-issue date is 1912–S. All of these coins were made at Philadelphia until Denver struck 8,474,000 in 1912 and San Francisco minted 238,000.

This must have been a popular coin, for several early dates' mintages are over 10 million and most later dates were struck in quantities of 20 million or more.

One of these coins could pay for a Cubanola cigar at the A. Kiefer Drug Co., in Logansport, Ind., in 1896. In 1904 a nickel would buy you a pound of dates from R. S. Place of Davenport, Iowa. And in 1910 F. O. Sherwood's store advertised "Mother's Bread, 5¢/loaf" in the Silverton, Colo., *Standard*.

Estimates of value for 1913 Liberty nickels vary. It's still not clear how these fabled coins came to be, or when—they may have been made in 1917 or 1918. In *The Numismatist* for December 1919, Samuel W. Brown—a former mint storekeeper—offered to pay $500 for each coin. In 1920 he exhibited all five at the ANA convention. He tried to sell them for $600 each, but nobody wanted them because of their questionable background. *Coin Prices* in 1974 specifically charged that the coins "were produced in secrecy at the instigation of Samuel Brown, a one time mint employee. . . ."

The late J. V. McDermott bought one in 1943 from coin dealer James Kelly (for $300, said *Coins Magazine*; for $900, said *Numismatic News*). Thanks to McDermott's tours and constant exhibiting, the 1913 coins remained well known. And the price kept climbing.

McDermott's coin now belongs to Aubrey Bebee of Omaha, Nebr., who paid $46,000 for it. King Farouk is supposed to have paid $3,750 for one of the coins and later bought another. One of his nickels brought $3,731 when auctioned at Cairo in 1954.

Don't waste your time looking for 1913 Liberties—all are well known and in collections. But it's not a waste to look for other dates. Your hunting will be in dealers' and auction catalogs. Every collector should own at least one Liberty nickel. The design is beautiful, artistic, and a credit to our coinage.

Star-Line dates are Proofs of 1907 and 1908. Marginals are 1894, 1900, 1901, 1904, 1908, and Proofs of 1887, 1902, and 1905.

16

Chief X Three-Names

The controversy made for a
crowded warpath.

In 1911, James Earle Fraser, son of a railroad construction engineer and pupil of Augustus Saint-Gaudens, proposed an Indian-and-buffalo design for the nickel. From travels with his father, Fraser was familiar with several Indian tribes.

Secretary of the Treasury Franklin MacVeagh gave the idea preliminary approval January 13, 1913. There was a delay of about six weeks before the design won final approval. Patterns were struck during January—possibly more as presentation pieces than as any necessary test—showing the design as it was adopted, except that there's no incuse F (for Fraser) below the date. The obverse has an American Indian facing right, with a hair braid at the right side of his head, and wearing three feathers in his hair; the tip of the third is visible past the two more prominent ones. LIBERTY is at the upper right rim and the date, horizontal, is at lower left.

The "buffalo" on the reverse—actually a bison—is a stylized portrait of then seventeen-year-old Black Diamond; Fraser must have seen him at the New York Zoological Gardens, where the bison was displayed as a gift of the Barnum & Bailey circus. His left-facing standing figure almost fills the coin's reverse. Around the top is UNITED STATES OF AMERICA, with a tiny E PLURIBUS UNUM just above the animal's sloping back. At the bottom is FIVE CENTS. Production of the new coin began February 21, 1913.

I call the Indian "Chief X Three-Names" because the evidence is overwhelming that no single man was "the Indian on the nickel." Two-Gun White Calf (Piegan) believed he was, but his

FIG. 16–1. Five cents, 1913, Type 1, reverse. Note the "mound" on which the bison seems to stand.

FIG. 16–2. Five cents, 1936–S, obverse. Who was the third model?

descendants have denied this. Chief John Big Tree (Seneca) believed for over 50 years that the coin showed him; when he died, newspapers honored his claim—until they began hearing from collectors who pointed out that he had no proof of the claim. (Some numismatists do think he was one of the models, so you might say they honor his claim with "reservations.")

I don't know whether it was a result of this claim, but *Coin World* reported (December 10, 1969) that John Big Tree posed for the Indian-head emblem of the Pontiac automobile.

Fraser once said he had made a composite portrait showing all the fine features of many Indians. That sounds like a public relations statement. In 1931 Fraser told the Bureau of the Mint he had used three models. One was Chief Two Moons (Cheyenne); the second was Chief Iron Tail (Sioux); and the third was—but Fraser *couldn't remember who he was!* Lee Martin once quoted Laura G. Fraser, the designer's wife, in *COINage*, as saying that Two Moons posed for the forehead and Iron Tail posed for the chin. The third model remained unidentified. It might have been John Big Tree—or it might not.*

Controversy over this coin began right on schedule. In January 1913 Treasury Secretary MacVeagh said the Indian-Buffalo design "will give this coin a place with the best modern work." But *The Numismatist* attacked the bison's rough surface, charging

---

* Tribal affiliations vary according to different references. I've listed tribes as they appear in most cases. If there's an error, my apologies to the offended tribe.

that the shaggy hide would encourage counterfeiters. Sure enough, cast counterfeits were reported in 1914. The ANA publication also warned that the exposed date would wear off quickly. As we know, this also proved correct.

Another problem was caused by the exposed FIVE CENTS below the bison. The denomination, which appeared to be on a mound on which the animal stood, quickly wore off. But until it did, and until the buffalo was somewhat worn, the coins were too thick for stacking and also, it's reported, for vending machine slots.

Other objections were that the designer's initial was too prominent, the E PLURIBUS UNUM was too crowded, there was no "In God We Trust," and the bison's face looked too much like that of a human being.

That was the Type 1 coin. Philadelphia made almost 31 million, Denver struck just over 5.3 million, and San Francisco released a little over 2 million.

On Type 2 nickels a straight ground line was cut across the base of the design and FIVE CENTS was lowered to the height of the rest of the surface. This feature, along with the large raised area on the bison, is why so many nickels have a reverse that grades better than the obverse. It's also why there are so many coins with clear mint marks, right below the denomination, but no date.

In the period 1913–38 one or more mints made Buffalo nickels every year except 1922, 1932, and 1933. Philadelphia, Denver, and San Francisco all made the coin in 17 out of its 26 years of issue. Top mintage came in 1936, when Philadelphia struck 118,997,000 regular-issue nickels plus over 4,000 Proofs. Lowest mintage is the 970,000 of 1926–S, which cost $12 to $15 in Fine. Some common dates cost only about 30¢ in Fine. Proofs were struck 1913–16 and 1936–37, with mintage from 600 in 1916 to 5,769 in 1937.

A nickel had pretty good purchasing power then. In 1914 one would buy a copy of the Sunday *New York Tribune*; in 1918, A. S. Hinds of Portland, Me., advertised a sample with three kinds of (ice?) cream for 5¢. In 1924 you could buy Coca-Cola for a nickel. I've used dateless Buffaloes to buy soft drinks, but it takes two of them now.

FIG. 16–3. Five cents, 1913, Type 2, reverse. Mint workers created a sunken area by cutting a ground line below the bison. By sinking the surface and putting the denomination there, they made the coin thin enough to fit into vending machine slots.

But there are consolations, and one is that a few Buffalo nickels *still circulate*. You won't find one every day, or even every week, but you'll spot some if you watch for them.

There are too many varieties to list—nickels struck on cent planchets, double dates from 1913 on, double mint marks, and others. Some are popular, some aren't. The 1938–D with D over S is well known, but the one with *double* D over S has only a small following. The 1937–D with the "three-legged buffalo"— caused by a die that was filled, damaged and poorly repaired, or simply overpolished, depending on your information source—is widely sought; but 1930–S with eight legs and 1935–D with two legs are less popular.

Star-Line dates are 1934, 1937–D, and 1937–S. Marginals are 1913–S Type 1, 1914–S, 1929–D, 1930–S, and 1931–S.

Whether you're an investor, nickel specialist, variety lover, or just plain coin collector, this is a coin you can enjoy adding to your collection. It's hard to find Buffalo nickels with clear dates— but doesn't that just add to the challenge?

17

The Man of Monticello

A switch in design, the "silver
nickels" of World War II and some
crime-fighting coins.

The Jefferson nickel was minted first in October 1938 and released in November. From then through 1949, Philadelphia, Denver, and San Francisco all issued these coins every year except 1968, 1969, and 1970. Since 1949 at least two mints made nickels each year; Philadelphia made the coins every year except 1968, 1969, and 1970.

Relatively few people know that only part of designer Felix O. Schlag's plan for the coin became reality. The contest rules specified that the obverse was to show an authentic portrait of Thomas Jefferson and that the reverse was to have Monticello. Schlag drew a left-facing portrait wearing wig and pigtail, based on a portrait in a second-hand magazine he had found in a used-book store. IN GOD WE TRUST is at left, LIBERTY and the date are at right. On the reverse is Jefferson's home seen from about a 45-degree angle; next to the building are shrubbery and a tree. UNITED STATES OF AMERICA around the bottom and E PLURIBUS UNUM around the top are separated by small dots. FIVE CENTS is below the building. The starkly modernistic lettering has R, S, and D uncomfortably narrow.

As you can tell, some changes were made. I'd guess patterns were struck with the original design, since it's said that the reverse caused problems for the mint's high-speed machinery.

Revisions may have been done by mint staff engravers, or by Schlag himself under government orders. Monticello became more stylized and the viewpoint was switched to head-on. MONTICELLO was added below the building, which was enlarged to

FIG. 17–1. Five cents, 1968–S, obverse. The 1968 coin was the first 5¢ piece since 1954 to carry the S mint mark.

stretch almost from rim to rim, and the denomination was lowered; the shrubbery and tree disappeared. National identification and motto were squeezed into less space.

Schlag left his initials off the design. He once said it never occurred to him to put them on, but later indicated he was tired of the whole matter by the time the government finally approved the coin.

A nickel would pay for a telephone call, a soft drink, or a greeting card in those days. Three would buy a pound of sliced bacon at the A&P Food Store in Central City, Ky., in 1938.

WARNIX

One coin that belongs in our collections is one of the 5¢ pieces known as "warnix." World War II rocked our numismatic boat, making copper and nickel too important to the war effort for use in coins. As with cents, the government considered recalling nickels, but decided to use a new alloy instead. On October 8, 1942, a new 5¢ piece appeared: 56 percent copper, 9 percent manganese, and 35 percent *silver*—our first silver 5¢ coin since the half-dimes of 1873. The new coins were called "silver nickels" and "nickelless nickels," but the term "wartime nickels" caught on, and eventually was shortened to "warnix" (one coin is a "warnick").

To mark the changed alloy, mint marks were enlarged and moved from their spot at right of Monticello to above the dome. Artistically this seems to me the place where they should have been all the time.

Philadelphia had made nearly 50 million nickels by changeover time. To mark new-type coins a P mint mark was used—making warnix the *only* U.S. coins to carry the Philadelphia mint mark.

(Denver made only Type 1—cupronickel—in 1942; San Francisco made only warnix, or Type 2.)

Warnix continued through 1945. Between 1942 and 1945 the three mints issued almost 870 million of them.

Many people are astonished to learn that warnix helped the Secret Service catch a counterfeiter. In 1958 the Secret Service caught up with sixty-two-year-old Francis L. Henning in Cleveland, and charged him with making counterfeit 1944 nickels. The obverse of his fakes was that of a 1944 coin, but the reverse was that of an *older* Philadelphia coin *which lacked the P mint mark.* Alert members of the Camden County (N.J.) Coin Club ran across some of the fakes in 1955, simultaneously with a bank teller. With two inquiries on hand, the Secret Service went into action. It discovered Henning's equipment when called by the new tenant of the room he had abandoned, and eventually caught up with him. Henning's counterfeits—struck in the correct prewarnix cupronickel alloy—earned him a three-year prison term.

The 1944 fakes still turn up in circulation. If you find one, *you are bound by law to turn it in to the U.S. Secret Service.* It's still a counterfeit, and illegal to keep. But check it first. A "1944 plain" nickel *is* a legitimate mint error *if* it's a warnick. A die whose mint mark was clogged with grease or dirt would produce such coins.

But that's not all—a warnick also helped trap a Soviet spy whose downfall was his lack of numismatic savvy. Colonel Rudolph Abel, the USSR's top man for the U.S. East Coast, used a "box" (hollow coin) to pass on information. In 1953 he accidentally paid newsboy Jimmy Bozart with this nickel. When the boy later happened to drop the coin, it split open. Jimmy picked it up, examined the two halves and the strip of microfilm and headed home. On his father's advice, the boy passed the box on to a

FIG. 17-2. Reverse of a "warnick" struck at Philadelphia during the 1942–45 period. Few of the "silver nickels" are circulating now.

policeman, who contacted the FBI—which put Abel under surveillance.

Half of the "coin" was the reverse of a warnick, with a large P mint mark over the dome. But the obverse was dated 1948! When a defecting Soviet agent mentioned a Colonel Abel in New York, the pickup was made and Abel went for an undesired vacation.

Warnix still circulate, but you won't often see one. It's a challenge to put together a set from pocket change.

One more point. Some collectors and dealers designate Philadelphia's coins by adding "P" to the date. Warnix are a good argument against this: it's bad practice to speak of 1944–P cents or dimes, which don't exist, when there are *real* 1944–P coins.

SINCE 1946

After the war, we went back to cupronickel nickels with small mint marks. These issues brought both high and low mintage figures for the series.

Top mintage *date* is 1964–D, but not all 1964–D nickels were made in 1964—about five out of seven were struck in 1965. The true high-mintage nickel is the one struck in Denver in 1965 but marked 1964–D, which I'd identify as 1964–D (65–D), with 1,331,475,320 struck. However, since there seems to be no way to tell when any single "1964–D" nickel was coined, we're left with 1974 as top-mintage identifiable date, with 601,752,000 minted.

The same problem exists for low mintage. The true low-mintage Jefferson nickel is 1965—only 972,000 1965-dated nickels were struck at Philadelphia that year. But there are 136,131,380 nickels dated 1965: which ones were made that year? The lowest-mintage identifiable nickel is 1950–D, with 2,630,030 minted.

Proofs were struck 1938–42, then discontinued because of the war. Minting resumed in 1950, dropped after 1964 because of the coin shortage and finally started again, at San Francisco, in 1968.

Varieties are everywhere. In 14 different years, at all three mints, nickels were stamped on cent planchets; double dates are known for several years; double mint marks start with 1938–D and continue up to today; the double dome is known on many dates, often together with a double profile portrait.

In 1966 a small FS was added in the exergue. To make room for the designer's initials a small slice was taken off the bottom of the portrait. Mint Director Eva Adams presented Mr. and Mrs. Schlag with the first two 1966 nickels struck with the FS, and *COINage* magazine called these the only Proof coins minted in 1966.

Two years later, mint marks were restored and moved to the obverse; all other lettering on the "heads" side follows the line of the rim, but the D or S is vertical.

There is no Star-Line date. Marginals are 1938–D, 1946–S, 1958, and Proofs of 1942 and 1953.

18

Early Dimes

From dixième to disme to dime.

The Act of April 2, 1792, provided for a "disme," a silver coin valued at one-tenth of a dollar. It would contain 37.5 grains of silver, with the rest of its 41.6 grains of weight made up by alloy.

A few dimes struck in 1792 in silver and copper were evidently all patterns. They have a left-facing Liberty head whose hair streams behind her as if in a wind. The date is below this portrait. At the rim is LIBERTY PARENT OF SCIENCE & INDUS. On the reverse is a not-at-all lifelike flying eagle much like the dove on some Vatican coins and on Canada's 1967 cent. UNITED STATES OF AMERICA is around the top and sides, and DISME is horizontal at

FIG. 18–1. Disme, 1792 pattern, copper, reverse. This almost certainly has been a museum piece since it was struck. However, dismes struck in silver probably circulated. Coin is in the National Collection, Smithsonian Institution.

bottom. The edge has diagonal reading. It's believed that only about 15 to 20 were struck.

Dimes of 1796 began the Draped Bust type, with a mintage of 22,135. They're the most expensive early dimes, costing approximately $215 in Fair, about $775 Fine, and about $3,000 to $6,500 Uncirculated.

Draped Bust dimes have Robert Scot's (or maybe Gilbert Stuart's) right-facing bust of Liberty with her hair lying down along the back of her neck in a free, flowing style. LIBERTY is at the top and the date is below the bust. On the reverse is a scrawny eagle perching inside a wreath, with raised wings. UNITED STATES OF AMERICA is around the rim. The coins are larger than today's dimes, but there's no "E Pluribus Unum" or denomination.

A new reverse came into use in 1798, the heraldic eagle holding an E PLURIBUS UNUM banner in its beak and arrows and an olive branch in its talons. A U.S. shield is on its chest. Clouds and stars are above the eagle. This design continued through 1807.

Mintage of early coins varied from 8,265 in 1804 to 165,000 in 1807. All of these coins were struck at Philadelphia. Most cost $115 or so in Good condition, and $175 or more in Fine.

There are varieties with different-sized numerals and numbers of stars. The only Star-Line date is 1800. Marginals are 1802, 1805, and 1807.

19

Capped Bust Dimes

The in-betweeners of our dime series.

The Draped Bust-Liberty Cap dime appeared in 1809, drawn by John Reich, and lasted partway through 1837. Like earlier coins, they were made by either manpower or horsepower, and all were struck at Philadelphia. None was made dated 1810, 1812, 1813, 1815–19, or 1826, but remember that mint records weren't always accurate nor kept by the calendar year. It has been suggested, for instance, that more than half the 100,000 "1822" dimes were struck with dies dated 1821.

On the obverse is a left-facing Liberty portrait shown to about shoulder length, wearing a liberty cap and low-cut gown; her hair cascades in waves down her neck. There are seven stars at the left rim, six at the right, and the date at bottom. LIBERTY is on the cap's headband.

FIG. 19–1. Dime, 1836, obverse. The Capped Bust design is about as big as a dime design can be without appearing too heavy for the coin.

FIG. 19–2. Dime, 1836, reverse.

A small eagle with U.S. shield on its chest looks to its right on the reverse; its talons hold an olive branch and three arrows; above is a banner lettered E PLURIBUS UNUM. Around top and sides is UNITED STATES OF AMERICA and at bottom is 10C.

In Richmond, Va., you could buy a pound of bacon for a dime in 1809. Some ladies probably found dimes handy in 1815 in Windsor, Vt., where three of the coins would buy a yard of calico from Abner Forbes.

These coins began with a weight of 2.7 grams (slightly more than that of today's nickel) and average diameter of 18.5 mm. From 1828 on, new mint equipment turned out slightly smaller coins.

Varieties are plentiful, including overdates (1823 over 2), large and small date sets (1814, 1821), different-sized denominations (1829, 1830), and others.

The low-mintage date is 1809, with 44,710 struck; but the rarest coin is actually 1822, which can cost $2,500 Uncirculated. Highest mintage came in 1835, when 1,410,000 dimes were made. Common dates cost about $15 to $18 Good and $20 to $26 Fine. Proofs were struck in 1820, 1829–33, 1835–36, and possibly other years.

Star-Line dates are 1814, 1828, 1836, and 1837. Marginals are 1829, 1834, and 1835.

Capped Bust dimes hardly are popular with collectors—but it's good to have one to represent the type, and with its low cost the 1835 is a prime candidate for the job.

20

Our Longest-Lived Dime

"Prices to suit the hard times."
—advertisement, 1843.

Our early dime designs lasted 13 years; later types were in use less than 30 years; but the Liberty Seated design was issued for 54 years!

The Act of January 18, 1837, cut the dime's weight from 41.6 to 41.25 grains and raised the fineness to .900. If we needed anything more to produce a new design, in 1835 Christian Gobrecht began working on the Liberty Seated type. One of his early drawings gained quick approval for use on small silver coins. The authorities probably reasoned that imperfections would be hidden by the small size.

The basic design is Liberty sitting on a rock, twisting her head to look back leftward, her right hand holding a U.S. shield across which is LIBERTY and her left holding a pole atop which is a liberty cap; the date is at bottom. The reverse has simply ONE above DIME in a laurel wreath, with UNITED STATES OF AMERICA around top and sides. The edge is reeded.

In addition to Philadelphia, mints at New Orleans, San Francisco, and Carson City made Liberty Seated dimes. From 1837–91, two or more mints made dimes each year, except in 1837, 1844, 1846–48, 1855, and 1879–83, when Philadelphia was the only dime-producer. Many dates cost only $5 Good and $6 to $10 Fine, thanks to mintages that despite their lowness were high enough to preserve plenty of coins for twentieth-century collectors. Proofs were struck as early as 1850. Top regular-issue mintage came in 1891, when Philadelphia struck 15,310,000 dimes for release. Low-mintage date is 1867, with 6,000 released, but only 20 specimens at most are known of 1842–O and 1860–O. Top price is about $8,000 for an Uncirculated 1860–O.

In 1838 a new subtype appeared, with 13 stars around the obverse rim.

You could have used dimes at Isaac M. Jones's dry goods and hardware store in 1843 in Clarksville, Tenn. He advertised in *The Clarksville Jeffersonian* that May, among his "prices to suit the hard times," a yard of calico for a dime and a yard of chintz for 20¢.

The dime's weight was cut in 1853 by the Act of February 21. The 41.25-grain coin contained more than 10¢ worth of silver, so to prevent wholesale melting it was reduced to 38.4 grains. Arrowheads were put next to the date to show the change; they remained on dimes through 1855. The weight change is why so many earlier dates were melted—their silver was worth more than 10¢.

Two of the lighter dimes would buy you an ounce of Chinese sugar cane seed in Brownsville, Nebr., in January 1857.

"Transitional patterns" similar to half-dime ones, without national identification on either side, were made—maybe for the same reason as the half-dimes. Starting in 1860, UNITED STATES OF AMERICA replaces the stars that formerly decorated the obverse rim. The wreath on the reverse expands into an ornate one of corn, cotton, tobacco, and wheat. Mint marks are at the reverse bottom.

Arrowheads at the date reappeared in 1873–75; the Act of January 12, 1873, increased the coin's weight slightly to 38.58 grains. Philadelphia made both types; San Francisco made only the heavier (Type 2); Carson City struck 12,400 Type 1 coins and 18,791 Type 2's, but only *one* 1873–CC "no arrows" is known

FIG. 20–1. Dime, 1853, with arrows type, obverse. The "arrows" are actually arrowheads and we should call them that, since use of the wrong term can confuse noncollectors and beginning collectors.

today—the rest probably were melted—and evidently only about 20 "with arrows" ones survive.

A dime would buy a cake of soap in 1883 from the Frank Siddalls Soap Co. of Philadelphia, which advertised in the January 25 *Youth's Companion* that its soap "never fails when it falls into the hands of a person of Refinement, Intelligence and Honor."

There are many varieties—1837 coins with large or small date, 1840 and 1841 with or without some drapery lines, 1853 with or without arrows, 1856 large or small date, 1875 branch mint coins with the CC or S within the wreath or below it—there are enough to please almost any collector.

As with other obsolete coins, Liberty Seated dimes won't pile up in your pocket change. Because of relatively low collector interest, it should be worthwhile to try auctions as primary sources. Careful bidding can bring you bargains.

Star-Line dates are 1863, 1864, 1865, 1866, 1867, 1879, 1881, 1885, and Proofs of 1862 and 1890. Marginals are 1846, 1847, 1849, 1857–O, 1858, 1860, 1872, 1873, 1877–S, 1886, 1886–S, 1888, 1891–S, and Proof 1877.

21

Barber Dimes

The smallest of the beautiful trio of 1892
includes one of our top rarities.

When William Barber died in 1880, his son Charles became Chief Mint Engraver. His work assisting his father for ten years and the coins he produced himself prove he earned the job.

After the competition of 1891 flopped (the full story is in Chapter 27), Barber's design appeared on the new dime with his incuse B on the truncation of the neck. Patterns of 1891 show the design substantially as on issued coins. The obverse has a right-facing Liberty head with UNITED STATES OF AMERICA around top and side rims and the date at bottom. Liberty wears a liberty cap, laurel wreath and tiny coronet inscribed LIBERTY. The reverse has ONE DIME in a corn-oak-wheat wreath. Barber wanted to include "In God We Trust" and probably also "E Pluribus Unum," but couldn't because of lack of space.

The first issue was in 1892, when Philadelphia released 12,-120,000 and also made 1,245 Proofs. New Orleans minted 3,841,-700 dimes and San Francisco struck 990,710. Mint marks are at reverse bottom. Top mintage came in 1907, with Philadelphia's 22.2 million; lowest regular-issue mintage is the 440,000 total of 1895–O. Proofs were struck at Philadelphia 1892–1915; top-mintage date is 182, lowest is 1914 with 425 coins. Denver began making dimes in 1906.

Thanks to many mintages over 10 million, some Barber dimes cost $2.50 or less in Fine. The highest-priced date is 1894–S, which brought $12,250 in 1965 and about $50,000 in 1972, and is likely to continue pushing higher.

This probably is our best-known Barber dime, but its origin is mysterious. The mint told Farran Zerbe in 1905 that San Francisco needed to show an additional $2.40 in struck coins at the end of the fiscal year. Dime dies were on hand, so 24 1894–S dimes were minted. There was plenty of time for the order to strike dimes dated 1894 to come through. But that order never arrived, and most 1894–S pieces were bagged and released with other dates. An auction catalog claims the coins are all Proofs and

FIG. 21–1. Dime, 1913, obverse. Barber's dime was the last to use the same obverse as quarters and halves.

FIG. 21–2. Dime, 1913, reverse.

adds, "Of the mere 24 pieces struck, we can definitely account for only five. . . . Two others are said to exist. . . . " Still another story claims the coins were made to test the dies or for assay purposes; one version says ten of them were melted at the mint.

New Orleans made its last dimes in 1909. Philadelphia and San Francisco made both Barber and "Mercury" dimes in 1916, while Denver made only the new type.

You could get the makings of a meal for one of these coins in 1908, when a can of Van Camp's Pork & Beans cost 10¢. Three dimes would buy a pound of sirloin steak in Saint Louis, Mo., in 1914.

This type offers a good selection for variety collectors; among others there are 1893 with 3 over 2, 1895-S with double S, and 1905-O with large or small mint mark.

I haven't seen a Barber dime in circulation since the 1940's, but there probably are a few around. However, you're likely to have better luck in coin shops, auctions, and other collectors' duplicates.

Star-Line dates are 1903-S, 1906-D, 1908-S, 1910-D, 1910-S, 1912-S, and Proofs of 1907 and 1909. Marginals are 1897-O, 1908-S, 1911-S, and Proofs of 1904, 1905, 1906, 1910, 1911, and 1912.

22

Is This Our Most Beautiful Coin?

When a collector looks awed
and speaks of a 1916-D, there's only one coin it can be.

Dimes had the same obverse as higher denomination silver until 1916, when Adolph Alexander Weinman's design appeared. He was one of several sculptors commissioned to submit designs.

FIG. 22–1. Dime, 1945, obverse. Miss Liberty, wearing a winged liberty cap. Since she's descended from the Greek goddess Athena, it's ironic that millions of Americans have mistaken her for the Roman god Mercury.

FIG. 22–2. Dime, 1945, reverse. Weinman's design combines the free, flowing lines of the olive branch with the stark discipline of the fasces.

On the obverse is a left-facing Liberty head wearing a winged liberty cap. LIBERTY is widely spaced around top and sides, with E and R partly hidden by the top of the portrait. IN GOD WE TRUST is in small letters at lower left, in front of the neck. It's balanced by the date, at lower right, and Weinman's monogram level with the motto.

The reverse has a vertical fasces with a battle-axe blade protruding from it at the top, bound by three horizontal and two diagonal bands; around this twines an olive branch. UNITED STATES OF AMERICA is around top and sides, with ONE and DIME at bottom separated by the fasces. Balancing an outthrust of the olive branch at left of the fasces is a small E PLURIBUS UNUM at right.

In 1916 *Numismatist* editor Frank Duffield queried Weinman about the design's symbolism. Weinman, then forty-six, replied that the fasces was for unity of strength, the battle-axe represented our readiness to defend the nation, and the olive branch symbolized our love of peace.

The wings on Liberty's cap cause a very slight resemblance to Mercury, Roman counterpart of Hermes, messenger of the Greek gods; but this is a *liberty cap*, not a helmet, and the wings stand for freedom of thought. Weinman's model is supposed to have been Mrs. Elsie Stevens, wife of poet Wallace Stevens.

What should we call this coin? "Mercury dime," the popular

name, is *wrong* and sounds to me like someone raking fingernails across a blackboard. *COINage*'s Lee Martin suggested "Weinman dime," which fits our custom of naming some coins for designers. Brown & Dunn call it the "Winged Liberty (Mercury)" dime. The Red Book uses "Winged Head of Liberty or 'Mercury' type."

I suggest the shorter "Winged-Head Liberty," or "WHL," as the shortest possible correct name. That's what you'll see in this book from here on.

Three mints produced WHL dimes; Denver's D and San Francisco's S are on the reverse, between ONE and the stem of the olive branch.

Back in my high-school days, I was riding a crowded local bus to school one morning and standing near the fare box. A man boarded the bus and dropped some coins into the box. I noticed that one dime looked old, so I asked the driver for it. He started cranking the machinery which counted change and totaled receipts. As we neared school, my tension grew: the less my chance of getting the coin, the more I wanted it.

Finally the bus pulled to the curb. The driver plunged his hand into the pile of change and came up with the dime. I handed him two nickels, thanked him and stepped off the bus.

Then I looked down and almost fainted.

In my palm lay a dime minted in Denver in the year 1916.

For two nickels I had purchased the fabulous 1916-D, rarest WHL dime of all.

This coin, only About Good, still is in my collection and I wouldn't sell it for any price. Collectors will understand my feelings. For those who don't know the coin's significance, Philadelphia minted over 22 million WHL dimes in 1916 and San Francisco made 10.45 million. But Denver produced only 264,000, lowest regular-issue figure for the entire series.

Issue was scheduled for May 1916, but Weinman was ill and this plus technical problems held up production until August. The first pieces were released in late October and were immediately successful. Typical comments were "excellent workmanship," "delighted," and "youthful, refined and of gentle expression." One collector wrote to *The Numismatist* that the WHL dime was "the best piece of work that the United States mint has turned out in a century."

The 1916–D's rarity, several varieties' popularity and many dates' high mintage combined to keep the public aware of the WHL dime. Even in the early years it was plentiful: Philadelphia struck more than 55 million in 1917. So the coin was available to many collectors.

One or more mints issued dimes every year between 1916 and 45, except for 1922, 1932, and 1933. Almost all silver dimes are out of circulation; the remaining few are probably 1942 and 1944 coins, whose mintages topped 200 million! Proofs were struck from 1936 to 42, at Philadelphia only, with totals increasing from 4,130 the first year to 22,329 the last.

During this coin's lifetime there were quite a few items you could purchase for "one thin dime." Macy's grocery department in New York sold 10-ounce cans of Italian style spaghetti for 10¢ in 1917. In the Loft candy stores' Sunday specials in June 1935 you could buy a chocolate ice cream soda for a dime. And in Central City, Ky., in March 1938, a dime would buy a dozen doughnuts, a 20-ounce loaf of rye bread or a pound of chocolate drops at the A&P Food Store.

Two controversial WHL dimes are 1923–D and 1930–D. Neither is mentioned in official mint records. Yeoman states in the Red Book: "Dimes dated 1923–D and 1930–D are counterfeit." A Secret Service spokesman told me, referring to 1923–D, "To the best of our knowledge, that is true." Ray Young wrote in *Coin Prices* that "Evidently the counterfeiters paired a Philadelphia or San Francisco 1923 obverse with a Denver reverse of another date." If they're not simply "business counterfeits," where do these coins come from? A few numismatists have expressed ideas, at least about 1923–D pieces.

Frank Spadone suggests they might be foreign-made. Numismatist Andrew Verbance once supposed that they were made with official dies and equipment but without official authority. Lee Martin of *COINage* reported a probable total of 14 to 50 such coins.

WHL dimes are a fertile field for variety collectors. Over 100 double dates are known; there are off-metal dimes and dime planchets struck with other coins' dies; there are loads of double mint marks and several large-and-small mint mark sets; and others. The best-known varieties are 1945–S with large or small S and the rare 1942 with 2 over 1. The latter evidently resulted when a die was struck late in 1941 with a hub dated 1941 and then given a second strike with a hub used for preparing the next year's dies.

Weinman's design is clean, dramatic, and expertly drawn. It wasn't his fault that Mussolini's fascists chose for their symbol the object he had pictured. But this did cause a drop in the WHL dime's popularity.

Star-Line dates are 1935–D, 1937–D, and 1939–S. Marginals are 1916–S, 1928–S, 1929–D, 1929–S, 1930, 1931–D, 1934–D, 1937–S, 1938, 1938–D, 1940–D, 1940–S, 1944–S, 1945–D, 1945–S, and Proof 1939.

Future collectors won't find these coins in circulation; the best hunting grounds already are auction catalogs and other collectors' duplicates, as well as coin stores. Several dates cost 75¢ to $1.75 in Fine, and $3 to $7.50 Uncirculated.

This is one of my favorite U.S. coins; for many years I considered it our most beautiful coin of all—as some collectors still do—and I'm certain its popularity will continue to grow.

23

FDR Dimes

A persistent legend, some discarded designs
and the switch to clad coins.

There's a legend concerning our current dime, which shows the late President Franklin Delano Roosevelt, that for some reason FDR agreed to put on a U.S. coin (often the FDR dime itself) the initials of Soviet premier Josef Stalin. Gullible people speak vaguely of a "secret political agreement" and close their ears when you demonstrate how ridiculous the story is.

Of course, FDR probably never even dreamed of a Roosevelt

FIG. 23–1. Dime, 1969–D, obverse. Though it was issued to honor the late President Franklin D. Roosevelt, this dime is a regular issue coin rather than a commemorative. The 1969–D issue includes both low-D (shown) and high-D varieties.

dime. The little JS below the left-facing portrait belongs to the late John R. Sinnock, the designer.

The dime was perfect for FDR's portrait. In 1921 he became a victim of polio (poliomyelitis), and for the rest of his life he was paralyzed from the waist down. From the late 1930's on, annual March of Dimes campaigns began on his birthday, helping fund efforts to conquer polio. The dime soon became a symbol of those efforts.

Unfortunately, the FDR dime is one of our poorest coins. The portrait is well drawn, but the total style approaches grossness. The reverse, with its liberty torch between oak and laurel branches, is more pleasing.

As issued the coin shows changes from ideas Sinnock tried out in preliminary sketches. His earlier portrait is grimmer and set lower, with LIBERTY at top instead of at the left rim. For the reverse he considered a hand holding the liberty torch, a figure of Liberty holding a lantern and a large building symbolizing the United Nations; the best of his discarded designs shows pillars representing the "Four Freedoms," two at each side of the liberty torch, and crossed branches behind the torch. Had Sinnock used this, E PLURIBUS UNUM would have been at the top instead of crossing behind the torch and branches, and would have been smaller; there'd be stars instead of dots flanking ONE DIME at bottom.

The first FDR dimes were released January 30, 1946, the anniversary of the late President's birthday. Mintage that first year after his death was 255,250,000 from Philadelphia, over 61 million from Denver, and almost 28 million from San Francisco.

Top mintage date is 1967, with over two billion struck, and top mintage coin is 1967 (67–D), with 1,156,277,320 made; unfor-

FIG. 23–2. Dime, 1962, reverse. The coin's reverse is better than its obverse, but it's far from being an outstanding design. Mint marks are on the reverse, above the E in ONE, 1946–64; from 1968 on, they're on the obverse, above the date.

tunately, there's no way to identify this due to the lack of mint marks on coins of 1965–67. Top-mintage identifiable date is 1970–D, with 754, 942, 100 made. Lowest mintage is the 6,890,000 of true 1965 coins; but these are indistinguishable from the other 1.5-billion-plus dimes dated 1965; so we fall back on the 1955, with 12,450,181 minted. Proofs were struck at Philadelphia 1950–64 and at San Francisco from 1968 on; totals range from 51,386 (1950) to 3,950,762 (1964).

You could buy a large bag of popcorn for a dime for many years at theaters and amusement parks. I recall when bus fares in Washington, D.C., were 10¢. And for many years, parents despaired at the number of dimes children spent for comic books.

Like quarters and halves, dimes changed to clad coins in 1965. Outer faces are 75 percent copper and 25 percent nickel; the core is copper; and the weight, unchanged since 1873, was cut from 2.5 to 2.268 grams.

One of the best-known varieties is 1962–D with a large dot between D in GOD and R in TRUST; evidently there was a pit in one of Denver's dies. Another is the dime (known with dates from 1966 to 1970) struck on an extra thick planchet punched by accident from clad metal strip meant for quarters. There also are 1968 (68–S) and 1970 (70–S) Proofs—coins struck by dies into which no mint marks had been punched.

Where do you find FDR dimes? Most that you see are clad, but many silver ones are around, even rare dates. For those who want only top-condition coins, sources will have to be auctions and dealers.

The only Star-Line coin is Proof 1959. Marginals are 1947–S, 1949–D, 1955, and Proofs of 1957 and 1960.

Part Three

Twenty Cents to Trade Dollars

24

Twenty-Cent Folly

"It is understood by all, I think, that the
coinage of the twenty-cent piece was originally
a mistake. . . ."—Congressman Morrill, 1878.

Our silver 20¢ coin has a beautiful design, the right amount of
precious metal and a firm place in our decimal-based coinage.
Yet it failed dismally.

The "double disme" proposed in 1803 wasn't issued, but in
February 1874 Senator John P. Jones of Nevada introduced a
new bill authorizing a 20¢ piece. (Four years later, Senator
Sherman would tell a House committee that the coin was created solely because Senator Jones had asked for it.) The idea
was supposedly to help solidify our decimal-based coinage, help
eliminate "bit-dealing" (the continued use of the one-eighth-
dollar fraction represented by the now-demonetized Spanish
real), and aid the West, where a shortage of 5¢ coins made it
difficult to give or get correct change.

Congress passed the Jones bill, disregarding the fact that two
dimes were better for all three stated purposes, and President
Ulysses S. Grant signed the Act of March 3, 1875.

Only one of the 1874 and 1875 patterns is really important.
This Barber design shows a pretty young Liberty head facing
left and wearing a coronet lettered LIBERTY, with 13 stars around
the obverse and the date at bottom. The reverse has a spade-

shaped shield with an incuse 20; at the shield's base are crossed arrows and two olive branches; above are rays. UNITED STATES OF AMERICA is around top and sides, and CENTS is at bottom.

If the coin had been issued with this distinctive design, it *probably would have succeeded.*

But the design approved in April 1875 is the same Liberty Seated design, by Christian Gobrecht, as on half-dimes, dimes, quarters, halves, and silver dollars; William Barber simply copied it. The reverse appears much like a squeezed-down Trade Dollar, with the same eagle and the same heraldic errors (arrows and olive branch in the wrong claws and the head facing the wrong way). At the reverse bottom is TWENTY CENTS. The coin weighs 77.16 grains.

Mintage for issue, begun in May 1875, lasted less than two years; Proofs were made for an additional two years. Philadelphia made both regular-issue and Proof coins; Carson City and San Francisco made small quantities of regular-issue pieces.

The short period and low mintage totals make varieties hard to find. There are 1875–S with double S and 1876–CC with doubled LIBERTY. There may be more, but not many.

You could use a 20¢ piece in Concord, N.H., in 1876 at the Woodworth Brothers Store, which sold candy for 20¢ per pound during the holiday season. Next July, in the same city, J. E. Clifford advertised a canvas slipper you could have bought with two 20¢ coins.

Before the year was out, it was clear that 20¢ coins were failing. Carson City melted almost all the 10,000 it made that year, and only about eight to 15 are known today.

"A great deal of annoyance is caused by this, in our country, uncommon subdivision of the dollar," complained F. W. Helmick in 1878, "as it approaches too nearly to the quarter dollar."

If you looked carefully you could see that the eagle is facing in different directions on the two coins, that there's a shield on its chest on the quarter but not on the 20¢, and that the quarter's edge is reeded while the 20¢ coin's is plain. But many of these were accepted for quarters by people who got more and more disgusted. The coin is known with the TWENTY removed, indicating widespread alteration to take advantage of its similarity to the coin worth five cents more.

<figure>FIG. 24–1. Twenty cents, 1875–S, reverse. The similarities between this coin and the quarter-dollar were much more prominent than the differences.</figure>

Finally, a bill was introduced to halt minting of the unwanted coin. On April 23, 1878, Congressman Morrill, representing the Committee of the Finance, told Congress, "I am directed by the Committee of the Finance, to whom was referred the bill (HR No. 4394) to prohibit the coinage of the twenty-cent piece of silver, to report it without amendment. As I presume there will be no objection, I ask the action of the Senate upon this House bill. It is understood by all, I think, that the coinage of the twenty-cent piece was originally a mistake, and that being so nearly the size and weight of the twenty-five-cent piece the two are often confounded."

The bill was passed and the 20¢ coin was dropped from our coinage. Today you can buy one in Good condition for about $45 to $55, and in Fine for $60 to $75.

Due to the brief issue period, Star-Line does not operate.

25

Early Quarters

Miss Liberty gained some weight in
the early nineteenth century.

Our first quarter-dollar coins, authorized by the Act of 1792, weren't issued for another four years. The Act said they'd be "one-fourth the value of the dollar or unit" and contain "ninety-two grains and thirteen sixteenth parts of a grain of pure, or one

FIG. 25–1. Quarter-dollar, 1796, obverse. In the National Collection, Smithsonian Institution.

hundred and four grains of standard silver." This weight, only a grain lighter than three modern clad dimes, would last until mid-January 1837, when it would be reduced to 103.125 grains.

Like several other early coins, the first type lacks any denomination. It has a Liberty head facing right, wearing drapery like the top of a flowing gown. The date is below and LIBERTY is at the top. Eight stars are along the left rim, seven at the right. The reverse has a scrawny eagle in a wreath, with UNITED STATES OF AMERICA around top and sides. The eagle's wings are inverted; the wreath is laurel and palm. This 1796 design by Robert Scot is a "single-year type," since the 5,894 (or 6,146 according to Yeoman) minted at Philadelphia are the only ones with this exact design. The coin costs about $900 to $1,000 in Good.

You could use two of these quarters in Portland, Maine, in July 1802, to pay your admission to the Union Hall for the performance of *Castle Spectre* (five acts) and *Lovers' Quarrels* (two acts).

In 1804, when the 13-star limit went into effect, a modified design by Reich appeared. Liberty's portrait is less puffy-cheeked, but otherwise similar to the 1796 one. There are seven stars at left and six at right. The reverse, though, switches to a "heraldic" eagle with 13 arrows in its right talon and an olive branch in its left (the talons are heraldically reversed); but the eagle's head faces correctly to its right. In its beak is a banner lettered E PLURIBUS UNUM. Above are 13 stars and an arc of clouds. The rim has UNITED at left, the eagle's right wingtip, STATES OF at top, the left wingtip and AMERICA.

This is the earliest quarter with a denomination on it, 25 at left of the eagle's tail and C. at right. The 6,738 mintage figure

FIG. 25–2. Quarter-dollar, 1805, reverse. This design, based on the Great Seal of the United States, seems more modern than you might expect from the coin's date. The reason is that the Barber reverse on quarters and half-dollars of 1892 also was based on the seal, and we automatically relate this older coin to the later one.

makes it our third rarest quarter, too, with a $325 to $350 price tag in Fine.

The Draped Bust/Heraldic Eagle design continued through 1807, with top mintage of 220,643 that year. All the coins were made at Philadelphia.

There's an 1806 variety with 6 over 5; an 1805 die probably was in usable shape at the end of the year and was redated.

Coins of 1804–07 were followed by a seven-year break. During this time you'd have used four of the old coins to pay your board for a day at J. S. Smithers's City Hotel, in Richmond, Va.

Next came John Reich's Capped Bust design of 1815–28. The left-facing Liberty on these is less lifelike than the one Reich drew for earlier coins; she's close to being chunky. Liberty wears a liberty cap with LIBERTY on the headband; her hair flows freely down the back of her neck. There are seven stars at left and six at right. The eagle on the reverse is slightly more lifelike than its predecessor, though its head is too large. It wears a U.S. shield on its chest, turns its head correctly right, and holds three arrows in its left talon and an olive branch in its right. UNITED STATES OF AMERICA is around top and sides and 25 c. is at bottom.

These quarters are slightly smaller; the diameter was further reduced in 1831. Both times, the planchets were made thicker to keep the weight at 104 grains. The coins were released in 1815, 1818–25, 1827–28, and then no more until the new subtype of 1831. During this period William Kneass succeeded Robert Scot as engraver in January 1824.

FIG. 25–3. Quarter-dollar, 1831, obverse.

The rarest Type 1 coin is 1827, but fewer than ten are known; the rarest date most of us can afford is 1822, with 64,080 struck and prices of about $18 to $25 Fair and $60 to $80 Fine. Top mintage is the 361,174 of 1818.

One of these coins would buy your breakfast at the S. Drew Tavern and Beef-Steak House in Washington, D.C., in 1821. Twenty-five cents was the fee for a Florida sheriff or marshal for recording an execution in 1829.

Varieties are plentiful; there are at least ten for 1818 alone. Among others are 1822 with 25 over 50¢, 1825 over various dates, and originals and restrikes for several years.

Proof-like presentation pieces were struck at least in 1817, 1821, and 1834. Some authorities consider these genuine Proofs.

On Kneass's redrawn design of 1831 the eagle appears more powerful, because its size remained the same while the rest of the design was reduced. To allow this, something had to give way, so the "E Pluribus Unum" banner was discarded. The Type 2 coins were issued 1831–38, and you could have used three of these in Savannah, Ga., in March 1835 to buy a gallon of Madeira wine from Scott & Balfour. Mintage of this type goes from 156,000 for 1833 to 1.9 million for 1835. Common dates cost $30 to $40 in Good condition and about $40 to $57 in Fine. A Proof-like Uncirculated 1822 with the $^{23}\!/_{22}$ variety brought $67,500 in November 1973.

FIG. 25–4. Quarter-dollar, 1831, reverse. The eagle looks large because it remained the same size while the rest of the coin was scaled down.

All of these quarters have to be bought or traded for. In view of the low prices, which indicate low collector interest, I'd recommend trying your luck with auctions before you visit dealers.

The Star-Line date is 1828. Marginals are 1833 and 1834.

26

Gobrecht's Quarters

These represent our longest-lived quarter-dollar design, first issued in 1838 and then issued every year through 1891.

Like half-dimes and dimes, Liberty Seated quarters show the early Gobrecht design: Liberty faces right, sitting on a rock, turning her head to look left; her right hand steadies a U.S. shield across which is a LIBERTY banner, her left holds a liberty pole. She wears a flowing Greek chiton which leaves her neck and arms bare. Thirteen stars line top and side rims; the date is at bottom. The reverse is almost exactly like that of Capped Bust quarters except that the denomination now is QUAR. DOL.

The coin was issued every year 1838–91. All four operating mints of that time which struck silver coins (Philadelphia, New Orleans, San Francisco, and Carson City) made Liberty Seated quarters. Mint marks are below the eagle.

You could use a Liberty Seated quarter to buy a bonnet from Isaac Churchill of Woodstock, Vt., in mid-May 1839. In February 1841, A. J. Foster was selling cast-steel hatchets to Freeport, Pa., residents for three quarters. When Larry O'Gig and Rose Redland starred in the drama *The Robber's Wife* at the National Theatre in Cincinnati, Ohio, the evening of Friday, February 26, 1847, a quarter would buy you a seat.

FIG. 26–1. Quarter-dollar, 1884, obverse. Like other silver coins of that time, this shows the Gobrecht obverse design.

FIG. 26–2. Quarter-dollar, 1844–O, reverse. When the New Orleans branch mint struck this coin, E PLURIBUS UNUM had been removed from the reverse and IN GOD WE TRUST hadn't yet been added.

In 1853 the coin's weight was cut slightly; arrowheads were added flanking the date, and rays were put around the eagle's head. The rays, which made the reverse look crowded, were dropped after a year but the arrowheads remained through 1855. At this time the mints didn't always release coins when the coins were struck. Some 1850, 1851, and 1852 quarters were melted after the new law changed the coin's weight.

Silver, copper, and aluminum patterns were made in 1863 to test the new "In God We Trust" motto. They have the regular obverse and a reverse showing the motto on a banner above the eagle. This was the regular-issue reverse beginning in 1866.

Various patterns were struck during this period with different versions of the Liberty Seated and Liberty head designs. One 1870 piece by William Barber has a reverse with 25 CENTS in a heavy wreath of cotton and corn and STANDARD at the top in small letters. This was part of the "Standard Silver" series proposed as replacements for fractional currency (paper money in low denominations) then flooding the country. This particular

FIG. 26–3. Quarter-dollar, 1884, reverse. The addition of a banner with IN GOD WE TRUST made the quarter's reverse too crowded.

pattern is interesting because it's evidently one of the few legitimate patterns lacking "United States of America."

Arrowheads again appeared on quarters in 1873, when the weight was raised from 96 to 96.45 grains. With the motto over the eagle, rays weren't used this time. The arrowheads of 1873-74 are the last design change.

Mintage of quarters ranged from 4,000 for 1873-CC to 17,816,000 for 1876. One of these 1876 coins would purchase six loaves of bread in Olympia, Wash., that August. Proofs were struck as early in 1842, and are listed in the Red Book 1855-91, with totals of 250 in 1879 to 1,355 in 1880. Many regular-issue coins cost $7 to $10 Good and $11 to $15 Fine.

Among the many varieties are 1840-O with or without drapery folds from the elbow, 1853 without arrows with recut date, 1877-S with S over horizontal S and others.

Our sources will be coin auctions, other collectors' duplicates and dealers' stocks.

Star-Line dates are 1857-O, 1863, 1865, 1871, 1890, and Proofs of 1873 No Arrows, 1875, and 1878. Marginals are 1858-O, 1859, 1872, 1875, 1876-CC, 1877-CC, 1880, 1881, 1884, 1885, 1886, 1887, 1888, 1888-S, 1889, 1891, and Proofs of 1863 and 1879.

27

Barber Quarters

"... Far more beautiful than
any which has yet appeared. ..."
—*The New York Times*, 1891.

Mint Director Edward Owen Leech mentioned in his annual report for 1890 that some new coin designs were needed, so legislation of September 26, 1890, authorized a change in design. One result was a report in *The New York Times* on May 23, 1891, that "about six weeks ago the Treasury Department . . . sent a circular letter to a number of New-York artists and sculptors, inviting designs" for new coins. The prize was $500 and all entries had to be in by June 1.

Several sculptors, as indignant as they were distinguished, met at Daniel French's home and decided they did want to work on new coins, but not under the government's announced conditions. Their letter to Leech complained that "the time given for the preparation of designs is too short and the compensation altogether insufficient. . . ."

The nearly 300 designs that were submitted by others all were blasted by contest judge Augustus Saint-Gaudens. The famed sculptor said only a few men living, including himself, were qualified to design the new coins. This did nothing for the pride of the official mint engravers. Finally, disgusted Treasury officials scrapped the contest and gave a go-ahead to Charles E. Barber. His design was approved by early November.

Most of his work went into the larger half-dollar patterns, but two or three silver pattern quarters were struck, and that November 6 the *Times* was able to comment, "The design for the reverse of the half-dollar and quarter-dollar is a return to the design of almost the first coinage of the country, while the female head on the face of the coin is far more beautiful than any which has yet appeared on our coins."

Barber drew Liberty facing right; she wears a triple head-dress formed of a liberty cap, wreath over that and a tiny coronet inscribed LIBERTY. There are six stars at the left rim and seven at right, IN GOD WE TRUST around the top and the date at bottom. Barber's tiny incuse B is at the base of Liberty's neck. The reverse, as the paper said, goes a long way back—a heraldic eagle with U.S. shield on its chest, olive branch in its right talon and 13 arrows in its left. The eagle's beak holds a scroll lettered E PLURIBUS UNUM. Above are 13 stars. The rim has UNITED STATES OF AMERICA at top and sides, QUARTER DOLLAR at bottom. The wingtips cover most of the E in UNITED and the E and part of the R in AMERICA. Mint marks are below the eagle's tail.

It's worth noting that obverse stars are traditional six-pointed

FIG. 27–1. Quarter-dollar, 1893–S, obverse. The Barber series was the last "set" the U.S. issued with a single obverse design for dimes, quarters, and halves.

ones but reverse ones are the first five-pointed stars on a U.S. coin. It has been suggested that this is because the Great Seal, on which the design is based, has five-pointed stars.

Like dimes and half-dollars, these were often in the past called the "Morgan" type, because of their slight resemblance to the Morgan silver dollar's obverse.

Minting of regular-issue quarters began Saturday, January 2, 1892. Next Monday, Mint Director Leech received a box with $50 in new halves, quarters and dimes. "Most of the visitors to Mr. Leech's office," reported the *Times*, "were enthusiastic about the designs, particularly of the half dollars and quarter dollars."

Philadelphia struck 8,236,000 regular-issue 1892 quarters, New Orleans made 2,640,000 and San Francisco minted 964,079. While 1892 costs $7 to $9 Fine, the 1892–S costs about $26 to $30.

Two or more mints issued Barber quarters every year 1892–1916. Denver began making them in 1906 and continued through 1916 except for 1912. All four mints issued quarters in 1907, 1908 and 1909. Mintage varies from 40,000 for 1913–S to 12,624,000 of 1899. Proofs were struck at Philadelphia every year through 1915, with totals from 380 in 1914 to 1,245 in 1892.

You could have used one of these quarters to buy a bottle of Modjeska Tooth Powder from the Larkin Soap Mfg. Co. of Buffalo, N.Y., in the early 1890's. In 1898 the Spatula Publishing Co. of Boston, Mass., would sell you a bottle of red or black lettering ink for 25¢. And in 1914 a quarter would purchase the current issue of *The Smart Set* magazine, which proclaimed, "One civilized reader is worth a thousand boneheads."

FIG. 27–2. Quarter-dollar, 1893–S, reverse. The design went a long way back.

Among the few varieties are 1892–S with double S, 1898 with double 98, and 1916–D, with double D.

These coins are out of circulation, and there's little point in searching for them. Get them from dealers, other collectors' duplicates, and coin auctions. Many dates still cost less than $3 Good and $10 Fine.

Star-Line dates are 1894, 1906, 1910–D, 1911, 1913, and 1914–D. Marginals are 1893–S, 1896, 1906–D, 1907–S, 1913, 1915, 1915–D, and Proofs of 1908, 1910, and 1911.

28

With Shield and Olive

Prudes didn't like the way Miss Liberty posed, but collectors appreciate the quarters of 1916–30.

Imagine the Goddess of Liberty striding toward you through a small gateway. Her head is turned to your right; her outstretched right hand grasps an olive branch and one end of the drapery which she's pulling off a shield. Her left arm raises the shield itself. She wears a filmy gown and her feet are bare. This is the scene on Liberty Standing quarters of 1916–30. (Some collectors prefer "Standing Liberty" quarter and the convenient abbreviation "SLQ." It's all the same coin.)

Hermon A. MacNeil's artistry shows Liberty offering peace but, as world tension grows, preparing to defend herself in war.

FIG. 28-1. Quarter-dollar, 1917, Type 1, obverse. Note the prominent beads-and-bars rim design. This was de-emphasized on Type 2 coins.

FIG. 28-2. Quarter-dollar, 1917, Type 1, reverse. The early "low eagle" design.

Realizing that the coin needed more than a vertical figure, Mac-Neil softened this with the horizontal lines of the low wall and its gateway. The combined verticals and horizontals add stability and depth. Thirteen stars line the gateway vertically, seven on the left wall and six on the right. IN GOD and WE TRUST are on the left and right walls, respectively. Around the top rim is a wide-spaced LIBERTY, with the figure's head between the B and E. The date is at bottom. At right and slightly above it is the designer's incuse M.

A soaring eagle with spread wings dominates the reverse. UNITED STATES is at the top, with OF AMERICA below it. Below this, directly above the eagle, is a tiny E PLURIBUS UNUM. There are seven stars at the left rim and six at the right, separating national identification from QUARTER DOLLAR at bottom. Some numismatists call this quarter our most beautiful coin; it's certainly among the top three or four!

Mixed use of the modern U and old Roman V sometimes leads people to think they've found an error coin: UNITED and QUARTER have U, while TRUST, PLURIBUS and UNUM have V.

This coin's "Miss Liberty" was thirty-four-year-old Doris (Dora) Doscher. The 5-foot, 4-inch young lady also posed for New York City's Pulitzer Memorial Fountain and the Metropolitan Museum of Art's "Diana," both figures by Karl Bitter. She also lectured and served as a trained nurse. Posing for this coin earned her the nickname "the girl on the quarter," a title she was deservingly proud to claim.

FIG. 28–3. Quarter-dollar, 1926–S, reverse. The second, or "high eagle," reverse.

FIG. 28–4. Quarter-dollar, 1926–S, obverse. This is the Type 3 obverse, with Miss Liberty fully clothed, less detail in the wall and gateway, and the date in a sunken area.

In 1917, the second year of issue, the eagle was raised and the stars rearranged five left, five right, and three below the eagle. This made the reverse less crowded and helped direct attention to the eagle.

It's interesting that a *1916* pattern has the eagle in this raised position. This has a laurel branch around the rim instead of stars. Judd says this was struck in silver with the regular obverse die and that more were struck with an earlier pattern die without the incuse M. He also says that the early patterns with the design as it appears on coins were struck with the regular-issue die—which means the "raised eagle, rim wreath" reverse must have been struck in 1916; this must have been an early idea first discarded and later used in a compromise between the two verse types.

This is the change everybody knows about—but there were several others, too.

On Type 1 coins Liberty's right breast is bare. This caused a flareup from various self-appointed guardians of the public morality. So shrill and vitriolic was their outcry that minting was halted early in 1917 and the design was "edited."

On Type 2 quarters—most of the 1917 mintage and all later dates—Liberty wore a chain-mail coat under her gown, covering her "upper body." The long lines of drapery from the shield to her right hand, and the material crossing her right arm, are wider and flatter. Her hair was windblown on Type 1 coins but is gathered up on Type 2's. Several lines which added to the wall and gateway's realism were removed, and the whole surface was made slightly more concave.

It developed that some people, including some mint officials, had claimed dirt and germs collected too easily in the thin incuse lines of the first design. Also the new quarter evidently didn't stack well.

You could have used a quarter in 1919 to buy a can of Faust Chile Powder, which C. F. Blanke Tea & Coffee Co. advertisements called a "different" seasoning. In 1923, Lambert Pharmacal Co. was offering a 25¢ package of Listerine throat tablets to cure bad breath (and, implied the ads, restore marital happiness, summon departed suitors, and turn bridesmaids into brides).

Dates on early quarters had no protection; as one of the highest spots on the coin, they quickly wore off. In 1925 the area around the date was deepened below the surface, allowing higher-relief dates. This overdue improvement makes it relatively easy to find quarters dated 1925 and later with readable dates. Some collectors consider these later coins a separate subtype, or even a wholly new type (Type 3).

One or more mints produced quarters every year 1916–30 except 1922. Mints involved were Philadelphia, Denver, and San Francisco. The branch mint's D or S is at left bottom of the gateway, next to the bottom star.

The low-mintage date is 1916, with 52,000 struck and prices of $225 to $250 Good and $350 to $425 Fine. Few were made because 1916 Barber quarters already were plentiful. Highest mintage came in 1920, when Philadelphia made 27,860,000 quarters. There are no Proofs.

The major variety is 1918–S with 8 over 7. Among others are 1920 struck on a nickel planchet meant for a foreign coin, 1926–S with 6 over 0 and several clash die coins.

Only a few of these beautiful coins are still circulating, but if you find one you can add it to your collection for face value. Several dates cost $4 or less in Fine condition and $60 to $80 Uncirculated.

Star-Line dates are 1917–D Type 1 and 1923. Marginals are 1929–D and 1930–S.

29

Continuing Commemorative:
The Washington Quarter

> ". . . First in war, first in peace, and first in the
> hearts of his countrymen."—Henry Lee, Resolutions
> Presented to the House of Representatives on the
> Death of Washington, December 1799.
> And second
> President on a regular-issue U.S. coin.

Part of the eight-month observance of the bicentennial of George Washington's birth was to be the issue of a commemorative coin. But instead of a one-year item, this would be our new regular-issue quarter-dollar. Since the Liberty Standing type had been issued for less than the required 25 years, Congress passed a special act March 4, 1931, to authorize the change.

One of the design competition rules was that the portrait must be modeled on the Houdon bust. After the Revolution, Virginia's Legislature passed a resolution providing for "a statue of General Washington, of the finest marble and best workmanship." French sculptor Jean Antoine Houdon was commissioned in 1785 to do the work. He came from Paris with Franklin and arrived at Mount Vernon late at night on Sunday, October 2, 1785. He made a preliminary bust there and took it back to Paris for completion.

Sculptor John Flanagan did several preliminary drawings, some showing Washington facing right; he also tried out various eagles. His accepted design shows Washington facing left, wearing a wig; Flanagan's JF is on the portrait's base. The date is at

FIG. 29–1. Quarter-dollar, 1969–D, obverse. Mint marks are on the quarter's obverse from 1968 on. The Washington quarter began as a commemorative, skipped a year, then went on to become a popular coin design.

FIG. 29–2. Quarter-dollar, 1969–D, reverse. The clad quarter has drawn plenty of public criticism from both collectors and noncollectors. Really well struck specimens are difficult to find.

the bottom, LIBERTY is around the top, and IN GOD WE TRUST is at lower left.

The reverse's relatively lifelike eagle perches on a bundle of arrows which at first looks like a fasces. UNITED STATES OF AMERICA around top and side rims extends down about half the length of the wings. E PLURIBUS UNUM is directly above the eagle's head. QUARTER DOLLAR at bottom is artistically controlled by the wingtips, which reach almost to the rim. Below the eagle is a partial wreath of crossed olive branches.

Although they marked the bicentennial of his birth, the quarters weren't released until August 1, more than five months after Washington's birthday.

No quarters were issued in 1933, but the Washington design returned as a regular issue in 1934. Philadelphia, Denver, and San Francisco all have minted the coin; at least one mint has struck quarters every year from 1934 on. San Francisco stopped making quarters after 1954, but resumed in November 1965, striking quarters dated 1964 but without the S mint mark. Coins that do have mint marks have them on the reverse above the R or ER in QUARTER 1932–64 and at lower right on the obverse beginning in 1968. Mint marks were omitted from coins dated 1965–67.

In March 1938 a quarter would pay for six pounds of rice at

the Red Front Cash & Carry Store in Central City, Ky. And today I can take a quarter into a Bethesda, Md., drug store and buy 65 sheets of typewriter paper or a package of 135 3 × 5 filing cards.

San Francisco's 1932 coin is the rarest, with mintage of 408,-000. Top mintage coin is the 1967 struck at Philadelphia, with mintage of 873,524,000—but because of the omission of mint marks, the top-mintage identifiable coin is 1970–D, at 417,-341,364. The high-mintage *date* is 1965—over 1.8 *billion*.

Quarters changed from .900 fine silver to cupronickel clad in 1965. The quarter was the first "sandwich coin" in production (on August 23) and the first released for use (on November 1). Some collectors think the coins are beautiful; many others call them hideous and a temptation to counterfeiters. I think that what counts is that clad coins are a fact of numismatic life: we might as well accept them.

Special Bicentennial quarters are dated "1776–1976." Their reverse, by Jack L. Ahr, features a drummer in colonial costume. Mintage of 1.4 billion is planned.

Variety collectors can enjoy Washington quarters as much as anyone: there are 1932–D with double mint mark, 1935 struck on a cent planchet, 1945–S with large or small S, 1954 with a die break turning the 9 into a backward R, 1966 with recut date and lettering, many dates with hairline die breaks along the bottom of the portrait, loads of double mint marks and others.

Star-Line dates are 1944–S, 1949–D, 1959, and 1960. Marginals are 1932–S, 1938–S, 1939–S, 1940–S, 1943–D, 1944–D, 1945–D, 1946–S, 1947, 1948–D, 1956–D, 1958, and Proofs of 1951 and 1960.

Almost every date is available in circulation; prices for Uncirculated coins range from about $1 to $450 or so. Proofs were struck 1936–42 and 1950–64 at Philadelphia, and from 1968 on at San Francisco.

30

Early Half-Dollars

Liberty took until 1801 to learn to smile.

The Act of April 2, 1792, provided for a "Silver Half-Dollar" weighing 208 grains. Our first issues came in 1794. These show Robert Scot's stringy-haired Liberty facing right, LIBERTY at top, the date at bottom, and 15 stars arranged eight at the left rim and seven at the right. A thin eagle perches in a wreath on the reverse. UNITED STATES OF AMERICA is around the rim. Like several other coins, these "Flowing Hair" halves have lettered edges: FIFTY CENTS OR HALF A DOLLAR.

Only 5,300 were made in 1794 and 317,844 in 1795. Today one costs about $100 to $200 in *Fair* condition! Probably fewer than eight Unc 1794's exist; one offered in 1974 was priced at $14,750.

The Draped Bust type of 1796–97, instead of cutting her off at the neck, shows Liberty down to below her shoulders. She wears a hair-ribbon but most of her hair still lies free along her neck. The reverse's eagle is slightly reworked, but not improved. A small ½ is added at the bottom.

The authorities planned to increase the number of stars on coins as states joined the Union; but it quickly became obvious

FIG. 30–1. Half-dollar, 1795, obverse. The Flowing Hair type. Coin is in the National Collection, Smithsonian Institution.

that they had to either abandon that plan or eventually issue coins covered with stars. Those in charge decided to limit stars to 13 for the original states. The policy went into effect on half-dollars in 1801, with seven stars at left and six at right. That year's reverse abandons the lifelike eagle for a heavy "heraldic" one and drops the wreath and fraction.

Liberty was improving with age: in 1794 she looked rather startled; in 1796 she appeared somewhat disdainful. But by 1801 she was learning how to smile.

That year seven of these coins would pay your fare on the stagecoach from "George-Town" in the District of Columbia to Port-Tobacco, Md. In June 1802, nearby Virginia's *Alexandria Gazette* noted that John V. Thomas had published "An excellent School Book" priced at a half-dollar and titled "A New Intro-duction to Reading, or, A Collection of Ea*f*y Le*ff*ons."

Mintage of halves stayed low, with several years' totals near 30,000 and nothing over a million until 1807 (and most of those were a new design). Yet 1805 (211,722 struck) catalogs at only about $35 Good, and some dates cost under $85 Fine. How come?

In the early nineteenth century so many gold coins and silver dollars were melted and exported that the half-dollar became the largest coin in substantial use. Halves were bagged and shipped from bank to bank, getting little use outside banks. The situation was rough on those who needed halves and couldn't get them—but it turned out to be a blessing for collectors. Many halves remained in Extremely Fine and even better condition, and today these are plentiful enough to keep prices, when you consider mintage totals, pretty low.

We should remember that records were kept on a fiscal year basis, that old dies in usable condition often were recut and reused, and that there was less precise order and method in the mint at that time. So we have not only unreliable records, but also many varieties, among which are 1795 with recut date, 1796 with 15 or 16 stars, 1803 with large or small 3, and 1806 with 6/5.

There are no Star-Line or Marginals for these early dates.

Robert Scot, the mint engraver, had working for him a former

German bondman named John Reich, who had been freed by a mint official. Reich was about to make his own mark in numismatic art.

31

Capped Bust Halves

Sharing the spotlight with the
first steam-powered coinage.

John Reich designed the Capped Bust half-dollars of 1807–39. These formerly were called Turban Head coins because their liberty cap looks a bit like a low turban.

The obverse shows Liberty facing left. She looks much as she did on the earlier Draped Bust coins, but the portrait is better centered and a little more lifelike. LIBERTY is on the liberty cap's headband. Miss Liberty wears her hair unbound along the back of her neck and over her shoulders. There are seven stars along the left rim and six at the right; the date is at bottom.

A small and only slightly lifelike eagle is on the reverse, with a U.S. shield on its chest; the wings are inverted, the head turns to its own right, and the correct talons hold the olive branch and three arrows. Above is a scroll inscribed E PLURIBUS UNUM; national identification is around top and sides.

The denomination is shown as 50 C. at the reverse bottom, but these coins still have a lettered edge.

In 1807 when 750,500 were struck, the coin still weighed 208 grains and was 89.24 percent silver. The diameter was 32.5 mm.

In 1810 a half-dollar would pay your admission to the gallery of the New Theatre in Philadelphia to see the December 29 performance of *Henry IV* by "Shakespear" and a comic opera called *Hit Or Miss*.

FIG. 31–1. Half-dollar, 1826, obverse. John Reich's repeated use of liberty caps on U.S. coins is understandable, since he was a former bondman who had been freed by a mint official.

FIG. 31–2. Half-dollar, 1826, reverse.

These halves are dated from 1807 to 39, omitting only 1816; all were made at Philadelphia until the New Orleans branch mint made 178,976 in 1839. The mint mark is on the obverse, above the date. Top mintage is that of 1836, when 6,546,200 were made; low mintage honors go to 1815, with 47,150 struck. New Orleans did strike 20 halves dated 1838 (reportedly in January 1839), but 1838–O coins were trial pieces made while testing a new coin press.

Six half-dollars would pay your stagecoach fare from Philadelphia to Allentown, Pa., on the Old Line Easton Mail Stage in 1828. If you traveled to Halifax, N.C., in February 1830, you could board yourself and your horse at the Farmers Hotel there for three halves per day.

At the second Philadelphia mint, the first steam-powered coining took place in 1836. That also was the year draftsman Christian Gobrecht became William Kneass's assistant.

Halves of 1836 were struck both with lettered and with reeded edges. The reeded-edge type costs $100 to $150 Fine, in contrast to the lettered-edge coin's $45 average price. Judd and Yeoman differ on the new coins' status. Yeoman lists them along with other regular-issue coins and makes no mention of any other status. Dr. Judd cites their .900 fineness and 206.25-grain weight as evidence that they should be classed as patterns struck as part of the process of readying the mint to work under the law that was expected to change the old .8924 fineness and 208-grain weight.

Steam-powered minting began November 8. The Director of the Mint sent the Secretary of the Treasury ten new coins, with a letter calling them the "first specimens of silver coinage by steam, executed this afternoon."

However, there's evidence for Yeoman's view in the Monday, December 5, issue of *Poulson's American Daily Advertiser*. The Philadelphia paper stated: (Official Text)

New coin.—The new fifty cent pieces about to be issued from the mint at Philadelphia, are spoken of as being of superior workmanship, and in the highest degree creditable to the artist, Mr. Gobrecht. The beauty and finish are equal to any thing of the kind in this country or Europe.

It's worth noting, too, that the reeded-edge coin's mintage of 1,200 is unusually high for a pattern.

The new modified coins of 1836 are smaller, with both obverse and reverse scaled down to a size of 30 mm.; since space is limited, the banner and motto were dropped from the reverse. The denomination is 50 CENTS this year and in 1837, but in 1838 it becomes HALF DOL. This type was issued through 1839.

Several years' dies remained in use, overpunched with new numerals: for instance, 1808 with 8 over 7, 1817 with 7/2, and 1822 with 2/1. There also are other varieties—large or small numbers, clashed dies, double dates, filled dies, and so forth.

Star-Line dates are 1811, 1817, and 1828. Marginals are 1810, 1813, 1814, 1821, and 1825.

32

Miss Liberty, Be Seated

Another of Christian Gobrecht's beautiful
Liberty Seated coins.

Development of the Liberty Seated half-dollar essentially follows that of the dollar; however, the first half-dollar patterns
didn't appear until 1838.

These show the usual obverse of a seated Liberty with U.S.
shield and liberty pole and a reverse eagle that's heavier than
Reich's and has no shield on its chest; this realistic eagle holds
four arrows in its left talon and an olive branch in its right, but
the head is turned to its left, an error I wouldn't expect from
Gobrecht. UNITED STATES OF AMERICA is around the top and
sides, separated by dots from HALF DOLLAR at bottom.

FIG. 32–1. Half-dollar, 1869, obverse. The Liberty Seated, one of
the most beautiful of U.S. coin designs, is made less appealing by
repetition. Gobrecht's design is on
the half-dime, dime, 20¢, quarter-
dollar, half-dollar, and silver dollar.

FIG. 32–2. Half-dollar, 1841–O, reverse. The change from earlier half-
dollar reverses is relatively minor.

There are more patterns with the Flying Eagle reverse and various differences in detail; more followed in 1839.

Like quarters, Liberty Seated halves started out with an obverse rim lined with 13 stars rather than a plain rim, as on dimes. On issued coins the eagle's head faces correctly to its right; the denomination is shown as HALF DOL.

The coins were issued first in 1839, then released by Philadelphia every year through 1891. New Orleans (1840–61), San Francisco (1855–78), and Carson City (1870–78) all issued these halves without a break. These coins continue with a 13.36-gram weight and 90 percent fineness, but are a trifle larger, 30.6 mm.

After four years as mint engraver Gobrecht died July 23, 1844. President Tyler appointed James Barton Longacre to the position. Among his assistants are two familiar names, Anthony C. Paquet and William Barber.

By now you could pay a half-dollar fare and ride from Wilmington, Del., to Philadelphia on the "Phil., Wil., and Balt. Rail Road." In Burlington, Iowa, a Liberty Seated half-dollar would buy the best bonnet ribbon in stock at J. G. Lauman & Brother's store in 1849.

In 1853 small arrowheads appeared at each side of the date, showing the reduction in weight to 12.44 grams. As with the quarter, rays were added around the eagle on the reverse but were dropped after a year; the "arrows" stayed on the coin through 1855.

Half-dollar patterns were made in 1861 with a banner above the eagle and the motto GOD OUR TRUST on the banner. Other patterns were struck with the motto in a plain field, along with "banner-type" ones, in 1862 and 1863. IN GOD WE TRUST was added on some 1863 patterns, and this motto on a banner was the one on patterns of 1864–66. Starting in 1866, IN GOD WE TRUST on the banner became part of the regular design.

Arrowheads reappeared for 1873–74, when the coin's weight was raised from 192 to 192.9 grains (12.5 grams). There were no rays this time.

Pattern and regular-dies trial pieces were struck in several years in various metals. One 1882 pattern is George Morgan's

FIG. 32–3. Half-dollar, 1869, reverse. As on other coins, half-dollars
added IN GOD WE TRUST on a banner above the eagle.

beautiful "Shield Earring" design: a right-facing Liberty head
wearing a headband lettered LIBERTY and an earring shaped like
a tiny U.S. shield.

Top mintage is that of 1876, when Philadelphia turned out
8,418,000 halves for release plus 1,150 Proofs. Low-mintage date
is 1884, with only 4,400 regular-issue halves and 875 Proofs.
However, the Red Book lists no mintage figure for 1853–O
without arrows, and the 1873–S without arrows evidently is
unknown today in spite of its 5,000 mintage figure. Proofs were
struck 1860–91, all at Philadelphia.

Many dates cost $10 to $13 Good and $15 to $24 Fine, so a
coin from this series is within reach of moderate budgets.

Star-Line dates are 1856–O, 1859–O, 1860–O, 1861, 1861–O,
1862, 1871, and 1878. Marginals are 1842, 1843–O, 1844–O,
1849, 1849–O, 1863, 1865, 1867–S, 1868–S, 1871–S, and Proof
1866.

Varieties are plentiful, including 1840–O with large or small
mint mark, 1843 with recut date, 1847 over 46, 1877–S with
double S, and others.

33

Barber Halves

"An ideal female head, representative of
liberty. . . ."—*The New York Times*, 1891.

Barber's obverse design shows, as *The New York Times* reported
November 5, 1891, "An ideal female head, representative of liberty, looking to the right, with a calm and dignified expression. . . ." She wears a liberty cap, laurel wreath, and tiny coronet
inscribed LIBERTY. Around the rim are six stars at left, IN GOD WE
TRUST above the portrait, seven stars at right, and the date below.

The reverse, basically, would show the eagle required by law;
it would be a "heraldic" one based on the Great Seal, with a
shield on its chest, an E PLURIBUS UNUM banner in its beak, an
olive branch in one talon and arrows in the other. UNITED STATES
OF AMERICA would be around the rim, with HALF DOLLAR at bottom.

But should there be clouds above the eagle or a 13-star constellation or both? Should the E PLURIBUS UNUM banner be sharply or
slightly curved? Should the eagle be large, medium, or small?
And if not large, then should it be inside a wreath?

Patterns were struck showing various possible designs. Some
show a medium-sized eagle; some show a smaller eagle and more
ornate olive branch and motto banner, with clouds; some have an
even tinier eagle and plainer olive branch within an oak wreath.
One shows a large eagle with a shield on its chest, holding the
gently-curved E PLURIBUS UNUM banner in its beak, an olive
branch in its right talon, and 13 arrows in its left; there are 13
stars over the eagle, an arch of clouds over the stars, UNITED
STATES OF AMERICA around top and sides and HALF DOLLAR at
bottom. A modification of this, with larger stars and no clouds,
was the adopted design.

FIG. 33–1. Half-dollar, 1892, reverse. Coin is in the National Collection, Smithsonian Institution.

The coin first was issued in 1892, when Philadelphia made 934,000, New Orleans released 390,000, and San Francisco struck 1.0 million. You might have used one of the new coins in Columbia, Tenn., that year to pay dentist S. A. Hays for pulling a tooth. Or you could have bought the Bridgeport Brass Company's "Bridgeport 50-Cent Wonder" lamp from the Connecticut firm.

Top mintage is 5,538,846 for 1899. The lowest figure is the 124,610 of 1914. Philadelphia, Denver, New Orleans, and San Francisco all made Barber halves, and two or more mints issued them every year 1892–1915. Philadelphia also struck Proofs every year. Some *1892–O* Proof halves were also struck, evidently to celebrate resumption of New Orleans half-dollar coinage.

Prices vary from the $4 to $6 range for several dates in Good condition to around $1,000 for an Uncirculated 1901–S. Some dates cost only about $10 to $15 in Fine.

The New Orleans branch mint wasn't making halves in 1915, so the 1915–O halves that exist are counterfeits. But there's some question about who made them and why. Some numismatists believe the 1915–O is of such good quality that it must represent an unfriendly nation's attempt at monetary sabotage!

The low demand level is reflected in the sparsity of known varieties. As with Liberty Seated coins, common design probably is a major factor in the lack of demand and generally low prices. There are, though, 1892–O with large or small I, 1892–S with some reengraved lettering, and a few others.

But that's no reason to ignore Barber halves. When a series is underpriced, that's the time to fill the empty spaces in your album or coin file!

Star-Line dates are 1908, 1911, and 1915–D. Marginals are 1905, 1905–O, 1910, 1911–S, 1912–S, 1913–D, and Proof 1914.

34

Liberty Came Walking

"... One of the most beautiful American silver coins
ever issued."—coin dealer's advertisement, 1973.
And a series that includes four of the silver half-dollars
with mint marks on the obverse.

The twenty-fifth year of the Barber design was 1916, and a new
half-dollar appeared that year. Patterns show the full-length figure of Liberty walking leftward toward the rising sun, around
which are 13 rays. She carries branches of laurel (military
power) and oak (civic glory) in her bent left arm; her right arm
is outflung, giving her spirit to the world. Behind her is a 13-star
U.S. flag. At right, in the field, are a large, crude LIBERTY and
smaller IN GOD WE TRUST. The date is at bottom.

On the reverse is an eagle with raised wings standing on a rock.
The left-facing bird is one of our most lifelike coinage eagles.
From a split in the rock grows a sapling of mountain pine, symbolizing the nation. UNITED STATES OF AMERICA is around top and
side rims in large letters; above the eagle, and following the curve
of the rim, is HALF DOLLAR. At bottom is E PLURIBUS UNUM.
Adolph A. Weinman's AW monogram is on some patterns. There
are similar ones with only minor changes.

On issued coins the AW is incuse, below the eagle's tail and at
right of R in DOLLAR. The denomination was moved to the reverse
bottom, its traditional spot, and E PLURIBUS UNUM was put at the
left center, but horizontal rather than along the rim. The motto is
artistically held in place by UNITED above, the eagle at right and
the sapling below, whose leaves fan out to form a base for the
words. On the obverse Liberty wears a flowing gown and sandals.
Weinman probably used Elsie Stevens as his model for the half-
dollar, as he did for the dime.

FIG. 34–1. Half-dollar, 1939, obverse. Some numismatists believe
the star-spangled object behind
Liberty is part of her gown, but
others say it's a flag. The arrangement of the material leads me to
believe that flag and gown are
separate.

FIG. 34–2. Half-dollar, 1917–D,
Type 1, obverse. Denver struck
765,400 coins before moving the
mint mark to the reverse. Type 2's
mintage was 1.94 million. This
Good condition coin was in circulation in the 1940's.

FIG. 34–3. Half-dollar, 1939, reverse. Like the Peace dollar, this
coin shows the American eagle
without arrows. But the raised
wings could be symbolic of the
nation's readiness to defend itself
in the coming war.

The Liberty Walking (or Walking Liberty) half-dollar was
issued first in 1916, when it was struck at Philadelphia, Denver,
and San Francisco. Mint marks are on the obverse, below IN GOD
WE TRUST on 1916 and some 1917 coins. But after part of the 1917
issue had been struck, they were moved to the reverse at lower
left, under the sapling.

You could use two of the coins that year to ride to Bridgeport,
Conn., from New York City on the New England Steam Ship
Company Sunday excursion steamer *City of Lowell*. Or you could
use a half-dollar to buy breakfast at the Hotel Theresa in New
York.

After an unbroken issue 1916–21 from all three mints, no halves were struck in 1922. San Francisco made some in 1923 and again in 1927 and 1928. In 1929 both branch mints made halves, but then came a break until San Francisco resumed minting the coins in 1933. Full three-mint coining resumed in 1934 and continued through 1947 except for 1938 and 1947, when San Francisco made no halves, and 1940, when Denver made none. Proofs were struck at Philadelphia 1936–42; mintage rose steadily from 3,901 in 1936 to 21,120 in 1942. Some Proofs cost in the $120 to $140 range.

It's a tribute to Weinman's skill that some of us treasure his Liberty Walking half as an outstandingly beautiful coin. "The Walking Liberty Half Dollar is certainly one of the most beautiful American silver coins ever issued," declared Paramount International Coin Corp. in a 1973 *Numismatic News Weekly* advertisement.

Many regular-issue dates' mintages are under 3 million, and several are below 2 million. Top mintage is 53,190,000 for 1943; lowest is 208,000 for 1921–D. Many dates cost $3 or less in Good, while several cost only $4 or so in Fine; Uncirculated common dates cost about $15 to $25. And though they're silver, a very few of these probably still circulate.

Among varieties are 1918–S with double S, 1934–D with large or small D, 1941 Proof with or without the AW, 1943 with double date and others.

Star-Line dates are 1934–D, 1938–D, 1939–S, 1945–S, 1946–D, and 1946–S. Marginals are 1916–S, 1929–D, 1935–D, 1937–S, 1939, and Proof 1939.

35

The Man with the Square Glasses

Here's a coin with a built-in controversy!

Comedian Bob Newhart, in a monologue on his record "The Button-Down Mind Strikes Back!" referred to Benjamin Franklin as "the one with the square glasses." John R. Sinnock's portrait of Franklin on the 1948 half-dollar omits the famed bifocals, but offers us a gentleman with a high forehead, long hair, and a relaxed appearance.

Franklin faces right, as if contemplating the date at right and below his portrait. Around the bottom is IN GOD WE TRUST and at the top is LIBERTY, both large. Sinnock's initials are at the base of the portrait, which is a composite of several Franklin portraits and is based on a medal the mint issued in 1933.

In the case of this large coin, in contrast to the small FDR dime, Sinnock's style is in scale with the available area. The relief is lower and the detail is less than I prefer, but the Franklin half-dollar is still a well-drawn and skillfully balanced coin.

But what's really interesting about these coins is that their reverse design is *adapted from another coin.*

Back in 1926 the U.S. issued a commemorative half-dollar to mark the nation's 150th anniversary. The obverse shows Calvin

FIG. 35–1. Half-dollar, 1961–D, obverse.

Coolidge and George Washington. The reverse features the Liberty Bell. At left and right of the bell, respectively, are the dates 1776 and 1926. The closely-spaced rim inscription is SESQUICENTENNIAL OF AMERICAN INDEPENDENCE, with HALF DOLLAR at bottom. And the designer? Chief Mint Engraver John R. Sinnock!

On the 1948 coin the bell again is in low relief, but it's slightly higher than in 1926. Sinnock replaced 1776 with E PLURIBUS UNUM, removed the 1926, and substituted national identification for the sesquicentennial rim legend. Since fewer letters are involved, rim lettering is larger and more readable on the Franklin half.

The portrait suffered from the low relief as much as, or more than, the bell; even a short period of circulation wore off the details in Franklin's hair. It's obvious that any coin is better in Proof or Unc than in a lower grade, but this is particularly true of Franklin halves. Only Proofs or well-struck Unc specimens show enough detail for collectors with high standards. On such coins you can, with a magnifying glass, read on the bell "Pass and Stow, Philadᵃ, MDCCLIII"—the name of the company that in 1753 (the Roman numeral date shown) recast the cracked bell. Above is a blurred portion of the bell's inscription, "Proclaim liberty throughout all the land unto all the inhabitants thereof," from Leviticus XXX:10.

The March 1948 *Numismatist* said only two Franklin halves had been struck by then; it's not stated whether these were patterns but I'd guess they were. Secretary of the Treasury Snyder showed one to President Truman, who was much pleased.

On April 30, 1948, the Franklin half was released throughout the country. As far as I've learned, neither the date nor the year had any special significance with respect to Franklin.

The official sendoff actually came the evening before, when a dinner was held for 200 guests at the Franklin Institute, in Philadelphia. Mint Director Mrs. Nellie T. Ross presented the museum with President Truman's gift of two of the coins embedded in plastic. In addition, each guest got one of the new halves.

In her address, Mrs. Ross explained that she long had hoped to see Franklin and the Bell on a U.S. coin. During World War II she had had Sinnock plan a coin showing these designs; it was held ready for use on the half-dollar or any new denomination that might be needed.

You'll note that I've omitted one feature from the description: a small eagle at right of the bell.

Franklin is generally believed to have disliked eagles. Mrs. Ross referred to his letter of January 26, 1784, to his daughter Sarah (Mrs. Benjamin Bache), in which he said, ". . . I wish the Bald Eagle had not been chosen as the Representation of our Country; he is a Bird of bad moral Character. . . . The turkey is a much more respectable bird, and withal a true original native of America." Another comedy record, "Stan Freberg Presents the United States of America," took note of this belief. Freberg included a scene in which two pilgrims, preparing the first Thanksgiving dinner, mistakenly cook the turkey centerpiece instead of the expected eagle. "You put our national bird *in the oven*!?" says one.

But Franklin was criticizing a proposed hereditary military society; he considered it a threat because it might create a hereditary military caste. I think it's far more likely that Franklin was writing allegorically than that he was seriously upset by the eagle's choice as our emblem.

Several writers have said that the eagle on the Franklin half is tiny because of Franklin's anti-eagle feelings. One even claimed that the bird's size proved Sinnock agreed with Franklin!

However, the fact is that Mrs. Ross was the one who ordered that the eagle be added, and that it be a tiny one. She hadn't planned on this, but decided it was necessary in view of the law requiring that an eagle be on the half-dollar's reverse. The small size was necessary to avoid conflict with the main design feature, the Bell. *Sinnock didn't even include the eagle*—it was done by Gilroy Roberts.

From 1948 to 1963 the Philadelphia mint struck Franklin halves every year. Branch mints made the coin, but less often: Denver made none in 1955–56; San Francisco only made halves in 1949 and 1951–54. Mint marks on branch mint coins are above the bell and below the E in STATES.

Very few Franklin halves are around now since they're 90 percent silver coins. If you do find any, they'll probably be 1963–D,

FIG. 35–2. Half-dollar, 1961–D, reverse. The small size of the eagle has misled many who see this coin. It has nothing to do with Franklin's reputed dislike for our national emblem.

the high-mintage date (Denver made over 67 million that year). Hardest to find is 1955, with only 2,498,181 released. Proofs were struck in Philadelphia between 1950 and 63, with mintage ranging from 51,386 in 1950 to 3,218,019 in 1962.

Among varieties are 1954–D and other years with double mint marks, 1957–D with double lettering, 1954–S and 1962–D with various die breaks, and others. The most famous variety probably is the 1955 "Bugs Bunny" coin, named for a die clash that makes Franklin appear as buck-toothed as that popular cartoon character.

Prices for Uncirculated specimens are about $4 to $8 for common dates and $25 to $40 for rare ones. Proofs cost about $7 up.

Star-Line dates are 1959–D, 1960, 1960–D, and 1961–D. Marginals are 1948–D, 1954, 1956, 1957, 1957–D, 1958, 1959, and Proof 1954.

Perhaps the Franklin/Liberty Bell half-dollar would have been issued for its full statutory 25 years, but we were never to know. A new half-dollar design was about to be conceived by tragedy on the afternoon of November 22, 1963.

36

Kennedy Half-Dollars

"This is a very dangerous and uncertain world."—President John F. Kennedy, last spoken address, Fort Worth, November 22, 1963

On November 22, 1963, the United States went into emotional shock. National grief at the death of a President was like nothing since the death of Lincoln.

High-level officials at once began considering using the late President's portrait on a coin. Only the quarter, half-dollar, and silver dollar were seriously considered. The dollar was discarded and widowed Jacqueline Kennedy herself wanted Washington kept on the quarter.

So on December 10, President Lyndon B. Johnson asked Congress to authorize replacement of the Franklin/Liberty Bell design. He signed the bill into law December 30. Three days later the Philadelphia mint received dies for striking 1964 Proof half-dollars.

Sculptors Gilroy Roberts and Frank Gasparro started with the Treasury Department Presidential Medal, which shows a left-facing bust with "Gilroy Roberts 1961" on the truncation. (A few writers' description of this as an "Inaugural" medal misled some collectors, including me, to think the official Inaugural Medal was used. It wasn't, and I regret the error in this book's first edition.)

The obverse, by Roberts, has JOHN F. at the left rim and KENNEDY at right. He substituted a widely spaced LIBERTY for the name, and raised the cutoff line, allowing better centering of the portrait and increasing its size in relation to the available area. He replaced his name and the medal's date with a stylized GR monogram. He reworked the forehead and made the mouth appear gently smiling. At Mrs. Kennedy's suggestion he softened the hair's part and added some hair lines. As a base for the neck's sharp point he added a horizontal IN GOD WE TRUST; the date is at the bottom.

Gasparro's reverse has two vertical torches of liberty flanking an inscription from Kennedy's inaugural address, "We shall pay any price, bear any burden, meet any hardship, support any friend, oppose any foe to assure the survival of liberty." Below is a smaller "John F. Kennedy." At bottom is "January 20" above "1961." At the top rim is "Inaugurated President" above a small Presidential Seal.

Gasparro put HALF DOLLAR, flanked by dots, at bottom and placed national identification around top and side rims. For the main design he used the Presidential Seal, a heraldic eagle holding an olive branch and arrows in its talons. A U.S. shield is on its chest, and a banner lettered E PLURIBUS UNUM is above, artistically held down by rays and an arch of clouds. Fifty tiny stars around the design represent the states and set off the rim inscriptions.

Philadelphia and Denver began minting halves February 11, 1964. The first distribution was March 24, when 26 million Kennedy halves were released—and promptly disappeared.

FIG. 36–1. Half-dollar, 1968–D, obverse. This was the first half-dollar since 1917 to carry the mint mark on the obverse.

FIG. 36–2. Half-dollar, 1964–D, reverse. The 1964–D is the only Kennedy half-dollar with a mint mark on the reverse.

They were put away as keepsakes by those who'd supported Kennedy and those who'd opposed him; millions were claimed as souvenirs by people abroad. One half-dollar reportedly brought $42 in an auction in Kenya. A man about to visit Europe phoned me long-distance, asking how many coins to take and what price to ask (I urged him not to profiteer). Many halves became pendants, watches, and other ornaments and novelties. Large-scale hoarding continued well into 1967; some hoarding continues even now.

Type 1 coins, .900 fine silver, were struck 1964–66 and dated 1964. Type 2's are part-silver with, says the mint, "a cladding of an alloy of 800 parts of silver and 200 parts of copper" and "a core of an alloy of silver and copper such that the whole weighs 11.5 grams and contains 4.6 grams of silver and 6.9 grams of copper. These were struck 1965–70. Their inner section is 21 percent silver and 79 percent copper. The total is 40 percent silver. Type 3 coins are the same cupronickel-clad type as quarters and dimes, and include the 1971–74 issues. Type 4 is the circulating commemorative with the date "1776–1976." Its reverse, by Seth G. Huntington, shows Independence Hall. Mintage of 400 million was planned.

Top-mintage coin is 1971–D, with 302,097,424 struck. However, the low-mintage coin poses a problem. The first Type 2 halves were struck December 30, 1965, but are included in 1966 production figures. We might never learn how many were made. During 1966 San Francisco minted only 470,000 regular-issue halves dated 1965, but 1965(66–S) bears no mint mark, and over 65.8 million halves are dated 1965. This leaves 1970–D, with its entire 2,150,000 mintage earmarked for that year's Uncirculated sets, as the low-mintage identifiable date.

Type 1 coins from Denver have the D mint mark at left of the olive stem and below the eagle's talon. Mint marks were omitted from coins dated 1965–67, but were restored in 1968 and moved to the obverse at lower right of the portrait and centered above the date.

Prices are in the $1.25 to $2.50 range for Unc coins, except Type 1's, which cost about $3 to $5, and 1970–D, which costs around $22 to $30. Proofs, struck 1964 at Philadelphia and 1968 to date at San Francisco, vary from about $3 or $4 up.

All dates are in circulation; I see more and more of these coins, even 1964 and 1964–D, in use. One will buy two standard 75-watt light bulbs or any of several magazines.

There are no Star-Line or Marginal dates for Kennedy halves.

37

I Have X Silver Dollars

Notes on one of our most popular
denominations.

Every so often, someone who hopes he or she has a rare silver dollar asks me to appraise the coin. Some silver dollars have been kept and passed from generation to generation. And most people are disappointed—for nine out of ten coins are *not* rare.

All early silver dollars *are* rare—in fact, up until 1878 the mintage totaled less than 8 million coins, and that's for 84 years! Of the regular-issue silver dollars from 1794–1935, over half had mintages under 1 million and another one-fourth were between 1 and 3 million.

Morgans' mintage soared to 44,690,000 in 1921; over 84.27 million Peace dollars were made in 1922. So why are coins so hard to find?

One reason is the infamous Pittman Act of 1918. It sent 270,-232,722 silver dollars to the melting pots, and we'll never know how many of which dates and mints were destroyed.

Another reason is increased interest in coins. Remember when the Treasury released most of its silver dollar reserve, in 1964?

People lined up for more than a city block to take part in the "silver rush" and the Treasury was crowded all day. You could buy rolls of 20 coins or bags of 1,000.

Part of the reason for the rush was a speech by Mint Director Eva Adams suggesting that no more silver dollars would be made. Gambling interests in Nevada, coin collectors, and speculators all piled on the bandwagon. Within days Treasury Secretary Douglas Dillon announced that (1) only minting of new dollars would prevent total exhaustion of the supply and (2) the Treasury wouldn't mind a cut in silver content if that concession would win approval for a new issue. By the time the Treasury called a halt it was down to about 3 million coins. Most of these later were sold to the public in a series of special government-run auctions. But after five sales, nearly a third of the coins remained unsold, in early 1975; it was suggested that the coins be stored for three or more years and offered again, but there could be an earlier sale in connection with the national Bicentennial.

Many years ago it was standard procedure for the Treasury to release these coins around Christmas to fill the seasonal demand. One December more than 3 million scarce coins flooded into the market: unaware of their $2 to $6.50 average value, mint officials had dumped 1884, 1886, 1887, and 1889 dollars into circulation.

Such "dumping" had dramatic (and for some collectors, catastrophic) effects on prices. The 1903–O, for instance, catalogued at $1,500 Unc in the 1963 Red Book. After a December release of this date, among others, the book value plummeted to $30 Unc! It's still below $75. The 1904–O, also in that December 1973 release, dropped from $350 to $3.50 Unc and remains well under $20.

By the way, the silver dollar and Trade Dollar share the honors as largest-sized regular-issue U. S. coin, with 38.1-mm. diameter. The only larger official issue is the Panama-Pacific 1915 $50 gold commemorative. The double-eagle's diameter actually is only 34 mm.

38

Silver Dollars of Early Days

Hundred Cents, One Dollar
Or Unit—edge inscription, early
silver dollar.

The silver dollar's pedigree goes a long way back, as we'll find in a later chapter. The U.S. coin was authorized by the Act of April 2, 1792, with weight of 416 grains and fineness of .8924.

For two years no dollars were made. The first are Robert Scot's Flowing Hair coins of 1794–95. These show a Liberty head facing right, with very straight and sharp nose, and wavy hair. She looks slightly upward, perhaps to symbolize the young nation's confidence and hope. LIBERTY is at the top and the date is below. There are eight stars at left and seven at right.

The reverse has an eagle so slim it's like a cross between a starved pterodactyl and a hungry vulture. It perches with raised wings on a bundle of arrows, looking to its left. Around it, in front of the right wing and behind the left, is a large olive wreath; outside the wreath is UNITED STATES OF AMERICA.

FIG. 38–1. Silver dollar, 1794, obverse. Scot's design, on a coin in the National Collection, Smithsonian Institution.

FIG. 38–2. Silver dollar, 1799, obverse. The Draped Bust design. Coin is in the National Collection, Smithsonian Institution.

Only 1,758 silver dollars dated 1794 were minted, making this the rarest date until 1836. Only about ten are known Uncirculated, and apparently only around 50 to 75 survive in *any* condition. A Very Fine specimen brought $20,000 in an August 1974 auction.

In 1795 there were some changes. In addition to some Flowing Hair coins the new Draped Bust dollars by Gilbert Stuart were minted. Some of Liberty's hair is bound by a ribbon on these, and the coins have been called the Fillet Head type. The portrait is larger and there's drapery at the shoulders. The reverse's wreath changes to laurel (left) and palm (right). The eagle is smaller but heavier. This type continued through 1798; in addition to the old type, a new reverse was used that year with a large "heraldic" eagle.

From then on, the coin was issued unchanged through 1803. Or should that be 1804?

The famed 1804 dollars are Draped Bust/Heraldic Eagle coins, but they also are the hobby's most expensive and overrated fakes. Official records show 19,570 dollars made during fiscal 1804. They were made before March 28, when President Thomas Jefferson ordered minting of silver dollars halted. The coins were worth more as silver metal than as coins, and stopping coining was the only way to prevent wholesale melting and exporting.

However, those 19,570 coins were struck with dies dated 1803. We've found, remember, that the calendar year date might be incorrect, and that coins were recorded according to the fiscal year. Since fiscal year 1804 began July 1, 1803, an 1803 date on "1804" dollars was correct in terms of mint records.

The dollars dated 1804 were minted for presentation purposes, and shouldn't even be dignified by the term "restrike." The Type 1's ("originals") probably were made in 1834 or 1835, and their reverse has the first s of STATES between two clouds. Most Type 2's ("restrikes") were made in 1859 and 1868; they have the s almost perfectly centered over the first cloud.

How were the early silver dollars received? One source says the Flowing Hair type was unpopular, and calls its eagle "sickly."

You've probably noticed that the coins' description omits a denomination. The value *is* on these coins, but not where most people would expect it. Early dollars have the edge lettered HUNDRED CENTS, ONE DOLLAR OR UNIT. As you know, there was some support for the idea of calling the currency unit just that, a "Unit." Mint authorities evidently played it safe: whether "Dollar" or "Unit" won in the end, the coins would be acceptable.

Some early silver dollars have what look like file marks. These "adjustment marks" were made by workers who filed away metal to bring overweight coins down to acceptable weight.

You could subscribe to *The Newbern Gazette*, in North Carolina, for three of these coins in 1801. In Savannah, Ga., Mr. G. L. Barrett proposed to teach "the elegant accomplifhment of FENCING" at one dollar per lesson. And in Charleston, S.C., George C. Bailey advertised that November that he'd sell you "Foolfcap writing Paper, from 3 to 4 dollars, per ream."

These coins cost around $150 up in Fair condition; a Fine specimen costs $500 and up. All were minted in Philadelphia, with mintage ranging from the 1794 figure up to 423,515 for 1799.

The only Star-Line date is 1802. Marginals are 1800 and 1801.

39

The Most Beautiful Dollar of All

*Here's the true story of the
1836 silver dollar.*

C. GOBRECHT F.

We often call the first Liberty Seated silver dollars the "Gobrecht type" or "Gobrecht dollars," but "Type 1" would be better. When we consider the entire issue with this design, we discover that three other men also earned credit—Sully, Peale, and Hughes.

Thomas Sully drew the basic Liberty Seated design which appears, in much improved form, on our coins. Titian Peale, son of Colonial artist Charles Willson Peale, drew the impressive flying eagle. Assistant mint engraver Christian Gobrecht revised the designs at the end of 1835.

His first version shows Liberty sitting on a large rock. She sits facing right but turns her head to look left. Her left hand holds a pole atop which rests a liberty cap; her right steadies a U.S. shield across which lies a banner lettered LIBERTY. The date is at bottom. Below the design's ground line is C. GOBRECHT F. The F is for Latin *fecit*, "made," so we can loosely translate this as "Made by C. Gobrecht."

On the reverse a massive eagle flies upward to the left through a field of 26 stars. UNITED STATES OF AMERICA is around top and side rims; ONE DOLLAR is at bottom. The edge is plain.

Another pattern, also dated 1836 and also plain-edged, shows the eagle in a starless field.

Delighted, Mint Director R. M. Patterson ordered that Gobrecht's name be on issued coins. When the design was released to newspapers, Gobrecht was the focal point of a fusillade of criticism. Some papers called him a "conceited German" for putting his name on the coin so obtrusively. Bitterly offended, he removed his name.

Then Patterson told Gobrecht that the engraver should claim his due credit. So Gobrecht restored his name—in extremely tiny incuse lettering on the ground line. This produced the "common" Gobrecht dollars, minted December 11 *and issued soon after*.

Those who call them patterns claim that the law changing the dollar's weight to 412.5 grains wasn't passed until January 18, 1837. But there is no merit in that claim in view of what the government itself said to the press and in official mint records.

These coins have national identification around top and sides of the reverse, and ONE DOLLAR at bottom. For the rest of the description, here's the story *Poulson's American Daily Advertiser* (Philadelphia, Pa.) reprinted on December 16, 1836, from the Washington, D.C. *Globe*: (Official Text)

THE NEW DOLLAR

It gives us pleasure to announce that the dollar of our own mint is soon to make its appearance. The face of the coin represents a full length figure of Liberty, seated on a rock, with the classic emblem of the *pileus* or liberty cap, surmounting a spear held in the left hand. The right hand rests on the American shield, with its thirteen stripes, crossed by a scroll, on which is the word Liberty.

The reverse represents the American eagle, on the wing, drawn accurately from nature; all the heraldic appendage of the old coin being discarded. Over the field are placed irregularly twenty-six stars; the entrance of Michigan into the Union, having been, it seems, anticipated.

The design of the face of the coin was drawn by Mr. Sully, and that of the reverse by Mr. Titian Peale, both under instructions from the Director of the Mint. The dies were executed by Mr. Gobrecht, one of the engravers of the mint.

This emission of dollars is the first coined at the mint since the year 1805. It is intended to adopt the same design in the other coins, as soon as it is practicable to do so.

The following day, Saturday, the Washington, D.C. *United States Telegraph* announced that "The U.S. Mint is about to issue new American dollars, the coining of which has been suspended for the last thirty years."

This time the reaction was against the coin. A letter to the Boston *Transcript* that December objected to the liberty cap, which symbolizes the liberty of the freed slave. "Now we, as American citizens," the writer pointed out, "do not admit that we were ever slaves. . . ." The paper agreed. In Philadelphia the *American Daily Advertiser* printed several opinions under the headline "Doctors Differ." The paper's own comments include, "If this coin is objectionable on the score of appearance, it is equally so on account of the faintness of the outline, which will soon be effaced by the wear and tear incident to circulation." The paper also notes that "The *E Pluribus Unum*, which was so significant of our union, which is our national peculiarity, has disappeared." It quoted the New York *American's* objection to the plain edge, "There is no milling on the exterior circle. . . ."

The New York *Commercial Advertiser*, one of the few defenders, praised the dollar as "classical and beautiful" and "eminently graceful," calling the eagle "a novel and delicate design, very beautiful, an improved race of that noble bird."

But the same city's *Evening Star* charged that "the dollar looks like a Brummagen medal made of britannia ware," with Liberty "a poor, shivering, half dressed figure" and the eagle "a huge turkey buzzard, all wings."

Many Proofs are available—perhaps the first silver dollar in over 30 years was considered a novelty worth saving. But many other specimens are advertised with evidence of wear. In *Numismatic News*, "coin grades VF but shield grade F, Field shows many circulation marks" (Fred Sweeney ad, December 2, 1969); and "1836 Gobrecht. Name on base; reverse with eagle in starry field. EF $995.00; Impaired Proof (it saw a few months of circulation!) Sharp in all details—1295.00" (Hathaway and Bowers ad, September 9, 1969). Then there are auction catalogs: "One of the original issue. . . . Always popular, and collected as part of both the pattern and regular series" (Harmer, Rooke, November 1969); and the flat statement that the coin "was placed into circulation" (Hollinbeck Kagin, 282nd mail bid sale).

Why were the 1836 and 1839 issues struck in Proof? Probably

in the hope of offsetting, by heavy striking pressure, the low relief. Mint Director Patterson probably wanted to get these coins issued on a priority basis. It would have been better to make new dies in higher relief, but he may have feared that any delay on the controversial coin would result in cancellation of plans to issue new silver dollars.

Only 1,000 silver dollars were released in 1836. Another 600 were released in 1837; these were struck March 31 from the previous year's dies. The 1836(37) coins are distinguished from "1836 originals" by their reverse—it's *not* rotated 180 degrees from the obverse, as with most U.S. coins. The restrikes were omitted from official mintage records, but were listed in Dr. Judd's book on patterns. Most 1836 dollars offered as never-used Proofs apparently are restrikes; one catalog may be correct in stating that nearly all originals went into circulation.

John L. Riddell, M.D., writing in 1845, listed the 1836 dollar as a regular issue; so did William Von Bergen, in 1889. John Dye wrote in 1883, "In 1838 the first reduced 412½ grain silver dollar was issued: it bore the device of the dollar of 1836, excepting on the Reverse the stars were omitted." However, Dye was only partly right—the issue after 1836 was in 1839, not 1838.

In 1838 Gobrecht added 13 stars around the obverse rim. Patterns of that and the following year continue the basic designs. And as we know, the Act of January 18, 1837, had by then lowered the weight and boosted the fineness.

Even the government lists these coins as regular issues. In the official mint records in "Domestic and Foreign Coins Manufactured by Mints of The United States" the Philadelphia list includes, in the "Dollars" column, an entry of 1,000 for 1836 and 300 for 1839.

In 1840 Mint Director Patterson hired Robert B. Hughes to prepare plaster models of the silver dollar. Hughes reworked Liberty, improving her proportions, changing the lines of her gown and increasing the total grace and style. He also went back to an older, pre-Gobrecht eagle for the reverse.

Gobrecht was not a sculptor; Hughes was. It's safe to assume that the relief of the latter's model was high enough to avoid the criticism caused by low relief on Type 1 coins of 1836. When

FIG. 39–1. Silver dollar, 1859–O, obverse. This is the Sully–Gobrecht–Hughes obverse, one of our most beautiful coin designs.

FIG. 39–2. Silver dollar, 1859–O, reverse. The small O below the eagle identifies this coin as a New Orleans branch mint "product."

Hughes was finished, the Liberty Seated dollar was ready for its Type 2 phase.

FROM 1840 TO 1873

New silver dollars of July 21, 1840, have what we could call the Sully-Gobrecht-Hughes, or Type 2, obverse. It's basically the seated figure of Miss Liberty from 1836, plus the stars added around the obverse rim in 1839, plus Hughes's reworking of 1839–40. The Type 2 reverse shows a small eagle with a U.S. shield on its chest, holding an olive branch in its right claw and three arrows in its left. The eagle is fairly lifelike despite its rather large head, which turns correctly to its right. UNITED STATES OF AMERICA is around top and side rims, limited by the eagle's right wing, at our left, and the arrowheads, at right. ONE DOL. is at bottom. Coins with mint marks have them on the reverse, below the eagle.

It might seem strange that Gobrecht would step back and let Hughes do final revisions, but William Kneass had suffered a stroke in 1835, and when Kneass died in 1840 Gobrecht became chief engraver. He probably had enough to do, and must have viewed the silver dollar with mixed emotions at best.

Philadelphia issued the dollar every year 1840–73, except that only Proofs were made in 1858. New Orleans struck dollars in 1846, 1850, 1859, and 1860. San Francisco made them in 1859, 1870, 1872, and 1873. And Carson City minted silver dollars 1870, 1871, 1872, and 1873.

If your horse lost a shoe as you rode through Clarksville, Tenn., in 1843 you'd probably visit blacksmith R. C. Beauchamp, who'd charge one dollar for a complete shoeing job. In 1852, in Fond Du Lac, Wis., a dollar would buy four pounds of chewing tobacco at Lowell's Fountain City Grocery; two of the coins could purchase a gallon of Old Irish Whiskey at Henry Rahte's New Liquor Store. But out in California, where the gold rush economy had skyrocketed prices, you'd have had to pay a dollar for ONE EGG.

In 1863, 1864, and 1865 patterns were struck in nickel, copper, silver, and aluminum with the regular obverse and the "reverse of 1866" with IN GOD WE TRUST on a scroll over the eagle. Starting with 1866 dollars, the first of the Type 3 issue, this banner and motto were part of the regular design.

Top mintage came in 1872, with Philadelphia's 1,105,500 plus 950 Proofs. The low-mintage regular-issue date is, as far as we know, 1839. However, those 300 coins (or as many as survive) aren't necessarily the rarest: neither Red Book nor official record lists a figure for 1870–S, and 1873–S is a mystery coin. Mint records report 700 of the latter were made, but apparently all were melted. A. G. Heaton advertised in *The Numismatist* in 1900, "Wanted. Standard silver dollar of 1873, San Francisco mint; Good premium will be paid." But there's still not one authenticated specimen known.

Ever hear of the "Crime of '73"? That's what some people called the Act of February 12, which revised our coinage. It put the nation on the gold standard and ended minting of the Liberty Seated silver dollar.

Many dates cost $65 to $85 Good, $80 to $110 Fine, and $450 to $750 Uncirculated. Of course, auctions and dealers are our best sources for these coins.

The Star-Line date is 1867. Marginals are 1849, 1863, 1864, and 1865.

40

Those Were the Days

"The preparation of new designs for the obverse of silver coins and other contemplated improvements, renders the present time a favorable one for testing the qualifications of a properly recommended person with a view to his permanent employment as assistant engraver, should the result of the trial prove entirely satisfactory to us."
—confidential letter, Mint Director H. R. Linderman to superintendent of Philadelphia Mint, August 14, 1876.

After four years without silver dollars, the Act of February 28, 1878, once again authorized these coins. This "Bland-Allison Act," a compromise bill, gave the coins one of their now rarely used nicknames, "Bland dollars."

Representative Richard P. Bland of Missouri twice introduced bills for resumption of the silver standard. His second bill was passed after a compromise with chief opponent Senator William B. Allison. President Rutherford B. Hayes vetoed it, but on February 28 the act was passed over his veto. That same day Mint Director Linderman approved the new Morgan dollar design.

On June 13, 1876, Linderman had written to the Deputy Master of England's Royal Mint to ask whether the man could find a candidate for the post of assistant engraver at Philadelphia. The man recommended was a young designer named George T. Morgan. After examining samples of Morgan's work, Linderman offred him a six-month appointment. Morgan accepted and that October became a "special engraver" at $8 per day.

His first assignment was the silver dollar but he also worked on half-dollar patterns. One of these shows the design he later used on the dollar patterns of 1878 and on issued coins—an eagle standing with raised wings, holding an olive branch and arrows, with IN GOD WE TRUST in Gothic ("old English") lettering above the eagle. This was the first pattern to use this type of lettering. A laurel wreath stretches from wing to wing below the eagle.

After finishing the reverse design, Morgan began looking for a girl to model for the Liberty portrait. He mentioned his problem to Professor Thomas Eakins of the Academy of Fine Arts, who said he knew a young lady with almost classic features.

Without mentioning why he was there, Morgan went with Eakins and was introduced to schoolteacher Anna W. Williams. He saw a slightly plump girl with a fair complexion, blonde hair, and a carriage that could only be called stately. Later he would call her profile the closest to perfect he'd seen in either England or the U.S. He studied her face and considered and reached a decision. Then he told her why he was there, that he wanted her to become Miss Liberty.

Miss Williams refused. But her friends—probably urged by Eakins and Morgan—finally persuaded her to consent. She sat five times, and the result was our best-known silver dollar.

It's noteworthy that she lived at ·13th and Spring Garden Streets, four blocks from where the third Philadelphia Mint would be located.

It's also worth noting that Miss Williams' friends later did an about-face and tried to conceal her identity. They obviously failed, happily for numismatists with a bit of the romantic in their makeup. The famous article "To Marry A Goddess," that *The Numismatist* reprinted in May 1896 from the New York *Mail and Express*, was prompted by an announcement that Anna Williams would be married. But the marriage never took place: she died at sixty-eight, still single, in mid-April 1926.

A photograph of Anna Williams appeared in *Ladies' Home Journal* in 1892 and was reproduced on page 34 of the March

1970 *COINage* magazine. I don't say, as some contemporary newspapers did, that the coin was an almost photographic portrait, but there certainly is a strong resemblance.

Now let's examine the issued coin, one that certainly should be in our collections.

The obverse shows a Liberty head facing left, wearing a liberty cap over which is a wreath of oak leaves, cotton bolls, and wheat ears. In front of this wreath is a slim coronet with incuse LIBERTY. Some of Liberty's hair shows in front of the coronet and at the side and back of her head, with several curls extending below the portrait's cutoff line. Around top and upper side rims is E PLURI- BUS UNUM with dots between the words. There are seven stars at the left rim and six at right; the date is at bottom and a tiny incuse M on the base of the portrait identifies the designer.

On the reverse is the American eagle, rather stylized, its wings raised as if for flight; it looks to its right and holds an olive branch

FIG. 40–1. Silver dollar, 1904–O, obverse. The portrait isn't really photographic, but it's recognizable. This is one of several dates that were considered rare until a year-end release of coins from Treasury vaults made prices plummet. Those who had bought at high prices earlier were hurt, but the coins at last were within reach of collectors with limited budgets.

FIG. 40–2. Silver dollar, 1904–O, reverse. This is the only regular-issue U.S. coin design with Gothic lettering.

in its right talon and three arrows in its left. A laurel wreath extends from wing to wing below the eagle, providing a base. Above, on a horizontal line limited by the wing surfaces, is the Gothic IN GOD WE TRUST, tiny enough to fit the coin without intruding on the style of the other lettering. UNITED STATES OF AMERICA is around top and side rims, with the first and last words set off by wingtips. At bottom is ONE DOLLAR flanked by stars. Mint marks are below the wreath.

The first issue was in 1878. Morgan dollars were minted by Philadelphia and San Francisco 1878–1904 and again in 1921. Carson City struck the coins 1878–93 except 1886–88. New Orleans made them 1879–1904. Denver issued this type only in 1921.

In 1892 J. Rosenthal of Columbia, Tenn., would sell you a pair of shoes for two of these coins. A year later, cigar makers Jacob Stahl, Jr., & Co., of New York, advertised a sample box of ten Hotel Brunswick Perfecto cigars for $1 ("equal to any imported cigar").

Morgan dollars circulated widely in the West and South, but never were popular in the North or on the East Coast. Many were held by the Treasury and Federal Reserve banks as a reserve against paper currency.

Coinage ended in 1904, when the bullion supply ran out, but the coins stayed in use.

In 1911 The Macmillan Company advertised Molly Elliot Seawell's book *The Ladies' Battle* for $1, calling it a new book on "Votes for Women." You could buy a box of chocolates for $1 in 1913 from Stephen F. Whitman & Son, of Philadelphia. And in 1918 the Howe Mfg. Co. of Chicago offered for $1 a 6" × 8" American flag mounted on a special automobile radiator cap and illuminated by an electric light connected to the car's headlights.

The Pittman Act of April 1918, one of our great numismatic tragedies, resulted in the melting of 279,121,554 silver dollars for export to India (after being cast into bars) and another 11,111,168 for recoining in lower denominations at home. More silver dollars were made in 1921 with minor changes in the design, but it was essentially the same coin as in 1878.

Variety collectors can go at it with full enthusiasm—1878 coins include seven, eight, and seven over eight tail feathers; there are overdates (1880–O with 80/79), double dates (1879, 1900) mint mark varieties (1900–O with O/CC, 1882–O with O/S), and others. Some Morgan dollars have a dot after the M on one or both sides. On the obverse it's on the base of the portrait; on the reverse it's on the left loop of the ribbon tying the wreath. These dots were added to keep track of the dies.

Top mintage of 44,690,000 is that of 1921. Rarest regular-issue date is 1895, with 12,000 regular-issue pieces struck, but the Red Book lists this in Proof only, and for years it was assumed that only the 800 Proofs survived. Nonetheless, at least one business strike has been reported and is believed genuine; perhaps others also survived. For all practical purposes, though, the rarest date is 1893–S, with 100,000 minted. Proofs were struck every year at Philadelphia. Proof totals peaked at 1,355 in 1880 and dropped to 50 in 1921; it's believed that from seven to ten 1921 Proofs exist.

Regular-issue coins cost about $5 to $7.50 for common dates in Fine condition, $10 to $16 Uncirculated. But prices go up to about $8,500 or so for an 1895 Proof. Other collectors with duplicates, coin auctions, and dealers will be our sources for these coins.

Star-Line dates are 1893 and Proof 1884. Marginals are 1878–CC, 1891–S, 1892, 1892–O, 1897–O, 1898–O, 1903, 1904, and Proofs of 1887, 1888, 1889, 1890, 1891, 1900, and 1904.

41

Liberty Crowned

> "Say, lissen!"—to the ring
> of our last .900 fine silver dollar.

At the 1920 American Numismatic Association convention Farran Zerbe suggested the U.S. issue a coin to mark the signing of peace treaties ending World War I. This would be a new type of commemorative—one that actually circulated.

An ANA committee headed by Judson Brenner contacted the House Committee on Coinage, Weights, and Measures. That December the House committee took up the suggestion. (After the initial contact, reported *The Numismatist*, the ANA committee was "entirely ignored" by the House committee, Secretary of the Treasury, and Director of the Mint.)

The resolution providing for the coin, introduced May 9, 1921, failed to reach a vote; dollars were issued under the old 1878 Bland-Allison law. The Fine Arts Commission held a design contest and invited eight sculptors to compete. The winner of the $1,500 prize was 33-year-old Anthony de Francisci, an Italian immigrant who worked as a medalist in New York. (He had become a naturalized citizen in 1913.)

He drew the Liberty portrait modeled on his wife, Teresa Cafarelli de Francisci, to keep the design secret. It was a perfect choice. She was a beautiful model; since coming from Italy at the age of five, she had been fascinated by the Statue of Liberty, was, in her own words, "always posing as Liberty," and reportedly several times *played the role of the Statue* in patriotic exercises at school!

On the obverse is the young Liberty head facing left, very lifelike and with her mouth slightly open as if starting to speak. Some hair is gathered at the back of her head but most of it is

FIG. 41–1. Silver dollar, 1922, obverse. This is one of our most beautiful portraits of Miss Liberty, and represented a dream's fulfillment for the model.

contained by a large crown of spikes or rays. These are mixed long and short, in a planned at-random appearance. Around the top is a wide-spaced LIBERTY with B partly covered by the crown. Horizontal and providing a steadying influence are IN GOD WE at left of the throat and TRVST at right. The date is at bottom and a tiny AF monogram is below the portrait.

The reverse shows a large, powerful and lifelike eagle facing right. It perches, with wings folded, on a rock. In the distance are mountains and clouds. A sprig of mountain laurel grows from a split in the rock. From lower right, extending to and beyond the eagle, are rays of the rising sun. UNITED STATES OF AMERICA is around the upper rim. Directly below it is E PLURIBUS UNUM, with s and the first U of "Unum" partly covered by the eagle's head and beak. Level with the eagle's leg are ONE at left and DOLLAR at right, superimposed on the rays. At bottom is PEACE. Mint marks are at lower left, between ONE and the wingtip.

Liberty's expression caused widely varying reactions. Some observers thought she looked "startled" or "frightened." *The Wall Street Journal* called her a flapper, and one numismatist suggested that if she were to speak she'd be saying, "Say, lissen!" But Zerbe himself was quoted in the February 1922 *Numismatist*, "With utility defects remedied, it should be a pleasing and satisfactory coin for long and good service, and the A.N.A. can deservingly call it its own."

But not everyone was pleased. *The Numismatist* quoted Judson Brenner, "It lacks the artistic design which such a dollar, issued by a great nation, should have. It has caused great disappointment to those who conceived the idea of having the dollar issued and who desired to have a Peace dollar represent that which Peace should represent, namely, beauty and delicacy, together with being symbolic of Peace."

That year, ANA president Wormser charged, "There is nothing emblematic of peace on it except the inscription of 'Peace' itself," and added, as quoted by *The Numismatist*, "The idea of a lasting world peace, or a peace after so many years of disastrous world war, could have lent itself to much better, more artistic and allegorical treatment than was used on the coin issued."

Really? What's wrong with the laurel, symbolic of military victory? Who can say the eagle's folded wings and the absence of the traditional arrows don't represent peace? How about the American eagle standing triumphantly on the height? What about the dawning era of peace? How about the appearance of nature's having sculpted the enduring word "Peace" while wearing away the rock of war?

This is a beautiful and stirring coin whose *primary* artistic thrust admittedly is not commemorative, but whose secondary theme certainly *is*. I see the prime emphasis as the watchfulness of Miss Liberty joined with the strength of the nation.

The first Peace dollars were struck in December 1921, but those 1,006,473 coins were held for later release until January 3. So the true issue dates are 1922–35.

Coins of 1921 were struck in high relief; so were some 1922 coins. Later 1922 dollars are in lower relief. In addition to 1922 "type of 1921," varieties include 1921 with double profile, 1922 with double date and profile, 1935–S with extra rays at left of the eagle, and various others.

FIG. 41–2. Silver dollar, 1926–S, reverse. The Peace dollar belongs to a select group of coins, since it shows the eagle with an olive branch but without arrows. It also belongs to the somewhat larger group of controversial issues.

Mintage was anything but continuous. All three operating mints made dollars in 1922–23; then only Philadelphia and San Francisco minted them in 1924–25. Denver joined in for 1926–27, but left the job to the other two in 1928. Then came a five-year break caused by reduced demand, followed by three-mint operations in 1934 and silver dollars from Philadelphia and San Francisco in 1935. Philadelphia struck only a few Proofs; four are known for 1921 and three for 1922 with the high relief of 1921. Peace dollar Proofs are dull-finish "Matte Proofs" rather than the bright, mirror-like coins we usually associate with the term "Proof."

The biggest year for the U.S. silver dollar was 1922, when the combined mintage total hit 84,275,000, with Philadelphia making nearly five out of every eight coins. That total of 51,737,000 makes 1922 the top-mintage coin. Lowest is the 1928, with only 360,649 made.

Prices begin at $5 to $7.50 for several dates in Fine condition and go to about $800 for an Unc 1934–S.

As with Morgan dollars, we'll find most of these in coin auction catalogs, dealers' lists, and other collectors' duplicates. Only a few are in circulation.

In 1926 Montgomery Ward's spring-and-summer catalog listed for $1 such items as a pair of brown or black leather slippers for women, a red coaster wagon with blue wheels, or a padlock of rust-resistant iron. In 1935 the Hudson River Day Line was advertising its "Vacation-ette" one-day trips and a dollar would pay your fare up the Hudson River from New York to Indian Point. Also in the last year of issue, five silver dollars would pay for a room at The Breakers, in Atlantic City, N.J., with meals and bath.

The Star-Line date is 1927–D. Marginals are 1924, 1925, 1925–S, 1927, 1928, and 1934–D.

When San Francisco struck its final issue, in August 1935, the mintage total was 1,964,000. By a singular coincidence, dropping the zeroes gives us the year in which Anthony de Francisci died (on October 20) and in which we almost got a new issue of Peace dollars.

4 2

The Return of the Dollar

Collectors once more were about to have
silver dollars around—or were they?

THE ALMOST-COIN OF 1964

There were abortive attempts in 1953 and 1964 to issue new
Peace dollars. In 1965, while the 1964 date was "frozen" on coins,
316,106 silver dollars were struck at Denver—apparently 30 trial
pieces, 76 die adjustment coins (while setting the machinery),
and 316,000 of the authorized 45 million 1964–D Peace dollars.

However, the coin shortage and silver shortage prevented the
issue. The limited number of coin presses were needed for lower
denominations that would help ease the shortage. The Bureau of
the Mint repeatedly stated that all dies and 1964–D silver dollars
were destroyed. Many numismatists, however, believe that at
least seven coins were saved.

THE RETURN OF THE DOLLAR

With the death of former President Dwight D. ("Ike") Eisenhower in 1969, everyone suddenly was asking, why not issue a
new dollar coin with Ike's portrait? As in 1873 and 1878, a battle
developed over whether the coin would contain any silver.

The coin finally appeared in 1971, with Proofs and special Uncirculated coins struck in the 40 percent silver clad composition
used for Type 2 Kennedy halves. Beginning in 1973, Proofs also
were struck on the cupronickel clad planchets used for regular-
issue Ike dollars since 1971.

On the coin's obverse is a slightly "edited" left-facing portrait
of the late President, with some hairlines added; it is extremely
lifelike. Designer Frank Gasparro's "FG" is on the cutoff line. A

large, wide-spaced LIBERTY extends around the upper rim, IN GOD WE TRUST is in two lines below Eisenhower's chin, and the date is at bottom. Mint marks are above the date.

The new dollar's reverse commemorates the July 20/21, 1969, landing of the Apollo 11 spacecraft (which was named "Eagle") on the moon. Gasparro adapted that mission's insigne for the coin's reverse—a naturalistic eagle, wings beating, about to alight on the moon's cratered surface. The eagle's talons grasp an olive branch, continuing the Peace dollar's concept of an eagle without arrows but with the symbol of peace. A small Earth is at upper left, and E PLURIBUS UNUM is above the eagle, limited by the lunar horizon and providing a base for UNITED STATES OF AMERICA around the upper rim. ONE DOLLAR is at bottom, superimposed on the lunar surface, and Gasparro's initials are below the eagle's tailfeathers.

Bicentennial dollars have the "1776–1976" date. Their reverse, by Dennis R. Williams, shows the Liberty Bell in the foreground and the moon, seen from nearby in space, in the background.

Regular-issue coins are struck at Philadelphia and Denver, with Proofs and special Uncirculated 40 percent silver coins made at San Francisco.

Varieties are plentiful, with die breaks, off-center coins, lettering style differences, and others.

FIG. 42–1. The Uncirculated Ike dollar's obverse shows a former President who was for many years a hero of the coin's designer.

FIG. 42–2. The new dollar's reverse, adapted from a space mission's insigne patch.

43

Chop Mark

"I send you specimens of trade dollar in tin struck today. We will commence the regular coinage of trade $ in a few hours."—letter, Mint Superintendent James Pollock to Mint Director Henry R. Linderman, July 11, 1873.

Though the U.S. Trade Dollar was issued first in 1873, its story begins with the first Liberty Seated design. For several years William Barber and James Longacre continued trying their own interpretations of this theme.

Trade with China and Japan had grown quickly, and American businessmen were learning an unhappy fact: we still were losing money. Orientals preferred Mexico's peso to our dollar. This, decided American commercial interests, had to end. It didn't help matters when silver was found in the West and the supply began catching up with the demand. New markets were needed.

Silver and commercial interests got the support of the California Legislature, which relayed their petition to Congress. Mexico's 418-grain peso was capturing trade from our 412.5-grain dollar, explained the merchants. How about a heavier coin?

Mint Director Henry Linderman supported the idea. He hoped a new coin would use Western silver and allow a change to a gold standard. Otherwise, growing supplies would force down silvers' price until our coins' silver was worth less than their face value.

At first the proposed coin was called a "commercial dollar," and patterns of 1871 have this denomination. They show a large olive wreath around COMMERCIAL with the word curved, center high; below are crossed cornucopiae and a horizontal DOLLAR. A small ornament sets off weight and fineness, 420 GRS. 900 FINE, below. At bottom is a small banner lettered GOD OUR TRUST—the early form of our religious motto got another chance. UNITED STATES OF AMERICA is around the upper rim.

FIG. 43–1. Trade dollar, 1877–S, obverse. The long series of patterns, the engravers' hard work, and all the fuss over the coin seem ironic now, in the light of the coin's dismal failure both at home and abroad.

Next year, with Congress still undecided, Barber copied Longacre's Liberty Seated design from the 1871 commercial dollar patterns and added a few touches of his own. He also drew his "Amazonian" Liberty Seated. Judd says this was rejected because it was "too military," with eagles on obverse and reverse and no olive branch. Another cause for criticism was that Liberty is shown with her left breast bare—which, you recall, would cause horrified gasps when the Type 1 Liberty Standing quarter appeared. But more important, this year also brought the first patterns with the denomination shown as TRADE DOLLAR. The cornucopiae disappeared, the old motto yielded to IN GOD WE TRUST and COMMERCIAL gave way to TRADE.

Almost 20 different types of Trade Dollar pattern were struck in 1873, most showing Liberty Head and Liberty Seated obverses with various eagles and Trade Dollar reverses.

One pattern shows essentially the adopted obverse: Liberty sits on two cotton bales, holding a large olive branch in her outstretched right hand with the leaves reaching to the coin's rim. Her left hand holds one end of a banner lettered LIBERTY which is draped over the cotton bales; a wheat sheaf is behind her. At far left and right are wave lines showing the sea in the background. IN GOD WE TRUST is incuse on the narrow base line. Liberty wears a coronet and her hair is gathered up in a bun.

William Barber's reverse has an eagle with wings raised and inverted (tips down), its head to its own left, holding three long arrows in its right talon and an olive branch in its left. Above is an E PLURIBUS UNUM banner; below, slightly curved with center

FIG. 43–2. Trade dollar, 1877–S, reverse. This coin probably never left the U.S., since it doesn't have a single chop mark.

low, is 420 GRAINS, 900 FINE. Around upper rims is UNITED STATES OF AMERICA. At bottom is TRADE DOLLAR. Coins from branch mints have the mint mark above the D of DOLLAR.

Trade Dollars were released in 1873 by Philadelphia, San Francisco, and Carson City. These mints made the coins every year 1873–77. Only Carson City and San Francisco issued the Trade Dollar in 1878, but Philadelphia struck Proofs every year 1873–83.

Most Trade Dollars were exported. They were legal tender in this country, but, like other silver coins, only up to $5.

For a while it seemed the coin would succeed. Over 200,000 Trade Dollars were in use in Calcutta in the first quarter of 1874. Then came the first warning that we had made a mistake.

Minister Seward warned in his 1875 trade report that it was proving difficult to get the coin into northern and central China. How come? Our Trade Dollar was 420 grains, .900 fine, and contained 378 grains of silver. Mexico's peso was 418 grains, but its .970 fineness gave it a silver content of 405.46 grains.

Coins that were used in China soon began gathering what's now the piece's symbolic feature—the "chop mark."

Chop marks sometimes are described as test cuts to check a coin's quality. It's more accurate to call them monogram counterstamps, which mark a coin as genuine silver. A merchant receiving the coin had to take it at face value unless he checked it himself. Not every merchant had the facilities, knowledge, or inclination to add his own chop, but enough owners did add chops to make these marks a factor today in collecting and grading the coins. Auctioneers and dealers often describe Trade Dollars with standard grades plus a comment on the presence, or even the number and size, of chop marks.

Because foreign demand was less than hoped, and the mints kept making Trade Dollars, the big coins began flooding the domestic market. *The San Francisco Bulletin* reported on January 31, 1876: "This coin is now being subjected to a heavy discount, from four to five per cent. being named as the rate." Trade Dollars were so confusing and inconvenient that, said the paper, "even conductors on the street cars now refuse to take them for their face, and subject them to a discount of ten per cent."

Speculators began shipping kegs of Trade Dollars to Nevada and selling them at a discount to miners. The miners used the coins when buying from local merchants—who suddenly found themselves without the gold needed to pay freight bills. The merchants had to go to the original money broker and pay him a premium to take back his Trade Dollars and give them gold.

Virginia City merchants held a mass meeting July 13 and resolved to value Trade Dollars at 90¢. But dissenters saw a way to attract business: the Ross Brothers Palace Clothing Store announced in the July 21 *Daily Territorial Enterprise,* "Trade-Dollars Will Be Taken At Par."

Meanwhile the coin was getting commoner. On July 10 a *New York Times* editorial reported that "Trade Dollars have already made their appearance in this City at the bar-rooms and restaurants, and in the course of a few days they will no longer be looked at as curiosities."

But it already was the start of the end. Minister Steward soon would report that "in Southern China it has not displaced the Mexican [peso]. . . . I doubt whether it ever can come into general or even extensive circulation."

As the price of silver bullion declined, the Trade Dollar became even more of a problem. On July 22, 1876, Congressional Joint Resolution No. 17 was approved. Its Section 2 declares: "That the trade dollar shall not hereafter be a legal tender, and the Secretary of the Treasury is hereby authorized to limit from time to time, the coinage thereof to such an amount as he may deem sufficient to meet the export demand for the same."

The next year, when some of the coin's supporters urged Mint Director Linderman to keep it, he wrote back, "There being no demand at present for this coin for export, the discontinuing of its coinage is manifestly proper."

For a few months the final issue continued, as stores posted signs "No Trade Dollars Accepted." The last officially made coins of the series are those of 1883. Fifteen 1884 and 1885 specimens were struck, apparently without official order or knowledge.

The Act of February 19, 1887 prohibited further minting and authorized the Treasury Department to redeem *unmarked and undefaced* coins for other silver dollars or other U.S. coins. After the six-month exchange period the last circulating Trade Dollars disappeared. At least 7,689,036 pieces had been redeemed at face value. About 5 million of them were later melted and recoined as Morgan dollars.

Top-mintage coin is 1877–S, with 9,519,000. The rarest regular issue is 1878–CC: 97,000 were made but 44,148 were melted on July 19.

Varieties include 1875–S with S over CC, 1876–CC with almost the entire reverse doubled, 1876–S with large or small S, and others.

Star-Line dates are 1874–S, 1877, and Proof 1875. Marginals are 1873 and 1876.

Today a sample of this historic issue, our only demonetized silver coin, costs about $45 to $57 in Good condition and about $60 in Fine. Proofs cost around $1,000 and up; an 1884 was sold for $30,000 in 1974.

Many counterfeits have been made in recent years, of all dates and mints. Your safest policy is to restrict buying of Trade Dollars to the persons or firms you know and can trust.

Part Four

The Romance of Gold

44

Tiniest of All

The tiniest U.S. coins, and
their big brothers, fought an uphill
battle for public acceptance.

The story of our smallest coin starts January 25, 1849, with Congressman James J. McKay (D–N.C.), who introduced a bill providing for a gold $1 coin. On February 1, the Senate Finance Committee reported out a bill to authorize the gold dollar—and a $20 piece.

James B. Longacre, meanwhile, had problems. He made pattern dollars with square center holes, engraving individual pieces because it was so hard to make the small die. Mint Director R. M. Patterson sent three gold and three gilded silver ones to McKay, who was chairman of the Ways and Means Committee, on January 30, along with a draft of a bill authorizing the coins. The dime-sized patterns have a laurel wreath around the hole and U. STATES OF AMERICA around the rim. On the reverse, outside a circle around the hole, are 1 DOLLAR at top and the date at bottom; the rim has 13 stars.

The bill didn't have as smooth a time as McKay and Patterson would have liked. In the House, Joseph R. Ingersoll (Whig–Pa.) attacked the gold dollar as a "toy coin," and "scarcely perceptible to the eye or touch. . . ." Charles Hudson (Whig–Mass.) warned that counterfeiters would find it easy prey. The bill's supporters objected to the "easy counterfeiting" claims, and argued that people really did want gold dollars. However, the bill was passed by what Senator Charles G. Atherton (D–N.H.) later called a large majority.

Sunday, March 4, after a long session with more debate in both houses, the Senate passed the House bill, the House agreed to that version, and President Polk signed the Act of March 3, 1849. The act exempted the dollar from the requirement that all U.S. gold show an eagle on the reverse.

Longacre, according to Dr. Judd, "apparently had learned very little about die sinking during the four years [that he had worked at the mint] and had great difficulty in executing the gold dollar dies because of the small size of the planchet." He had to make three sets of dies. It's questionable whether these reports are accurate, or if they are true, whether they're fair to Longacre. "In the United States, techniques were available" for reducing coin designs to small size, according to Dr. C-Stefanelli. The Philadelphia mint had French-built reducing machines as early as the 1830's, he notes. However, Longacre sometimes couldn't get access to the machinery—he *had* problems with other employees. In any case, it was May 8 by the time the first coins were struck.

The coin shows a Liberty head facing left, wearing a coronet ornamented with rounded prongs and lettered LIBERTY. The hair is combed back into a bun with a few curls hanging down the neck. Thirteen stars line the rim. The reverse has a large 1 above DOLLAR with the date below. Around these is a laurel wreath, open at the top, and outside the wreath is UNITED STATES OF AMERICA. Mint marks are at the reverse bottom. Longacre's L is on the base of the portrait.

This Type 1 gold dollar is the smallest-sized of all U.S. coins, only 13 mm. in diameter. Because it's so tiny it feels very light— you have to hold one for several seconds before you feel the downward pressure of its 25.8-grain weight. Type 1 was issued from 1849 to 54, and also is called the Coronet Type, Liberty Head, or just small-size type.

In 1852 you could purchase a six-month subscription to *Scientific American* magazine for a gold dollar. That October J. F.

FIG. 44–1. Gold dollar, 1851, obverse. Longacre's portrait of Miss Liberty on this tiny coin is basically the same as that on the double-eagle.

FIG. 44–2. Gold dollar, 1851, reverse.

FIG. 44–3. Gold dollar, 1874, obverse. Note the similarity between this coin and the $3 gold piece.

FIG. 44–4. Gold dollar, 1874, reverse.

Tallant of Burlington, Iowa, was selling his best quality Young Hyson or Gun Powder No. 4 tea for $1 per pound.

The coin's tiny size proved a major problem so it was decided to make it larger. To keep the weight constant the authorities made the planchet thinner. Philadelphia made both Type 1 and Type 2 in 1854, while Dahlonega and San Francisco made only Type 1.

On the newer coins Liberty wears a feathered headdress with LIBERTY on the headband. Several long curls of hair lie along the back of her neck. Her profile is more angular. National identification shifts to the obverse, replacing the 13 stars, and the reverse's wreath becomes a larger, more ornate and less pleasing one of corn, cotton, tobacco, and wheat. This sometimes is called the Feathered Headdress, Indian Head, or large-size type.

Either type coin would serve to pay your board for a day at Johnson's Hotel, in Detroit, Mich., in 1854.

Type 3 coins appeared in 1856, with San Francisco making only Type 2 and Philadelphia and Dahlonega producing only the new style. The portrait is enlarged to use more of the available space; the hairdo and headdress are slightly revised.

By around 1859 many old Type 1 dollars were piled up in banks. The unpopular coin was getting solid competition from new silver coins and $1 bank notes. About 8 million Type 1 coins were shipped back to the mint and recoined as Type 3's.

In September 1860 two gold dollars would buy a barrel of rosin from L. Merchant & Co., in Mobile, Ala. That December 27 P. H. Peppe & Co. advertised in the *Mobile Daily Advertiser* that, "in consequence of the severity of the time," they'd sell $1.25 silks for $1. G. B. White offered corsets for $1 to Baltimore, Md., ladies in 1875. And for two gold dollars you could ride the daily stage-coach from Morgantown to Fairmont, W. Va., in 1880.

In 1872 the mint produced a remarkable pattern set—the only gold set with a uniform design for all denominations. Barber drew a young Liberty head facing left wearing a liberty cap with an incuse LIBERTY on the band. The date is at bottom and 13 stars line the rim. The reverse is the one from his "Amazonian" design, a large, fierce eagle standing with wings spread and inverted. The eagle looks toward its right; its right talon holds three long arrows and its left has a spade-shaped U.S. shield held slightly right of the vertical; a banner crossing the shield in a slim S-curve is lettered IN GOD WE TRUST. Around top and sides is UNITED STATES OF AMERICA, separated by stars from the denomination at bottom.

Philadelphia issued the gold dollar every year 1849–89. Dahlonega issued it 1849–61. Charlotte made gold dollars 1849–59, except 1854, 1856, and 1858. New Orleans missed only 1854 in making the coins 1849–55. And San Francisco's 1854–60 mintage omitted only 1855. From 1862 on, all gold dollars were struck at Philadelphia.

Proofs were struck 1856–89, all at Philadelphia, with mintage from 20 in several years to 1,779 in 1889.

Highest mintage, 4,076,051, is that of 1853. Lowest is 400 coins, for the 1875. Several regular-issue-dates cost $130 to $160 Fine.

But you had to beware of counterfeits. On Friday, October 22, 1852, *The Eddyville Telegraph* warned Kentuckians that "a large number of spurious gold dollars are said to be in circulation." Some of the predictions by the McKay bill's opponents obviously had come true.

Not all counterfeiters escaped, though. In 1878 F. W. Helmick reported in *Helmick's New Illustrated Counterfeit Detector* that "United States Detective Finnegan arrested on the 10th inst., at San Francisco, California, one C. F. Mohring for manufacturing and uttering [placing in circulation] counterfeit gold dollars. Several thousand blank pieces, five hundred finished gold dollars, and a quantity of dies and stamps were seized."

Varieties include 1849 and 1849–C with either open or closed wreath, 1855 with recut date, 1856 with upright or slanting 5, 1856–S with double S, 1861 with 1 DOLLAR doubled, and several more.

Since gold coins aren't circulating, our sources will be auctions and dealers. Probably few collectors have duplicate gold coins.

Star-Line dates are 1876, 1878, 1879, 1883, 1885, and Proofs of 1873, 1874, 1877, and 1878. Marginals are 1853–C, 1853–C, 1858–S, 1865, 1868, 1872, 1880, and Proofs of 1862, 1870, 1871, 1872, 1879, 1881, 1882, and 1883.

45

Our Five Quarter-Eagles

Princess, CAL and Coronet—and
quite a few more beauties!

TYPE 1, 1796–1807—CAPPED BUST RIGHT

Our $2.50 gold coin was authorized by the Act of April 2, 1792, which specified a 67.5-grain weight and a fineness of *not* .900 but .916-⅔. Since the coin was valued at one-fourth of the eagle, or $10 coin, the natural name was "quarter-eagle."

FIG. 45–1. Quarter-eagle, 1796. On this first type, the rim is plain. After a short time, more 1796 coins were struck, but those have stars at the rim. Coin is in the National Collection, Smithsonian Institution.

The first coins, designed by Robert Scot, are slightly larger than today's cents. The obverse shows Liberty facing right, wearing a tall, high-peaked liberty cap. Much of her hair lies along the side and back of her head. At the top is LIBERTY and at bottom is the date 1796. The reverse is the "heraldic" eagle type. The eagle looks to its right, but the talons are reversed—arrows in the right one and olive in the left. Only 963 coins were made with this design; another 432 were struck after stars were added around the obverse rim.

There are minor changes in the portrait in most years. Planchet size was increased slightly in 1797 and stayed large through the issue. All of these coins were minted at Philadelphia, and the only dates not appearing are 1799, 1800, 1801, and 1803.

Top mintage of 6,812 belongs to the 1807; low-mintage date is 1797, with 427. Prices start about $1,600 for a Fine 1807 and go as high as $25,000 for an Uncirculated 1796.

You could have used one of these coins at Nashville, Tenn., in 1801 when *The Tennessee Gazette* advertised in mid-April, "For ʃAEE [sic] at the Upper Ferry, Good ʃalt at 2⁵⁰ centʃ per buʃhel."

Varieties include 1796 with or without stars, 1804 with 13 or 14 stars on the reverse, and others.

There are no Star-Line dates. Marginals are 1805 and 1806.

TYPE 2, 1808–34—A CHANGE IN HAT SIZE

After 1807 came a switch in design followed by a long break in coinage. Reich's 1808 design shows Liberty facing left, wearing a large liberty cap that's folded so that it looks crushed by the coin's rim. LIBERTY is on the headband. There are seven stars at left, six at right, and the date at bottom.

On the reverse is a new eagle, more realistic than the old heraldic one in spite of the small U.S. shield on its chest. It looks to its right and correctly holds an olive branch in the right talon and arrows in the left. Above, on a curved scroll is E PLURIBUS UNUM, incuse. As before, UNITED and AMERICA are set off from STATES OF by the wingtips. At the bottom is the value, shown as 2½D.

Only 2,710 of these were made, and apparently most were remelted. Today one costs about $6,000 or more in Fine condition. Yet in 1810 you might casually spend one in order to travel from Boston to Plymouth, Mass., on the Boston, Plymouth & Sandwich Mail Stage.

The next quarter-eagles were struck in 1821, when their size was reduced to 18.5 mm. and their design modified by Robert Scot. Liberty's cap has a lower peak, and her profile is more Roman.

The portrait is enlarged and cut off at the neck; the stars are evenly spaced around the rim, with the date at bottom. On the reverse the only change is a slight thinning of the eagle's wings.

These were issued in 1821, 1824–27, and 1829–34; all were made at Philadelphia. High mintage is the 6,448 of 1821; low figure is the 760 of 1826. Prices range from about $1,200 to $1,800 for several dates in Fine up to $15,000 or more for an Uncirculated 1808 or 1834.

Varieties include 1824 over 21 and 1826 over 25 if you count all overdates as varieties, but there probably were usable dies left over that were redated; I don't know of any "normal" 1824 or 1826 coins. There probably are some legitimate varieties yet to be discovered.

Again there's no Star-Line date. Marginals are 1827 and 1829.

FIG. 45–2. Quarter-eagle, 1808, obverse. This coin, in the National Collection, Smithsonian Institution, shows John Reich's Capped Bust design.

TYPE 3, 1834–39—CLASSIC HEAD

On 1834–39 coins the portrait by William Kneass drops the liberty cap and wears a hair ribbon lettered LIBERTY with hair curls shown above it. The face is sharper and more lifelike than those on earlier coins. The eagle's wings again thin out, and the motto and ribbon are omitted.

Philadelphia made both types in 1834, but for every one of the old type it struck 28 new ones. Mintage was unbroken during this period. Charlotte's first issue was 1838, followed by another in 1839, when Dahlonega and New Orleans issued their first quarter-eagles. The coins of those two years have mint marks on the obverse, above the date.

Two of these coins would provide you with a month-long, 12-lesson fencing course in St. Louis, Mo., in 1834. The instructor was a Professor Stanley, a former British Army instructor.

The coins' fineness changed to .900 when the Act of January 18, 1837, went into effect.

Varieties include 1839 with 9 over 8, 1839–C with recut date and others.

Top mintage is the 547,986 of 1836; lowest is the 7,880 of 1838–C. Prices for some dates are $150 to $175 in Fine and $1,250 to $1,600 Uncirculated.

Once more, no Star-Line date. Marginals are 1837, 1838, and 1839.

TYPE 4, 1840–1907—PRINCESS, CAL AND CORONET

The Coronet Type quarter-eagle's 1840–1907 mintage period is the longest for any quarter-eagle design—68 years when at least one mint struck $2.50 coins every year!

Liberty is smaller on these coins. Her hair ribbon becomes a coronet and the portrait looks younger and lighter. The hair is better controlled, with most of it gathered at the back of the head. The cutoff line is higher and more level. On the reverse the eagle is a bit smaller and the olive branch in its right talon now curves upward instead of being splayed out with leaves pointing in three directions. This leaves space at the denomination, so dots

FIG. 45–3. Quarter-eagle, 1843, obverse. Gobrecht died the year after this beautiful coin was struck. Coin is in the National Collection, Smithsonian Institution.

are added beside the 2½D. to separate it from UNITED and AMERICA.

Philadelphia issued $2.50 gold pieces yearly except 1841 and 1863, when it struck only Proofs. Dahlonega released quarter-eagles 1840–57 and again in 1859. Charlotte made the coins 1840–60, except in 1845, 1853, 1857, and 1859. New Orleans' dates are 1840–57, with none issued 1841, 1844, 1848–49, 1853, or 1855. And San Francisco struck the gold pieces 1854–79, skipping 1855, 1858, 1864, and 1874. Mint marks are on the reverse, below the eagle.

The 1841 Proof-only issue is a special case. There's no official mintage total, and only about ten pieces are known. It's possible that fewer than 30 were struck, all for special sets, yet some did circulate: one is known worn down to VG. The coin is known as "The Little Princess," and the least enthusiastic comment I've seen calls it an "American classic."

For the story of the 1848–CAL coins credit goes to Richard S. Yeoman, who dug out the facts and calculated how many coins could have been made:

Military governor Col. Richard B. Mason collected samples of gold from California to send to Washington as proof that gold-rushers' fabulous claims were well within the range of truth. He sent over 230 ounces with military courier Lt. Lucien Loeser, who traveled to Washington via Peru, Panama, Jamaica, and New Orleans.

From the Capital, Secretary of War W. L. Marcy sent the gold to Philadelphia, suggesting to Mint Director R. M. Patterson that some be reserved for medals "and that the remainder be used in striking quarter eagles, bearing a distinguishing mark," which would be given to any applicant at face value.

Yeoman's calculations produced the accepted total of 1,389 coins. CAL was punched above the eagle while the coins lay in the dies, presumably to avoid any mistake about which coins were native California gold and which were from the mint's regular supply.

Adams and Woodin noted in 1913 that "the coins are readily distinguishable from the average United States gold pieces as they contained a large percentage of silver, which gave them the brassy color always shown by gold bearing a large percentage of silver."

A single gold, 2 or 3 aluminum, and 4 to 12 copper patterns were struck with Barber's uniform design in 1872.

A $2.50 coin would buy a day's stay for a transient at the New Marboro Hotel in Boston in 1879. Ten years later the Palmer Mfg. Co. of New York was advertising "The Oxford" five o'clock tea stand, 1½-pint kettle and brass tray and lamp for $2.50. And in 1899 a quarter-eagle could purchase a man's summer bicycle suit with reinforced bloomers and coat with four patch pockets from Strawbridge & Clothier in Philadelphia.

Proof striking, we know, began earlier but the Red Book's figures start with the 112 of 1860. Proof mintage ranges from 223 in 1901 down to 20 in several years; however, only *two* CAL Proofs are known.

Regular-issue mintage peaked in 1853, when Philadelphia struck 1,404,668 quarter-eagles. Low-mintage date is 1854–S, with 246 coins! Many dates cost about $85 to $100 Fine.

A quarter-eagle planchet got into the wrong hopper in 1900 and was struck with cent dies. Among other varieties are 1843–C with small or large date, 1843–O with double O, 1851–O with double date, 1862 with 2 over 1, and others.

The Star-Line dates are 1877 and Proofs of 1871, 1872, and 1891. Marginals are 1874, 1876, 1891, 1898, and Proofs of 1866, 1868, 1869, 1873, 1874, 1878, 1879, 1882, and 1884.

TYPE 5, 1908–29—THE VANISHING QUARTER-EAGLE

The obverse of our final quarter-eagle design shows a dignified Indian head facing left, wearing a large war-bonnet. There are six stars at the left and seven at right, LIBERTY at the top and the date at bottom. Above the date is a tiny BLP, for designer Bela L. Pratt.

FIG. 45–4. Quarter-eagle, 1915,
obverse. This incuse coin had a
tough time winning public acceptance.

FIG. 45–5. Quarter-eagle, 1915, reverse.

On the reverse a large, lifelike eagle stands on a bundle of
arrows across which is an olive branch; the eagle faces left and
holds its folded wings close to its body. At right is IN GOD WE
TRUST; at left, slightly lower, is E PLURIBUS UNUM. UNITED STATES
OF AMERICA around top and side rims artistically holds the eagle
in place. Below the eagle is 2½ DOLLARS.

This coin has no milling (raised rim) to protect the raised
design because there *isn't* any raised design. The Indian, date,
eagle, and all the lettering are incuse. I'll have more to say about
this when we discuss Pratt's half-eagles, for his $2½ and $5 coins
were our last to use one design for more than one denomination.

Philadelphia issued these coins 1908–15, skipped 1916–25,
then released more in 1926–29. Denver's coins are 1911, 1914,
and 1925 only. Top regular-issue mintage is Philadelphia's 722,-
000 in 1913; lowest is 1911–D's 55,680.

Because the coins are relatively recent, most are available in
Very Fine for $100 or less. Philadelphia struck Proofs from 1908
to 15; these cost over $2,000, with mintage of 100 (1915) to only
682 (1910).

In 1915 another "gold cent" was struck when a quarter-eagle
planchet was mixed up with blanks headed for cent dies.

You could use a quarter-eagle in 1916 to buy a Waterman's
Ideal Fountain Pen from the L. E. Waterman Co. In 1917 the
coin would buy you a pair of the best imported kid gloves at
Lord & Taylor in New York.

There's no Star-Line date. Marginals are 1914, 1927, and Proofs
of 1909 and 1913.

46

Three-Dollar Gold

"... Frequently mistaken for a quarter-eagle
and often counted as a five-dollar
piece."—Dickeson, 1859.

The $3 gold piece was introduced in 1854 in order to make it easier to buy postage stamps. It's beautiful in design and unusual in denomination—and it was *very* unpopular.

Top mintage of 138,618 was in the first year of issue. It showed unfounded optimism. Later years' mintages often were 3,000 or less.

On the obverse is a Liberty head (some numismatists call it an Indian princess, some refer to it as Sarah Longacre) facing left and wearing a feathered crown with the tips of the feathers curling outward and LIBERTY on the headband. At the rim is UNITED STATES OF AMERICA. James Longacre's JBL is on the portrait's base. This side is considered the obverse despite the absence of date and presence of national identification. Collectors view the portrait as the determining factor in this case, as on the $1 gold coin.

Like most other U.S. gold pieces, this coin has a reeded edge.

On the reverse is a large 3 above DOLLARS and the date, in a wreath of corn, cotton, tobacco, and wheat. DOLLARS is slightly larger from 1855 on. Mint marks are at the reverse bottom.

This coin is .900 fine gold. It weighs 77.4 grains—less than two modern cents—but feels a *lot* heavier. It's almost exactly the diameter of a nickel but a bit thinner.

Three-dollar gold pieces never were particularly well liked. They had some use, but didn't circulate widely. Mints at Philadelphia, Dahlonega, and New Orleans issued them in 1854 and counterfeiters quickly pounced on the coins as models.

FIG. 46–1. Three dollars, 1874, obverse. Longacre evidently took this design from the Type 2 gold dollar, improved it on this coin, then returned it to the dollar to produce the third type.

FIG. 46–2. Three dollars, 1874, reverse. Like half-cents and trimes, $3 gold coins probably are more popular now than at any time during their issue period.

In 1855 only Philadelphia and San Francisco made $3 coins. After that the only branch mint making them was San Francisco in 1856, 1857, 1860, and 1870. Mint officials either decided to quit issuing the coins at San Francisco in 1860 or else had a priority requirement for gold for other coins. Though 7,000 1860–S pieces were struck, 2,592 were remelted.

In 1859 Dickeson wrote that the $3 piece was less than a favorite. "As a coin it is very unpopular," he said, "being frequently mistaken for a quarter-eagle and often counted as a five-dollar piece." One place where this may have happened was Yankton, Dakota Territory (now South Dakota), where A. S. Chase & Co. sold shingles for $3 per thousand in 1862.

Some coins were made into love tokens; others were used as pendants, bracelet ornaments, and other jewelry.

You could board for a day at Gilmore House in Baltimore, Md., for one of these coins in 1869, or do the same at The Ebbitt House in Washington, D.C., in 1880. Out West, in Virginia, Nev., Titus Jepson would sell you nine meal tickets for his Colombo restaurant for $3 in 1876.

Philadelphia issued the coins yearly 1854–89, except 1873, 1875, and 1876, years when only Proofs were struck. The rarest regular issue is 1881 (500 made). Prices for some dates in Fine are in the neighborhood of $300.

In 1870 San Francisco struck only two coins. One was put into the cornerstone of the new mint building.

The 1872 Barber pattern in the uniform design series has THREE DOL. at the reverse bottom. Otherwise, except for its size, it's exactly like the other coins.

Proof minting began at least as early as 1858; totals go from 290 in 1888 to 20 for several years. Only ten of the 1875 Proofs are known, and one was sold for $150,000 in 1974. However, restrikes are known of the 1865, 1873, and 1875 Proofs.

Several varieties exist; best known is 1856–S with small, medium, or large S. There also are 1864 struck on a cupronickel cent planchet, 1854–D with clashed dies, 1869 with recut 9, 1873 with closed or open 3, 1882 with doubled 2, and others.

Star-Line dates are 1860–S and Proofs of 1865, 1878, and 1879. Marginals are 1871, 1879, 1880, 1884, 1886, and Proofs of 1868, 1869, 1872, 1882, 1883, and 1884.

The last $3 gold coins were the 2,429 that Philadelphia released in 1889. The next year the Act of September 26 discontinued the denomination. Probably the nation's coin collectors were the only ones sorry to see the coin go.

47

That Was the Coin That—Wasn't!

Planning, politics, and patterns—and
a coin that might have changed history.

One of the best-known items ever to come from the Philadelphia mint is a nickel-sized gold $4 pattern called a *stella*.

The man who suggested this denomination was John A. Kasson, our minister to Austria and formerly chairman of the Committee of Coinage, Weights, and Measures in Congress. The $4 piece would have been more than an American coin—it would have been an international one, and might have changed the course of history.

This coin was to be equivalent to Austria's 8 florins, France's 20 francs, Holland's 8 florins, Italy's 20 lire, and Spain's 20 pesetas. In other words, it would bring the United States actually, if not officially, into the Latin Monetary Union.

Charter members of the Union (1865) were Belgium, France, Italy, and Switzerland. Greece joined in 1868 and Monaco later issued coins minted to LMU standards. The purpose was to standardize Europe's coinage systems and avoid a threatened worldwide financial panic. The flow of gold from Australia and the western U.S. had caused a major drop in the price of silver.

Union members went on the gold standard and agreed to base their currencies on the French franc. Several meetings held later in an effort to widen membership and influence failed.

De facto Union membership of the U.S. could have sparked a series of joinings by other countries. It would have brought us politically, economically, and socially closer to Europe. Would an American have been there to save Archduke Ferdinand? Would U.S. leadership have united Europe to crush Hitler at the start? But history turned another way.

Before the coin could be issued it needed approval by the Committee on Coinage. Patterns were struck to give committee members something solid to examine. It was the committee which suggested the name "stella" (Latin for "star") for the coin.

George Morgan and chief mint engraver Charles E. Barber both submitted designs for the coins, and patterns were made in 1879 and 1880 showing each artist's work.

Both portraits face left. Barber's has long, flowing hair, and the date at bottom in small numerals. Around the rim are the weight and fineness, with 13 stars separating letters and numbers. Barber based this on an 1878 pattern half-eagle his father had designed. His pattern is called the "Flowing Hair" type, while Morgan's is the "Coiled Hair."

Morgan showed Liberty's hair coiled tightly in a style like the one ladies wore in the early 1880's. The rim inscription is the same but the date is slightly larger than on Barber's patterns.

Barber's flowing hair points a downward artistic direction with

FIG. 47–1. Pattern $4 coin, gold specimen in the National Collection, Smithsonian Institution. This is Morgan's obverse, in my opinion the more beautiful of the two.

FIG. 47–2. Pattern $4 coin, gold, in the National Collection, Smithsonian Institution. This is the Barber design. Coin was acquired as part of the Lilly Collection.

a minimum of discipline; Morgan directs the eye upward with a tone of power and control.

There's only one reverse: Barber's large five-pointed star inscribed ONE STELLA 400 CENTS in four lines. Around top and sides is UNITED STATES OF AMERICA. The value is repeated at bottom, as FOUR DOL., maybe because we were used to seeing a denomination there on U.S. coins. Within the circle formed by the main rim inscription are a tiny E PLURIBUS UNUM and a not-so-familiar DEO EST GLORIA ("To God Is the Glory," or "Glory to God").

Fifteen gold patterns were made with Barber's design and ten with Morgan's each year. These actually were "goloid," a gold-silver-copper alloy developed and patented by Dr. W. W. Hubbel. There also were 15 copper and 4 aluminium specimens each year with each design, plus a single white metal piece with the 1879 Morgan design. Dr. Judd disputes these figures, suggesting a maximum of 12 for the 1879 copper and Morgan gold and 3 for Barber's 1879 aluminum and white metal; he lists a top of 12 for 1880 Morgan gold and both copper and 3 for both copper and aluminum. In 1911 Edgar H. Adams reported an extremely rare 1879 Barber variety with a smaller portrait; he said in the March *Numismatist* that no mintage figure was known but that this existed in copper, silver and possibly gold.

Sets of 1879 patterns were available to Congressmen for about $6.50 per set. The legislators didn't storm the mint but there was enough demand for the Committee on Coinage to ask for more samples early in 1880.

The new year's dies weren't ready yet, but the 1879 dies still were handy. So mint authorities made 400 gold restrikes with the 1879 Barber dies. Originals weigh 108½ grains; restrikes, which should be written 1879(80), weigh about 103.

You could buy an 1879 flowing hair pattern for $100 back in 1911. By 1959 it cost $2,000 and by 1967 it was $6,000. Catalog value for the coiled hair type went from $4,500 (1879) and $4,750 (1880) in 1959 to $16,500 for either date in 1967. The flowing hair type has been sold for $24,000 recently; an 1879 coiled hair stella brought $29,000 in the Champa Sale in mid–1972. It's hard to say what the real value of these coins might be—like other major rarities, they frequently set new records.

Since this is a pattern, Star-Line doesn't operate. But if you can purchase *any* stella, then go ahead! With one of these beautiful pieces your collection will include a real treasure.

As for the final outcome—after all the planning, politics, and patterns, the $4 gold coin that might have changed the course of history never was issued.

48

Half of an Eagle

"The Oldest And The Best"—motto of
the aircraft carrier *USS Intrepid.*

I've quoted my old ship's motto here because it's just as appropriate to the $5 gold coin: *first* gold coin struck by the U.S. and *only U.S. coin of any kind* issued by every one of our seven official mints.

TYPE 1, 1795–1807—THE EARLY YEARS

On July 31, 1795, 744 half-eagles were turned over to the Treasury. These 135-grain coins, .916-⅔ fine, were authorized by our most often cited coinage law, the Act of April 2, 1792.

The coins show Liberty's portrait drawn by Robert Scot, facing right and wearing a tall liberty cap, with her hair lying free along the back of her neck. LIBERTY is at upper right, just past the peak of the cap; the date is at bottom; varying numbers of stars fill out the rim.

On the reverse a small, scrawny eagle stands on a palm branch, holding what looks like a laurel wreath in its beak. Around the rim is UNITED STATES OF AMERICA. As with several other early coins, there's no denomination shown. You had to tell its value by weight and size (a little larger than today's quarter-dollar). A second reverse, used simultaneously with the first, shows a large "heraldic" eagle, with the same lettering.

Philadelphia, our only mint at that time, struck half-eagles between 1795 and 1807, except 1801. Over the design's lifetime there are minor changes in such points as the hair lines in the portrait.

Mintage varied from 3,609 in 1797 up to 64,093 in 1806. I know of no Proofs. Some dates cost $700 to $800 in Fine, some cost more; the top price is around $12,500 for an Uncirculated 1795 with the heraldic eagle reverse.

FIG. 48–1. Half-eagle, 1802, obverse. Either dies were prepared and never used, or a workman punched a 1 into the die and had to correct his error by punching a 2 over it. All of the year's coinage has this overdate, so it's not a variety. The date is read 1802 over 1, and can be written 1802/1 or 1802 2/1. Coin is in the National Collection, Smithsonian Institution.

FIG. 48–2. Half-eagle, 1802, reverse. In the National Collection, Smithsonian Institution.

Seven of these coins would buy a barrel of two-year-old brandy from Henry Cotten of Northampton County, N.C. He advertised it in *The North-Carolina Journal* May 11, 1801, as "ſuperior to any I ever ſaw."

Varieties include the two types of reverse used, 1795 with the last S in "States" over D, 1798 with large or small 8, and others.

The only Star-Line date is 1798. Marginals are 1796 and 1799.

TYPE 2, 1807–34—LIBERTY CAPS

In 1807 John Reich's design appeared, showing Liberty facing left, still a rather puffy-faced portrait. Liberty wears drapery and a low liberty cap with LIBERTY on its headband. As on other coins with this design, the cap appears crushed by the rim. Around the rim are seven stars at left, six at right, and the date at bottom.

The small and rather lifelike eagle on the reverse is handicapped by its long neck and the U.S. shield on its chest. It looks to its right and holds an olive branch in its right talon and arrows in its left. Above, following the curve of the rim and controlled by the wingtips, is a banner lettered E PLURIBUS UNUM. Around the rim, with wingtips setting off the first and last words, is UNITED STATES OF AMERICA. The denomination is at bottom, shown as 5 D., and separated from the national identification by olive leaves at left and the period after the D at right.

Philadelphia struck this type in 1807 in addition to the early one, and continued minting through 1812 without a break. With the 1813 issue Robert Scot (or possibly Christian Gobrecht or another artist) stepped in, and the Liberty portrait changed from a Draped Bust to a plain Liberty head. The head is larger and the cutoff point is moved to partway down the neck; this allowed the artist to center the head on the obverse and permitted an even

FIG. 48–3. Half-eagle, 1813, obverse. In the National Collection, Smithsonian Institution.

spacing of the 13 stars. The reverse was unchanged. This subtype was issued from 1813 to 28 except in 1816–17.

If coins of 1813–28 are a subtype, so are those of 1829–34; the diameter was reduced slightly and so was the scale of the entire design. Mintage ranged from 635 in 1815 to 263,806 in 1820. But many coins were melted, and of the 17,796 dated 1822, only *three* survive. Prices go from around $575 to $650 in Fine up to $50,000 or more!

In 1811 a $5 gold piece would buy a framed mirror from Norman Hayden & Co. of New Haven, Conn. In 1830 you could use one of these coins to subscribe for a year to the *Florida Herald*, of St. Augustine.

Varieties include 1809 with 9 over 8, 1810 large or small date, 1820 with square or curved base on the 2, 1834 plain or crosslet 4, and several more.

Star-Line dates are 1808, 1812, and 1823. Marginals are 1813, 1814, and 1834.

TYPE 3, 1834–38—THE ABSENT MOTTO

Like quarter-eagles, half-eagles were issued with William Kneass's Classic Head design after the Act of June 28, 1834, cut the weight to 129 grains and the fineness to 89.9225 percent. The

FIG. 48–4. Half-eagle, 1834, reverse. The motto was gone, but the coin still was beautiful. The eagle's head is much too large, but its lifelike appearance makes up for that flaw. Coin is in the National Collection, Smithsonian Institution.

only difference between the smaller coins and these $5 pieces of 1834–38 is size and the 5 D. at the half-eagle's reverse bottom. As on smaller coins, E PLURIBUS UNUM was dropped when the size was reduced, partly due to lack of space on the reverse and partly as an easy way to identify the lighter coins.

The single Star-Line date is 1838–C. There are no Marginals.

If you lived in Savannah, Ga., in 1835, you could pay a half-eagle and receive the local newspaper, *The Georgian*, for a year.

This type introduced branch mint half-eagles, as Charlotte and Dahlonega struck their first $5 gold pieces in 1838. Philadelphia issued the coin every year. Mintage ranges from 17,179 for 1838–C to 658,028 for 1834, but only 1838–C and 1838–D are under 200,000 and most dates cost about $125 in Fine.

Star-Line does not operate for this type.

TYPE 4, 1839–66—FIRST SERIES CORONETS

From 1839 to 1866, Coronet half-eagles have the same design as current quarter-eagles. The denomination changes to FIVE D.; the eagle is thinner and holds its head higher. Christian Gobrecht drew the olive branch pointing upward, so he added dots flanking the denomination to set it off from UNITED and AMERICA.

Philadelphia made the coins every year 1839–65. Charlotte's dates are 1839–61, except for 1845. Dahlonega's 1839–61 issue was unbroken. New Orleans issued its first half-eagles in 1840 and continued through 1857 except for 1848–50 and 1852–53. This makes a total of four issuing mints. The fifth was San Francisco, which issued the coins 1854–66.

There's no Star-Line date. Marginals are 1845–O, 1851–O, 1855, 1857–S, and 1860–S.

FIG. 48–5. Half-eagle, 1902–S, obverse.

Varieties in this series include 1839 with 9 over 8, 1846–D with double D, 1849 with recut date, 1861 large or small date, and others.

A $5 gold piece would buy you a barrel of flour in Scott County, Iowa, in June 1841. In Trenton, N.J., in 1846, the coin could purchase a pair of fine pants from Combs & Wakely; and over in Philadelphia you could buy the best window shades in stock from Hartley & Knight.

Regular-issue mintage dips to the 268 coins of 1854–S and rises to the 915,981 figure of 1847. Proofs are known as early as 1855, and Red Book figures range from 25 in 1865 to 66 in 1861.

Prices start under $125 for some regular-issue dates in Fine; top-price coin is the XF 1854–S sold for $16,500 at the Wolfson Sale.

TYPE 5, 1866–1908—SECOND SERIES CORONETS

In 1865, patterns were struck with the "reverse of 1866." They have the regular obverse but the reverse adds to the usual design a banner lettered IN GOD WE TRUST above the eagle. These 2 gold and 4 to 12 copper patterns are the earliest $5 pieces to use this motto. From 1866 on it appears on regular-issue half-eagles, providing a convenient break between what I've called First and Second Series Coronets.

Patterns struck in the 1872 Barber uniform-design set have FIVE DOL. as the denomination. Other trial pieces and regular-die trial pieces were struck in various metals and amounts in several years.

A half-eagle would buy a boy's suit in 1894 from the Putnam Clothing House in Chicago. In 1898 it would buy the Bench Drill

FIG. 48–6. Half-eagle, 1886, reverse. The IN GOD WE TRUST banner makes this coin's reverse a bit crowded, but it's still a beautiful design. Note the die break from the E of FIVE through the D and into the last A of AMERICA.

No. 8 (powered by hand crank) from the Goodell Bros. Co. of Greenfield, Mass. And in 1899 the Plume & Atwood Mfg. Co. of New York, Boston, and other cities offered its Banner Oil Heater for $5, "for that cold room of yours."

Philadelphia issued these coins every year except 1887, when it struck only Proofs. San Francisco issued the coins 1866–1906, skipping 1889–91. Carson City issued half-eagles 1870–93, missing only 1885–89. New Orleans produced only 1892–94 coins. These four plus the now-closed Charlotte and Dahlonega made a total of six mints. The seventh was Denver, which struck half-eagles 1906–07.

Regular-issue mintage dropped to 200 in 1875, the lowest mintage for the entire half-eagle series. High mintage for all half-eagles is the 5,708,760 of 1881. Proofs were struck in all years 1866–1907; mintage ranged from 20 in several years to 230 in 1900; all Proofs were made at Philadelphia.

Varieties include 1866–S with large or small S, 1873 with closed or open 3, 1880 with recut date, 1901–S with the second 1 over 0, 1902–S with double S (sometimes written S/S), and several more.

Prices for many dates are below $100 in Fine; but an 1875 in AU brought $60,000 in the ANA 83rd Convention auction in August 1974.

Star-Line dates are 1883, 1883–S, 1888–S, 1903, 1905, and Proofs of 1881, 1882, 1883, and 1885. Marginals are 1867, 1873, 1873–S, 1874–S, 1878, 1882–CC, 1883–CC, 1890–CC, 1892–CC, 1892–S, 1893–S, 1894–O, 1894–S, 1895–S, 1896, and Proofs of 1868, 1873, 1886, and 1891.

TYPE 6, 1908–29—INCUSE INDIANS

As with Coronet coins, half-eagles of the final type are the same as quarter-eagles except size and denomination, which is spelled out as FIVE DOLLARS at the reverse bottom.

It was Dr. William S. Bigelow's idea to make the design incuse, and Bela L. Pratt drew the design, which is why these sometimes are called the Bigelow-Pratt type. The idea didn't exactly win immediate approval.

FIG. 48–7. Half-eagle, 1909–D, obverse. The Bigelow-Pratt design is one of the few U.S. "Indian Head" designs whch really show an Indian rather than Miss Liberty.

FIG. 48–8. Half-eagle, 1909–D, reverse. This is very much like the Saint-Gaudens reverse on the 1907 eagle. This coin represents one of those little-known years when a branch mint out-produced the main one: Denver struck five half-eagles in 1909 for every one that Philadelphia made.

Numismatist Samuel H. Chapman wrote to President Theodore Roosevelt to charge that, as *The Numismatist* quoted him, "the Indian . . . portrays an Indian who is emaciated, totally unlike the big, strong Indian chiefs as seen in real life." He went on, "The placing of the design below the surface . . . can . . . be closely imitated by any metal chaser with the graver, without dies or moulds." The eagle looked like the golden eagle, which is found in Europe as well as the U.S., he said. And the incuse lines "will be a great receptacle for dirt and conveyor of disease. . . ." To top it off, he added, the coins wouldn't stack well.

The President sent Chapman's letter to Dr. Bigelow, who retorted that the Indian's portrait was of a man "whose health was excellent," that Mr. Pratt *had* drawn the American white-headed eagle, that forgers weren't likely to waste time engraving individual counterfeits, and that the warped die which caused stacking problems would be corrected. As for the hygienic problem, he said he'd never yet seen a dirty gold coin.

The insistent Chapman wrote back to claim his own arguments still were valid and saying he, at least, *had* seen individually made counterfeits and dirty gold coins.

For a while it looked as if Chapman were right. During the

Christmas season many people seeking gold coins as gifts refused the new ones and insisted on older Coronet pieces. But eventually the new incuse design became the one everybody was used to seeing, and I think this made a major difference.

Philadelphia, Denver, and San Francisco were the main producers; New Orleans made half-eagles only in 1909. Philadelphia issued them 1908–15, then made no more until the final 1929 issue. Denver made the $5 coins 1908–11 and again in 1914. San Francisco minted half-eagles 1908–16 without a break.

Unfortunately, counterfeiters like these coins as much as coin collectors do. The crooks have made fake 1908–S, 1911, and other dates—even 1915–D, despite the fact that Denver *did not make half-eagles* that year!

There's no new record mintage. Top figure is 3,423,560 for 1909–D and the low one is 34,200 for 1909–O. Proofs were struck at Philadelphia only, 1908–15, with mintage ranging from 75 in 1915 to 250 in 1910.

You can buy some of these coins in Very Fine condition for about $80 to $100; but the price can go to $4,500 or more for an Uncirculated 1929. Despite mintage of 662,000, this date is hard to obtain.

In 1910 the Culebra Hat Co. was advertising genuine Panama hats at $5 ("We gather these hats direct from the South American Natives"). And in 1929 a half-eagle would buy a Valet AutoStrop Razor from the New York maker.

I've yet to see *any* listing of varieties, so the field appears wide open for discoveries.

Star-Line dates are 1908–D, 1910–D, and Proofs of 1909 and 1913. Marginals are 1908, 1915, and 1915–S.

49

The Earliest Eagles

Including a counterfeit "bearing confiderable
refemblance to the real federal coin."

Our first $10 gold pieces are big coins—big and heavy. They're
larger than half-dollars, and glow as only gold can glow.

The first 400 were made September 22, 1795. They weighed
270 grains and were .91675 fine. There are one basic obverse and
two reverses, all by Robert Scot.

Coins of 1795–1804 feature a large Liberty head facing right,
her hair lying in waves along her neck. She wears a high, turban-
like liberty cap. LIBERTY is at the top, the date is below and the
rim is filled out with 13 to 16 stars.

The first reverse has a scrawny eagle perching on a palm
branch and turning its head to its left. Its beak holds a laurel
wreath. UNITED STATES OF AMERICA is at top and sides and, as we
might expect, there's no denomination. Only a few thousand were
made in 1795 and 1796. With 1797 came a new "heraldic" eagle
looking to its right but with the olive branch and arrows in the
wrong talons; this error lasted through 1804. Both reverses were

FIG. 49–1. Eagle, 1796, obverse.
This is one of several coins on
which Miss Liberty wears a liberty
cap with a high peak. Coin is in the
National Collecton, Smithsonian
Institution.

FIG. 49–2. Eagle, 1796, reverse. The palm on which this eagle perches is an unusual feature of U.S. coins; it appeared on only a few early issues before the olive branch replaced it. Coin is in the National Collection, Smithsonian Institution.

FIG. 49–3. Eagle, 1797–1804 type, reverse. This heraldic eagle replaced the more lifelike one after two years. Coin is in the National Collection, Smithsonian Institution.

used in 1797, but of the 14,555 struck, the mint made nine heraldic eagle coins for every small eagle one.

Mintage ranged as high as 44,344 for 1801 and as low as 1,742 for 1798. All the coins were struck at Philadelphia, and have a reeded edge.

Counterfeiters were quick to get busy faking the $10 gold piece. On Wednesday, July 1, 1801, the *Washington Federalist* published under the headline "More Forgeries" the following news item: (Official Text)

Where will villainy end!—An eagle bearing confiderable refemblance to the real federal coin, was cut at the Office of Difcount and Depofit on Monday, and found to be compofed principally of brafs with a thin wafh of gold. The falfe coin is greatly dificient in weight, and the body of the bird is confiderably more flim than that of the true eagle. Others of the fame die it is fuppofed are in circulation.

That August, you could have paid Samuel Ames two of these earliest eagles for a mirror. The Rhode Island merchant announced in *The Providence Gazette* on Saturday, August 8, his receipt of "an *affortment* of elegant Gilt-Frame LOOKING-GLASSES."

Speculators and hoarders were yanking gold and silver out of circulation at a frightening rate. The world ratio of silver to gold prices had changed, and our $10 coin was undervalued in terms of silver. In 1804 the authorities halted minting. Many of the year's eagles were melted; probably fewer than ten Unc examples survive, and perhaps fewer than 50 specimens in all conditions. The break would last until 1838.

You might expect our earliest eagles to cost a lot. They do. The Act of June 28, 1834, which cut the weight to 258 grains and the fineness to .899225, made earlier coins worth more as gold bullion than as coins. Many were melted, and now a Fine condition specimen may cost $1,100 to $1,700; an Unc coin usually costs $5,000 or more.

There's no Star-Line date. The only Marginal is 1804.

Varieties include 1797 with small or heraldic eagle, 1798 with different arrangements of stars, 1800 with a die break on "Liberty," and a few others.

50

Eagle and Coronet

$10 would buy you a buggy whip in 1879.

Like other gold coins of this period, these can be split into First and Second series, with dates of 1838–66 and 1867–1907 respectively. All of them are 27 mm. across, have a reeded edge, and weigh 16.718 grams.

First Series coins show Gobrecht's rather young Liberty head,

FIG. 50–1. Eagle, 1876, Proof, obverse. Coin acquired by the National Collection, Smithsonian Institution, in 1969, as part of Lilly Collection.

with rounded features, facing left. Most of the hair is gathered into three large buns at the back of her head by what Yeoman poetically calls a "cord of pearls," with only a few curls falling down the side and back of the neck. The portrait shows a coronet lettered LIBERTY. The date is slightly left of center at bottom and the rest of the rim is filled out with 13 stars.

On the reverse is the usual eagle wearing a U.S. shield on its chest and standing with wings raised and held out from the body. The head and neck are too large for the bird's size, and prevent it from being as excellent as it could be. The head turns to its right, the right talon has an olive branch, and the left has three arrows. UNITED STATES OF AMERICA is around top and side rims, with first and last words set off by the wingtips. At bottom, between dots, is TEN D. Mint marks are below the eagle's tail.

Philadelphia issued these 1838–65 without a break. The first branch-mint eagles appeared in 1841, with the O mint mark; New Orleans continued striking eagles yearly through 1860. San Francisco made the coins 1854–66 and was the only mint striking both "no motto" and "with motto" eagles in 1866.

With one of these coins you could board and lodge yourself and your horse for a week at the Victoria House, in Victoria, Tex., in 1859.

In 1861 patterns were made with the regular obverse and a reverse with GOD OUR TRUST on a scroll above the eagle. Other patterns have the motto without the scroll. In 1862 from 200 to 500 of each type were made in copper. More of each type were made in 1863, but 1864 patterns show IN GOD WE TRUST on the scroll, the "reverse of 1866."

Among varieties are 1839 with large or small letters, 1845–O with double date, 1849 with recut 1, 1865–S with the date over an inverted 186, and others.

There are no Star-Line dates. Marginals are 1845, 1846, and 1859–O.

With 1866 the Second Series Coronets begin, with changes on both sides. The portrait is sharper-featured; though it's still curved, the cutoff line is more level, and the date is better centered. As we've seen, the IN GOD WE TRUST banner is added above the eagle.

Philadelphia struck these coins 1866–1907, making our main mint the only one to strike eagles every year of the Coronet design. San Francisco made the coins 1866–1907, but missed 1875, 1890–91, and 1904. New Orleans didn't resume minting operations after the Civil War until 1879; it struck eagles from then through 1906 except for 1884–87, 1889–91, 1896, 1898, 1900, 1902, and 1905. The new Carson City branch mint began making $10 coins in 1870 and continued through 1893 except for 1885–89. Denver struck this type only in 1906–07.

As with other coins, trial pieces were struck with regular dies in several years, usually in copper and aluminum and usually with four to 12 specimens struck in each metal. Eagle patterns also were made with Barber's uniform design in 1872.

You could board and lodge for a week for $10 in 1872 at the Boonville Hotel, in Boonville, Idaho Territory. M. C. H. Dexter would charge you the same amount for board in 1875, at The Sea-Side House in Portland, Ore., and you could get the identical rate in 1876 at W. W. Tate's New Era Restaurant and Chop-House in Santa Fe, N.M. A gold eagle would buy you the best buggy whip in stock in 1879 at J. J. Smokey's, in Natchez, Miss. In 1879, saddle and harness maker George Cooper, of Fargo, N.D., would make a one-horse harness for as little as $10.

Top mintage is the 3,877,220 of 1881; lowest is the extremely low 1875 figure of 100. Proof mintage, which began at least as early as 1855, varied from 15 in 1884 to 120 in 1900. Regular issues cost about $130 to $170 for many dates in Fine, and from $180 to the $600 to $700 range Uncirculated. Most Proofs cost around $5,000.

Varieties are relatively few; about the best known is the 1881 with double profile.

Star-Line dates are 1878–S, 1892–O, and Proof 1865. Marginals are 1880–CC, 1882–O, 1883–CC, 1894–S, and Proofs of 1881, 1882, 1883, 1889, 1891, 1893, 1894, and 1895.

On August 7, four days after Saint-Gaudens died, President Roosevelt ordered Treasury Secretary Cortelyou to get the new $10 and $20 coins finished and released. But it was around November 1 before the new eagle was put into circulation.

51

Miss Liberty Goes Indian

"Can any of the clergymen now so bitterly condemning President Roosevelt say offhand . . . on which pieces of currency the motto 'In God We Trust' is and is not to be found?"—1907 letter to the editor.

The same 1905 dinner meeting that resulted in the beautiful Augustus Saint-Gaudens $20 coins also brought us his gold eagles. This involves the obverse which Saint-Gaudens planned originally for use on a new cent.

Liberty at first was shown wearing an olive wreath, her hair drawn up at the back of her head. LIBERTY was across the bottom and 13 stars lined the rim. Urged by President Roosevelt, Saint-Gaudens gave Liberty a feathered headdress. Late patterns show

FIG. 51–1. Eagle, 1913, reverse. Saint-Gaudens' Standing Eagle reverse appeared on the eagle in 1907. The following year, Pratt's quarter- and half-eagles appeared with an almost identical design.

the left-facing portrait wearing this Indian bonnet with LIBERTY on the headband, the date at bottom, and 13 stars at the rim.

For the reverse Saint-Gaudens used the standing eagle he had wanted to use on the $20 coin. The eagle faces left, perching on a bundle of arrows against which it holds an olive branch. E PLURIBUS UNUM is at right, behind the eagle and level with its shoulder. UNITED STATES OF AMERICA is around top and side rims; TEN DOLLARS is at bottom. There are dots before and after inscriptions.

Unlike most coins, even patterns, this piece has a *decorated edge*—46 stars representing the states.

According to *The Numismatist*, the model for Liberty was Miss Mary Cunningham.

Because of the sculptor's failing health, his friend and assistant Henry Hering did most of the physical work on this coin, as he did on the $20.

Branch mint coins have the mint mark on the reverse at left of the arrowheads.

According to *COINage* magazine's Lee Martin, President Roosevelt's removal of IN GOD WE TRUST from coins was *not* because he considered its use blasphemous, but because he *wanted to protect the religious motto from ridicule and criticism* to which its use on coins exposed it. Whatever the true reason, eagles of 1907 lack the motto—and the result was a wave of cutting criticism directed at the President.

The Washington Post defended him, reprinting on Friday, November 15, a letter from the *New York World* in which the writer challenged, "Can any of the clergymen now so bitterly condemning President Roosevelt say offhand, without examining the coins, on which pieces of currency the motto 'In God We Trust' is and is not to be found?"

Congress passed a bill in 1908 ordering the motto "inscribed upon all such gold and silver coins of said denominations as heretofore," which ended the brief rebellion. The motto was put at the reverse lower left, where it nicely balances E PLURIBUS UNUM.

The starred edge was modified in 1912 when two more stars were added to represent the new states of Arizona and New Mexico.

Naturally there were some who objected to what they considered inappropriate headgear for Liberty. In an address at the Corcoran Gallery of Art in Washington, quoted by *The Numismatist*, the President pointed out, "There is no more reason why a feather head-dress should always be held to denote an Indian than why a Phrygian cap should always be held to denote a Phrygian. . . . It is idle to insist that the head or figure of Liberty shall only appear in the hackneyed and conventional trappings to which conventional and unoriginal minds have gradually grown to ascribe to her."

Philadelphia released 239,406 eagles in 1907, the first year of issue. Philadelphia and Denver issued both "no motto" and "with motto" eagles in 1908.

You could purchase a Victor phonograph for $10 in 1910 from J. W. Jenkins' Sons Music Co., in Oklahoma City, Okla. Two years later, the United Clothes store of Minneapolis, Minn., was advertising, "Choice of any Suit, Topcoat or Raincoat in our store always . . . $10." And in 1915 you could use a gold eagle to pay for a man's suit at Raphael's, in Cheyenne, Wyo.

Philadelphia continued making the coins every year through 1915, then stopped until 1926, and after that made no more until 1932 and 1933. Denver made the coins 1908–11 and 1914; San Francisco struck eagles 1908–16, 1920, and 1930.

Top mintage is 4,463,000 for 1932; lowest is 30,100 for 1911–D. Proofs were minted 1908–15, with totals of 50 in 1914 to 204 in 1910; all Proofs were made at Philadelphia. The 1933 was released, but its legality was in dispute for years and some specimens were confiscated. Most of the 312,500 minted probably were melted, and the coin rates a $30,000 price now. Many other

FIG. 51–2. Eagle, 1913, obverse. One of our finest "Indian Head" coins actually shows Miss Liberty wearing the feathered headdress that symbolizes the nation.

dates, happily, cost far less—about $200 to $250 Fine and $275 to $350 Uncirculated.

Counterfeits exist for 1908, 1910–D, 1915, and almost certainly several other dates.

The only varieties I know of are 1908 and 1908–D with or without motto, which you really could class as subtypes, and 1910–S with double S.

The only Star-Line date is 1909–D. Marginals are 1913–S and Proof 1914.

52

Double Puzzle of the Double-Eagle

Here's the amazing saga of our $20 gold coin—and the true story of the priceless 1849 pattern that has been missing for over 120 years!

At the start of 1849 the President was James K. Polk, a Democrat. His successor would be Zachary Taylor, a Whig, who'd take the oath of office March 4. Robert M. Patterson was in his fifteenth year as Director of the Mint, William M. Meredith was Secretary of the Treasury, and James B. Longacre was chief mint engraver.

On January 25, chairman James J. McKay (D–N.C.) of the House Ways and Means Committee introduced a bill authorizing the gold dollar. On February 1, Senator Charles G. Atherton (D–N.H.) reported a bill from the Senate Finance Committee authorizing both the gold dollar and the $20.

We've seen part of the debate which followed. On February 20, the same day the House Ways and Means Committee reported out its amended bill authorizing both coins, Joseph Ingersoll attacked both proposed pieces, the $1 as a toy and the $20 as a "ponderous and unparalleled" coin. "Ponderous coinage once existed among a simple and a warlike people," he added acidly. "If it is to be introduced again, iron or tobacco will suit as well as gold." Joining him in the attack was Charles Hudson (Whig–Mass.), a member of the Ways and means Committee, who said that the Director of the Mint had admitted that a $20 coin was unwanted and useless. Henry Nicoll (D–N.Y.) supported the bill, telling the House he believed the country needed both coins.

A tabling move by Representative Rockwell of Connecticut failed by 127 to 37. The $20 amendment to the original bill passed and when the entire bill was voted on, it was passed and sent to the Senate. Two days later came the Senate Finance Committee's favorable report.

Saturday, March 3, "was destined to be a long one," said Elston G. Bradfield in the April 1949 *Numismatist*. Among those for whom it was the final day in office were President Polk, McKay, Atherton, Ingersoll, Nicoll, and A. Lincoln of Illinois. (Lincoln voted against the tabling attempt, and I agree with Bradfield that he probably "voted for the act itself when it was up for passage.")

This Senate session of Saturday, March 3, lasted through a wearying afternoon and on into the evening. Midnight came and passed. At last the coinage bill was up for action, and Senator Atherton demanded immediate consideration. To Senator William R. King (D–Ala.), who objected that there'd be little use for a $20 gold coin, Atherton replied as McKay had to similar objections in the House, that the coin could be dropped if the objection proved correct.

FIG. 52–1. Double-eagle, 1849, Pattern, obverse. The only located survivor out of the 8 or 9 gold double-eagle patterns struck in 1849. In the National Collection, Smithsonian Institution.

The Senate amended its bill, the House agreed and the newly-passed Act was sent to President Polk, who signed it.

Longacre got to work, but was hampered by personal and technical problems. Chief coiner Franklin Peale was one of the former—and he precipitated one of the latter by denying Longacre access to such vital equipment as the reducing machine. Longacre finished a double-eagle reverse die in June, but didn't complete the obverse die until December 22.

His basic design is a Liberty head facing left. Liberty wears a coronet (the coin is called the Coronet Type or the Liberty Head type); the tiny crown is ornamented with pearls and lettered LIBERTY. The date is at bottom and 13 stars are around the rim.

On the reverse is a large heraldic eagle with U.S. shield on its chest, an olive branch in its right talon, and arrows in its left. In the eagle's beak is one end of an elaborate scroll which circles below the bird and is lettered E PLURIBUS UNUM. Above are rays and 13 stars with the upper six stars superimposed on the rays. Around top and side rims is UNITED STATES OF AMERICA. The value is at bottom, shown as TWENTY D. The edge is reeded.

Since "In God We Trust" hadn't yet reached our coinage, it wasn't part of the original design.

Eight or nine gold patterns and at least one brass one were struck on an old screw press. These bought a problem to light: the regular steam-powered coinage presses didn't have enough power to produce the design's high relief. The coins would become as controversial as they were beautiful; already they reflected months of work and months of conflict.

Fifty-eight years in the future, the first patterns of a new double-eagle would be in too high relief for regular coin presses, would lack "In God We Trust," and would become the center of controversy!

But that's the minor part of the puzzle. The real question is about the 1849 patterns.

We know the brass one was restruck for one R. C. Davis and was last located in 1892. Where is it now? Good question.

We know that *most* of the gold patterns were melted. That's why most collectors never heard of them, and why it's widely believed that only one gold pattern was struck.

Two gold patterns were not melted.

One is in the Smithsonian Institution, and is one of my favorite displays when it's on view, despite the label describing it as "unique."

The second surviving 1849 gold pattern was presented to Treasury Secretary William M. Meredith. And this priceless numismatic treasure, as of this writing, may be *anywhere in the world!*

When writing about the $20 coin in *Coins Magazine,* I interviewed Dr. C-Stefanelli at the Smithsonian. "The possibility exists that another piece may turn up one day," he said; but he noted that the missing pattern "can be hidden *anywhere.*" Nobody came forward to say he had it, when the article appeared. I retold the story in a short article in *McCall's.* Still nobody claimed to own the long-missing pattern.

It may be in a safe-deposit box owned by a noncollector who's unaware of what a gem he has. It may have been—either accidentally or purposely—destroyed. Someone may have taken it to another country. Or a descendant of Meredith may be keeping the pattern and guarding its secret for fear of government seizure and in the hope of privacy.

On January 12, 1850, Longacre finished a second obverse die with larger coronet beads, a slight shift in position of the Liberty head, some different hair lines, a flatter cheek, and a tiny JBL on the cutoff line. Silver, pewter, and white metal patterns were struck, but this die, too, failed to make the grade.

On March 12 he finished the third die, which was usable.

Double-eagles are the highest-denomination U.S. regular-issue coins; they're the second largest, slightly smaller and thinner than the silver dollar. The .900 fine gold double-eagle weighs 516 grains (33.436 grams), just under 1¼ ounces, but feels much heavier. Mint marks on branch mint coins are on the reverse, below the eagle.

In 1852 you could take a $20 coin to Henry Rahte's New Liquor Store in Fond Du Lac, Wis., and buy a thousand of any of several types of cigars. In 1857 $20 was the cost of a student's tuition in the Classical Department at Arkansas College in Fayetteville.

Longacre's fourth die (1859) has only minor changes. The

FIG. 52–2. Double-eagle, 1864, Proof, obverse. The Longacre obverse design, as issued. This coin is in the National Collection, Smithsonian Institution.

portrait's cutoff line is slightly wider and smoother and the JBL is moved a little to the left. Four to 12 patterns were struck with this and a reverse by Anthony C. Paquet. This follows Longacre's closely, but the eagle and shield are slightly larger, the stars are clearer and all are below the rays, and the letters are larger and heavier. Similar patterns were struck in 1860.

Philadelphia and San Francisco both minted Paquet-reverse coins in 1861. Only a few were issued, though, and San Francisco withdrew its issue almost immediately.

Some patterns were struck in 1865 with the regular obverse and "reverse of 1866" with IN GOD WE TRUST in the ellipse of stars above the eagle. This became the regular-issue reverse starting in 1866. The shield changes from straight-sided to almost lyre-shaped. San Francisco made both "no motto" and "with motto" coins in 1866; the earlier type is rarer.

A double-eagle played a role in journalistic history in 1865. According to Sidney Kobre's book *The Yellow Press*, the *San Francisco Chronicle* was founded that year as the tabloid *Dramatic Chronicle*—by two young men *whose total capital consisted of a borrowed $20 gold coin.*

Pattern-class double-eagles include the usual die trials, most of them copper or aluminum, most with mintage of from 4 to 12 and most costing several hundred dollars. The 1872 uniform design series includes a double-eagle with the denomination shown as TWENTY DOL.

In January 1875 you could travel from Yuma, Ariz., to San Francisco, including cabin passage on the C. S. N. Company's steamer, for $40. Six months later a cabin cost $90 and the price for steerage was $40. Advertisements in *The Arizona Citizen* specified "$40 Coin."

In 1876 mint authorities decided to improve the coin's appearance. William Barber rotated the Liberty head a few degrees counter-clockwise to put the coronet's top between two stars. The reverse has a larger E PLURIBUS UNUM and scroll, and shows the denomination as TWENTY DOLLARS. This became the new regular-issue design in 1877. If you were in West Virginia three years later, you could use a double-eagle to purchase "the finest dress suit in Wheeling" from M. Salinger's Atlantic Clothing House.

Variety collectors will find several interesting double-eagles. A cent planchet was struck with the $20 dies in 1851, and there also are 1853 with 3 over 2, 1854 with recut date, 1873 with open or closed 3, and others.

Philadelphia made Coronet double-eagles 1850–1907 without missing a year, but 1883, 1884, and 1887 coins all are Proofs. New Orleans, first branch mint to make these, struck $20 coins 1850–61 and again in 1879. San Francisco minted the gold pieces 1854–1907, omitting only 1886. Carson City dates are 1870–93, except 1880–81 and 1886–88. Denver made these only 1906–07.

The highest mintage is the 6,256,699 of 1904, while the lowest is 590, for 1882. Proofs were struck 1858–1907 at Philadelphia, with totals ranging from 20 in several years to 158 in 1903.

Many Coronet coins cost around $250 to $270 in Fine condition, $300 to $350 Unc. Some Proofs cost about $2,200.

Star-Line dates are 1889–S, 1891, and Proofs of 1875 and 1891. Marginals are 1868–S, 1873–S, 1874–S, 1875–S, 1876, 1879–S, 1880–S, 1881–S, 1882–S, 1890–S, 1891–S, 1894, 1894–S, 1895, 1895–S, 1896, 1897, 1899–S, 1900–S, 1906–S, 1907–S, and Proof 1867.

In 1907, while Denver and San Francisco made Coronet type double-eagles, Philadelphia also made a new design whose story echoes 1849. The idea for the second design came during a dinner conversation in 1905 between President Theodore Roosevelt and sculptor Augustus Saint-Gaudens. The artist mentioned that ancient Greek coins were almost the only ones with any real artistic value (I disagree emphatically!), and the President suggested that he design some new coins.

FIG. 52–3. Double-eagle, 1907–D, reverse. This coin, in the National Collection, Smithsonian Institution, represents the final year of the Coronet type and Denver's second year of issuing double-eagles.

Because of Saint-Gaudens's failing health, Henry Hering did the physical work under his direction. Before this was finished, President Roosevelt saw some gold coins of Alexander the Great; impressed by their high relief, he suggested that new double-eagles also be high-relief coins. Neither he nor Saint-Gaudens, in their enthusiasm, realized that the mint's coin presses couldn't strike such coins with one blow.

An early design shows a standing *winged* Liberty facing the viewer. She wears an Indian bonnet over flowing hair, and a loose gown which billows in the wind. She holds a liberty torch in her right hand and an olive branch in her left. Her left leg is bent, resting on a rock. LIBERTY is around the top. Far in the lower left background is a tiny Capitol with a rising sun at left. A small sprig of what looks like laurel is at bottom, in front of the rock. The date is above the rock, in Roman numerals. There are 46 small stars around the rim.

The model for Miss Liberty is supposed to have been the same Mary Cunningham who modeled for the $10 coin. According to the story, she worked as a waitress and was serving the sculptor in a restaurant when he was struck by her beauty.

On later patterns the sculptor enlarged the Capitol, hid the sun but left its rays, changed Liberty's hair to let it stream freely in the wind and removed the wings and Indian bonnet. He added his ASG monogram below the date. This more disciplined and compact design has a better tone than the earlier one; it certainly has more impact.

An eagle with outspread wings soars across the reverse. Below and behind it is the rising sun, whose rays highlight the national

FIG. 52–4. Double-eagle, 1926–S, obverse.

emblem. At top is UNITED STATES OF AMERICA and immediately below it is TWENTY DOLLARS.

Saint-Gaudens wrote to the President May 16, 1907, that a *standing* eagle would be better than a soaring one. This stationary design, he said, would be in closer scale to Liberty, appear more dignified, and avoid using the rays on both sides. But Roosevelt strongly preferred the flying eagle, and this was the design used.

The Saint-Gaudens $20 coin has our only modern lettered edge: E PLURIBUS UNUM with stars between the words, plus 11 more stars for a total of 13, symbolizing the original states.

Of 22 high-relief patterns, two were remelted, one is held by the American Numismatic Society, two are in the Smithsonian and the rest rate a $32,500 value in Dr. Judd's book. These early strikes were in such high relief that regular coin presses couldn't strike them. Because of the high relief, the coins wouldn't stack. And they do not have "In God We Trust."

Shades of 1849!

Saint-Gaudens's health was failing rapidly. In the summer of 1907, President Roosevelt urged the mint to get new coins into production. Not practical yet, objected mint officials—the high relief meant stamping each piece three or more times to bring up all design details, and this took too long.

The President ordered them to issue the double-eagle even if it took all day to stamp one coin! But Saint-Gaudens went into a coma on August 1. Two days later, Saturday, August 3, he died. He never saw his $20 coin in use.

Not until the end of November did high-relief double-eagles

FIG. 52–5. Double-eagle, 1908, no motto type, reverse.

FIG. 52–6. Double-eagle, 1908, with motto type, reverse.

enter circulation. Those 11,250 coins have the date as the artist planned it; another 361,667 released later have lower relief, and a Western ("Arabic") numerals date. Evidently many persons found the Roman numerals hard to read. When branch mint coins were struck, the mint mark was put above the date.

But one item still was missing: "In God We Trust." We explored why in "Miss Liberty Goes Indian," so I won't repeat that. But word of the design, released when the designer died, caused a furor over the $20 as well as the $10.

The public, for the most part, agreed. The new coins were in such demand that in some cities they brought $30 each in January 1908. Many numismatists call these the most beautiful of all U.S. coins; even we who prefer other coins agree that the Saint-Gaudens $20 is *one* of the nation's best.

Congress passed a law in 1908 restoring the motto to our "Godless" coins, but more than 90 percent of the 1908 issue was struck before IN GOD WE TRUST was added around the sun on the reverse. Philadelphia and Denver made both "with motto" and "no motto" coins, while San Francisco struck only "with motto" pieces.

Philadelphia issued the Saint-Gaudens design 1907–32, but skipped 1916–19 and 1930. Denver made double-eagles 1908–31, except in 1912, 1915–22, and 1928–30. San Francisco issued the coins 1908–30, omitting 1912, 1917–19, 1921, 1923, 1928, and 1929. Proofs were struck at Philadelphia 1908–15, with mintage from 50 in 1915 to 167 in 1910. Low-mintage date is 1908–S, with 22,000. Top production came in 1928, when Philadelphia struck 8,816,000—high for the Saint-Gaudens design, the $20 denomination and U.S. gold coinage as a whole!

Prices for several dates are in the $260 to $275 range VF. The 1927–D and an "ultra-high relief" 1907 repeatedly break price records; in January 1975 the latter was sold for over $225,000.

Abraham and Straus, in Brooklyn, N.Y., would sell you a $25 Library Chair for $20 at their 1917 Harvest Sale. That same year a double-eagle would buy you a man's suit at Lord & Taylor in New York.

Varieties are relatively few: 1909 with 9 over 8, 1909–S with double S, and 1911–D with double D. Probably there are others still undiscovered.

In 1933 Philadelphia did strike 445,500 double-eagles, but the coins were never released. Only about ten specimens are known. A perfect BU gem was the final lot in the Col. James W. Flanagan Collection catalog by Stack's; the catalog called this specimen "the first that ever came up in any public auction" and referred to private sales at prices from $1,000 to $2,200—and that was in the 1940's! The Treasury Department has confiscated several of these coins. How many actually survive today? I wonder. . . .

With President Franklin D. Roosevelt's Gold Surrender Order of March 16, 1933, the active life of the double-eagle ended. Some numismatists list the $20 coin's issue period as 1849–1933, but double-eagles were not actually released until 1850, and were never officially released in 1933; so the true issue period is 1850–1932.

Star-Line dates are 1910, 1910–S, 1923–D, and Proof 1914. Marginals are 1908–D With Motto, 1909–S, 1910–D, 1913–D, 1914–S, 1922, and Proofs of 1909 and 1912.

Part Five

Let's Collect These, Too!

53

Medals for Our Collections

"Houston, Tranquility base here. The Eagle has landed."—Neil Armstrong, first words spoken by man from Earth's moon to Earth, July 20, 1969.

Some medals are issued by the government, some by cities, some by local or national associations—including numismatic groups—and some by individuals.

Some medals have close ties with coins—for instance, medals created by coin designers. Anthony C. Paquet designed the U. S. Medal of Honor used 1862–96. And Anthony de Francisci produced a bronze 2⅞-inch medal titled "Creation" in 1935, commissioned by the Society of Medalists; the group reissued that medal in silver in 1974.

There simply are too many different medals to describe, so let me share a very few with you. To start let's go aboard. . . .

FIG. 53–1. This copper medal was issued to mark the centennial of the city of Prescott, Arizona, in 1964.

THE FRIGATE *Constellation*

The frigate *Constellation,* oldest surviving U.S. Navy ship, has been inspiring medals since her launching in 1797. "Connie" was decommissioned in 1955 and handed over to the Constellation Committee. Maryland recommissioned her in 1967 as the state flagship. She is berthed at Constellation Dock in Baltimore, where thousands visit her each year.

"Connie"'s best-known medal is a 1¼-inch copper piece first struck in 1959 by Bastian Brothers Co. of Rochester, N. Y. The Constellation Committee salvaged copper spikes from the decaying vessel, and these provided enough metal for over 650,000 half-dollar-sized souvenir medals.

One side shows the first "Connie" under full sail, heading toward the left, seen from off the port bow (landlubbers read "seen from far ahead on the left side"). Around top and side rims is U.S. FRIGATE CONSTELLATION and at bottom is the launch date.

The reverse has a smoothly stylized eagle holding a tilted shield above a parchment navigation chart lettered THIS COIN STRUCK FROM PARTS OF THE FRIGATE CONSTELLATION THE FIRST SHIP OF THE U. S. NAVY. Two cannon barrels hold down the chart. The medal's edge is plain.

Donald F. Stewart, great-great-great grandson of Capt. Charles Stewart, Connie's commanding officer in the War of 1812, designed this and also a National Medal struck in several sizes at Philadelphia. It shows the ship heading to our right, with gunsmoke drifting past the stern. The rim has PER MARE INVICTUS MANEO ("At Sea I Was Invincible") and OLDEST SHIP OF THE U.S.

FIG. 53–2. The "Connie" medal is a stirring one, especially for coin collectors who were in the Navy.

NAVY. Her name and launch date and Philadelphia's mint mark are in the exergue. The reverse has an eagle perched on a stern-post dated 1797 and 1972, surrounded by 15 stars with inward-pointing rays. The rim has CENTENNIAL DIAMOND JUBILEE and BY ACT OF CONGRESS.

SERIES MEDALS

Whether you favor famous men, historic events, or science and the arts, somebody is issuing medals for you.

One of the top firms in this field is Presidential Art Medals, which issues medals in series with subjects such as Presidents, signers of the Declaration of Independence, and so forth.

For the ladies, the Société Commemorative de Femmes Célèbres produces medals showing famous women of history. Its medals have shown such honored ladies as Joan of Arc, Florence Nightingale, Amelia Earhart, and Queen Isabella I of Spain.

The National Commemorative Society's medals pay tribute to various aspects of life in this country; for instance, its thirteenth medal in the second series marked the centennial of professional baseball. It was issued the week of the 1969 World Series.

One society has two sets of members, two mints, and two headquarters. The Britannia Commemorative Society has offices in England and the United States. British members' medals are struck by John Pinches & Co., while Americans' medals are made at The Franklin Mint.

The American Negro Commemorative Society's medals, slightly larger than a silver dollar, honor such men as Frederick Douglass, Dr. Martin Luther King, Jr., William C. Handy, and others.

In addition to societies, private firms and organizations also issue medals. Cities issue medals for various civic anniversaries (San Diego, Calif., and Memphis, Tenn., for example). In 1969 Fulton, Mo., was the issue point of a National Medal commemorating the late Sir Winston Churchill's "Iron Curtain" speech of 1946, which was delivered there.

The International Numismatic Agency, World Proof Numismatic Association, fraternal groups, the ANA, and even local coin clubs and coin shops have issued medals at one time or another.

"THAT'S ONE SMALL STEP . . ."

Our space exploration has inspired enough medals to keep a collector busy for a long time. Let's look at a couple.

President Richard M. Nixon presented astronauts Aldrin, Armstrong, and Collins with three of four two-and-a-half-inch medals struck by Medallic Art Co. for Presidential Art Medals, Inc. (the fourth is the President's copy). On the obverse are the men's portraits and names, the National Aeronautics and Space Agency (NASA) insigne, a large 11 below and APOLLO at bottom (to designate the eleventh mission of the Apollo series). The reverse shows the landing craft "Eagle" on the Moon, with two astronauts walking nearby and Earth at upper left. Balancing the planet and spacecraft is MAN'S FIRST LUNAR LANDING, JULY 20–21, 1969.

The Franklin Mint's silver "Eyewitness Medal" also shows a lunar scene—Armstrong's first step onto the surface. Behind the figure is ONE SMALL STEP FOR A MAN . . . ONE GIANT LEAP FOR MANKIND. The one-and-a-half-inch medal's reverse shows the "Spirit of Apollo" plaque left on the moon.

As those who watched the moon landing on television or later heard tape recordings of it know, we heard Armstrong say ". . . one small step for man . . . ," not "for *a* man." NASA told me in 1974 that Armstrong confirmed that he did say "for a man," but I've never heard a satisfactory explanation of the missing "a." Most medals that quote the astronaut's words show the NASA version rather than what we read in *The New York Times* or heard on tapes.

There are many more "space medals" issued by societies, clubs, and private firms.

MINT MEDALS

Medal collectors will enjoy looking at the official U.S. Treasury publication *Medals of the United States Mint.* The 311-page, well-illustrated catalog includes order blanks that collectors can use to buy available medals.

About a century ago the mint began collecting dies used for

FIG. 53–3. The large, high-relief inaugural medal of 1961 is too large for standard coin envelopes. It must be kept in either a special extra-large envelope or, for better protection, the box it came in.

medals previously authorized by Congress. Collectors have been able to buy bronze copies of these since the 1860's.

Medals in the catalog are divided into Presidents, Secretaries of the Treasury, Directors of the Mint, Army, Navy, and Miscellaneous. There are biographies and other information that make the catalog worth its $5.25 price.

KENNEDY INAUGURAL MEDALS

Inaugural medals have been struck since 1901 but have been available to the public only beginning with Hoover's inauguration in 1929. The traditional obverse is the President's portrait.

Reverses showed the Great Seal of the U.S.; until 1945 the eagle faced its own left, but President Harry Truman ordered the heraldic correction. Another change came in 1961, when President-elect Kennedy ordered that his medal's reverse show the Presidential seal.

Paul Manship visited the Kennedy home and made four or five sketches of the President-elect, then modeled the medal in plaster of Paris. The design was reduced to 2¾ inches in diameter and medals were struck.

The original plan was for 7,500 silver and 15,000 bronze medals, in addition to the single gold one that's stuck for the President. But the serially numbered silver medals sold out quickly at $35 and the $4.50 bronze issue had to be raised to 20,000.

On the obverse is a left-facing portrait. Around the top is JOHN FITZGERALD KENNEDY and below the shoulder is PAUL MANSHIP © 1961. The reverse shows the Presidential Seal, featuring a heraldic eagle like the one on many coins. Above it are rays, stars, and clouds. Around the eagle is a circle of 50 small stars for the 50 states. The rim has PRESIDENT OF THE UNITED STATES OF AMERICA at top and JANUARY 20TH, 1961, at the bottom with INAUGURATED above it.

Running lengthwise around the edge are fine grooves which resemble reeding except for their direction and size, and which were produced by the lathe which removed excess material ("flash") from the medals. Incuse on one side is the number; across from it is MEDALLIC ART CO. NY .999+ PURE SILVER.

Bronze medals are smaller and have plain edges.

54

Tokens

A token may be issued for any of several
purposes, but the ones we're most familiar with in
daily life are those issued by local
transportation companies.

A FARE DEAL

Transit tokens are small bits of Americana that have been around
since the 1840's. Some of them have played additional roles.
Shortly after World War I, people near Buffalo, N.Y., were using
a Buffalo company's tokens as small change; and the Transit
Authority of New York City once tried to persuade local merchants to accept its 15¢ tokens as coins in the course of business.

Tokens may be brass, cardboard, copper, lead, nickel, tin, or
other materials. Some are square, some oval, some octagonal, and
probably some are other shapes; most, of course, are round.

Most of the tokens I've seen and collected are about the size of
a dime, but some are close to quarter size.

These have been issued for use on boats, buses, elevated trains,
horsecars, jitneys, streetcars, subways, and "trackless trolleys"
(electric-powered buses that get power from overhead wires).

If there's any single preferred design, it's the cutout type with a
center initial or symbol; this may be itself a shaped empty space
or it may be metal outlined by space. Many tokens of Washington, D.C., have a W in the center; some from San Diego have an
S. There's a Los Angeles Railway Co. token with a bell in the
center. Tokens issued for the Atlantic City, N.J., jitneys have a
large J with the metal cut out around the letter. The United Ry. &
Elec. Co. of Baltimore, Md., once issued tokens with a central
cutout outlining a U.

Real designs are scarce. One nice one is the trackless trolley on

FIG. 54–1. Transit token, Honolulu, 1924. One of the few dated vectures (transit tokens). This appears to be nickel; the same design was struck in a zinc alloy, or similar metal.

FIG. 54–2. Transit token, Des Moines, Iowa.

obverse *and* reverse of the small token issued by the Des Moines Railway Company. The Oakland, Brooklyn & Fruitvale R. R. Co., in California, issued a token dated 1871 showing a horse pulling a horsecar. This is one of the few dated transit tokens I've seen. Another is the small piece of the Honolulu Rapid Transit Co., Ltd., dated 1924; this has an H cutout in the center.

There's plenty of room for variety in this field—for there are over 8,000 different transit tokens.

The basic reference for vecturists (transit token collectors) is *Atwood's Catalogue of United States and Canadian Transportation Tokens*, 3rd ed. published at Boston by the American Vecturist Association in 1970.

TIMES WERE HARD

From around 1830–45 and 1860–65 people were hoarding coins. The gap between supply and demand was filled with copperheads, Jackson tokens, storecards, Civil War tokens, and other private issues. I group all of these as "Nineteenth-Century Tokens"; however, token collectors will prefer their own classifications. There are over 11,000 such pieces, and discoveries are made constantly.

Most are cent-sized and made of copper, but there also are cupronickel, silver, lead, and zinc ones from the size of the (small) cent to that of a quarter.

On November 23, 1837, the weekly edition of *The Globe* (Washington, D.C.), stated in an item headed "Copper Coin" that "there are great quantities of copper pieces in the market which circulate as cents, but which are not so. They are too light; but the worst part . . . is the bad metal. . . . Worst of all, they are a vile debasement of the current coin, by which individuals very improperly make a large profit at the public expense, their spurious coins being generally sold by the bushel, at 50 to 62½ cents the hundred."

There definitely was a need for *some* substitute for the missing coins. Most people accepted privately issued tokens gladly: they weren't government issues, but they had some value, and *anything* was better than the paper fractional currency!

Hard-times tokens often were political. Most are copper, the size of the large cent. Many resemble cents except for a satiric motto.

Jackson tokens deal with Andrew Jackson's campaign for the Presidency and his battle against the Bank of the United States. These flourished around 1837–41.

Nonpolitical hard-times tokens often were "storecards"—tokens with a store's name or name and address, issued both as advertisements and as a way to provide customers and potential customers with small change.

Civil War tokens, often called "copperheads," are the size of small cents; they flourished around 1861–64. Among the favorite designs were Indian heads, Washington, Lincoln, Franklin, and famous generals. On political or patriotic ones the motto sometimes has a bitter twist, but often it's simply an expression of sentiment: "Union Forever," "Army and Navy," and "The Federal

FIG. 54–3. One of the private tokens which aroused editorial ire—but which provided cent-like "coins" during a nineteenth-century coin shortage.

Government Must and Shall Be Preserved" are among the most popular.

The Director of the Mint saw tokens as illegal because they were unauthorized substitutes for coins. But there was no law against issuing trade tokens or private coins that didn't imitate official issues. Where U.S. coins said "One Cent," tokens usually added a tiny "Not" above it. The issuer could point out that *denying* value hardly was imitating the government's coins!

So the government passed laws in April and June 1864 to prohibit *all* private coinage. The new Indian Head cent and 2¢ coin helped ease the small-change shortage.

You can buy many nineteenth-century tokens for $2 to $3 in the lower grades and $5 to $10 Uncirculated. Auctions and other collectors are excellent sources.

MODERN "SEMI-STORECARDS"

Like some nineteenth-century merchants, several companies have issued tokens with an advertising function. Though they've little or no monetary status, they're descendants of storecards of the last century.

The Mohawk Airlines bronze "Gold Chip," 1¾ inches in diameter, shows conjoined portraits of a pilot, ground crewman, and stewardess. The rim has MOWHAWK AIRLINES, GOLD CHIP SERVICE. The reverse has WE'RE ON YOUR SIDE! MOWHAWK in large letters and the manufacturer's name at bottom in tiny letters: METAL ARTS—RICH., N. Y. The edge is plain. Passengers dissatisfied with the airline's service could demand a token and redeem it for $1 at ticket offices—or add it to a collection.

Braniff International's plastic "Fastbuck" is a little smaller than a silver dollar. One side has a clock face showing 11½ minutes past 9, with TIME IS MONEY across the center. The reverse has GOOD FOR A FAST BUCK in three lines; around the rim is REDEEMABLE 'TIL 12–31–68 AT BRANIFF TICKET OFFICES. The edge has very close reeding. When planes arrived late, each passenger received a token, which could be cashed in, spent later for a cocktail, or added to collections.

"Antique Car Coin" and "Mr. President" tokens have no monetary function, but they're interesting.

These are a little larger than a quarter, and there are three sets of auto pieces, struck by The Franklin Mint. The car's name is at the top rim. Each token pictures a car and has in the exergue a date when that automobile was made. Sets were struck in bronze, silver, and platinum, with plain edges.

The Type 1 reverse (December 1968) shows each car maker's trademark. Sunoco's "Antique Car Coin Game" (January 1969) brought aluminum tokens and two more reverses. Type 2 has Sunoco's trademark, two rosettes, and ANTIQUE CAR COIN SERIES 1. Type 3, on tokens entitling owners to various prizes, has INSTANT WINNER at top and bottom, and four rosettes. Series 2 tokens have reeded edges and improved reverses—a square shield lettered ANTIQUE CAR COIN SERIES 2, plus trademarks top and bottom. Its Type 3 reverse has the shield lettered YOU ARE AN INSTANT WINNER.

Issue prices were $5,000 for platinum, $75 for silver, and $10 for the immensely popular bronze. Aluminum tokens were free at participating gasoline stations. Early in 1975, sets of silver Proofs were selling for about $100 for Series 1, $85 for Series 2, and $80 for Series 3.

Shell Oil's "Mr. President Game" tokens picture U.S. Presidents. The Franklin Mint struck these 35 tokens in a special alloy to foil would-be counterfeiters of winning tokens. Each piece shows the portrait, the ordinal number of that President's term, dates of office, and his name. Reverses of winning tokens were marked SHELL'S INSTANT WINNER. Bronze sets were among the prizes.

LOVE TOKENS

Love tokens are coins ground down on one or both sides to remove the official design, then engraved for presentation to the loved one.

These have been presented to relatives, friends, and others on birthdays, anniversaries, even funerals! Some love tokens have just an initial, some have names, and many show dates, carefully drawn scenes, ornate floral bouquets, or other designs. Among the most popular designs are hearts and arrows, roses or other flowers, and lovebirds.

FIG. 54–4. Love token on reverse of a Type 1 gold dollar. "F.C.L." evidently wore this on a chain or bracelet.

Love tokens have been made in this and other countries, in just about any metal and on almost any denomination you can name. The favorite U.S. coin for this purpose is the dime—but *every* denomination has been used.

Making of love tokens dates back to before 1792; the fad reached its height in the last half of the nineteenth century, but it's continuing today.

The workmanship of love tokens ranges from crude to expert. Some have been done by novices, others by professional engravers; many were made by jewelers, to customers' requests.

Since love tokens no longer belong to the class of coins, the condition of the side that still has an official design is not a factor in pricing. All that counts is how much the prospective buyer wants to own the token.

55

Variety, Yes! Variety, No!

You can pay high prices for variety coins—or hunt for recognized ones in circulation—or even make your own discoveries.

VARIETY, YES! VARIETY, NO!

Varieties are coins of the same denomination, date, and mint—but with differences in design, lettering size or almost anything else. Some collectors love them, others can't stand 'em.

If you'd like to try this aspect of collecting, look at some Lincoln cents. On the first type (wheat ears reverse) you can find coins with blobs of extra metal on the wheat ears; on 1959 and later cents there are many varieties with bits of metal which resemble animals crawling on the Lincoln Memorial's columns.

Some varieties result from breaks in the dies which stamp the coin's design; a popular type is the "cracked skull," a coin with a die break on the head of the portrait.

Another common cause is the use of several dies with minor differences; typical examples are the large and small dates on both cents and nickels of 1960.

When dies are recut for longer use, the coins they make show double or even triple lines. Take a good look at several Jefferson nickels and you'll find some with the popular "double dome" variety. Many half-dollars dated 1960 and later have the denomination recut.

Sometimes a mint worker picks up a wrong date punch, or puts the date too high or low on a die; coins produced by a corrected die will show both the error and the correction. If a working die is struck by a hub with an error, it would have to be repunched to correct the mistake. If two sufficiently different hubs are used on a die, the die produces coins showing the difference, such as the 1942 and 1942–D dimes with $\frac{2}{1}$.

How big or small should a variety be? Some collectors include tiny differences such as the "micro double date" coins. But there seems to be the convention that a collectible variety should be one that's visible under, at most, a ten-power (10X) lens.

Mike Kolman, Jr. and Dr. J. H. Litman devised a scale to describe off-center coins that's now generally used for locating varieties. This "Kolit" setup is a clock face with the coin posi-

FIG. 55–1. One cent, 1955–D, obverse, BIE variety. This extremely popular variety is caused by a die break or pit in the die, which produces the "misspelled" word by apparently adding an I after the B in LIBERTY.

tioned in normal viewing attitude, with the top toward the 12 o'clock point. The direction or position of an error on the coin, or the area of a variety, is identified by the position of the hours on the clock face. Thus a Lincoln cent with a blob of extra metal at the rim in front of Lincoln's face might be K2 or K3.

U.S. coins' reverses are "upside down" from the obverse, a 180-degree rotation. Since that's our starting point, it's zero rotation *from normal.* All measurements start from this position.

Some varieties are "recognized" in the Red Book; many more are listed in the *V&O Guide.* These references can help you get acquainted with common varieties, and tickle your imagination toward going out and making your own "finds" to add to the list.

LARGE AND SMALL MINT MARKS

Coins with mint marks larger or smaller than usual are among the most popular varieties. These should be represented in collections by two coins, one showing the mint mark in normal size and the other showing the variety.

There are several possible causes. After a die is finished the mint mark is added with a separate punch. If more than one mint mark punch is used and the punches are of different sizes, they'll produce different-sized mint marks on coins. A single punch can produce different-sized marks if it's punched hard into one working die and lightly into another. If a light punch is corrected by a heavier one immediately afterwards, then this might produce coins with a double mint mark with such names as "light over heavy" or "small over large." And if a workman should use a mint mark punch intended for another denomination, the mark would be noticeably larger or smaller than that punched into other working dies with the correct punch.

56

Commemorative Coins

From 1892 through 1954 the U.S.
issued coins commemorating states,
cities, events and men.

OUR FIRST COMMEMORATIVE

Back in 1892 Chicago celebrated the 400th anniversary of Columbus's voyage to America and the U.S. issued its first commemorative coin. Charles E. Barber designed the obverse, which
shows a right-facing portrait representing Christopher Columbus;
the top rim has UNITED STATES OF AMERICA and the bottom has
COLUMBIAN HALF DOLLAR. Coinage laws specified that national
identification and denomination were to be on the *reverse*, so you
could make a case for calling this the reverse rather than the
obverse; however, as with the Type 2 and Type 3 gold dollar and
$3 gold piece, collectors accept the portrait side as the obverse.

George T. Morgan's reverse features the *Santa Maria* under sail
and headed to our left. Below is the date 1492 split by two globes
showing maps of the world. The date 1892 is at bottom. At the
rim is WORLD'S COLUMBIAN EXPOSITION, CHICAGO.

Priced at $1, the 1892 coins sold quickly. Philadelphia struck

FIG. 56–1. Columbian commemorative half-dollar, 1892, obverse.
Since Columbus's appearance is a
mystery, the portrait on this coin
was a guess. Charles E. Barber
drew the dignified portrayal.

more in 1893 but many of these *didn't* sell. Some unsold coins were released into circulation after the exposition and actually were used. Some of these wore down to Good condition! But they're so obviously different from the Barber halves used at that time that probably all now are in collections.

Many 1893 coins were hoarded for two years, in hopes that their value would rise. The September 1895 *Numismatist* reprinted a *New York Sun* report that "now they have been thrown upon the market and are freely circulated."

Both 1892 and 1893 cost about $8 to $10 Extremely Fine and $25 to $35 Uncirculated. Proofs were struck both years, and these cost several hundred dollars; the 1893 Proof is rarer.

FIG. 56–2. Columbian commemorative half-dollar, 1892, reverse.

PILGRIM HALVES

The Pilgrim Tercentenary coin was meant to mark the 300th anniversary of the Plymouth Rock landing. Boston sculptor Cyrus E. Dallin did the work with designs the commemorative commission supplied. The coin was released in November 1920.

On the obverse is a half-length portrait of solemn Governor William Bradford facing left and wearing the characteristic tall Pilgram hat with a buckle. In the crook of his arm he carries a large Bible. Above the shoulder is IN GOD WE TRUST. Around the rim are UNITED STATES OF AMERICA at top and PILGRIM HALF DOLLAR at bottom.

The reverse shows the *Mayflower* heading left under sail on a rough sea. Around the rim is PILGRIM TERCENTENARY CELEBRATION and at bottom are the dates 1620 and 1920.

Philadelphia was the only mint making these coins. In 1921 it struck more, adding "1921" at left of the portrait.

Today the 1920 coin costs about $40 to $50 Uncirculated; the rare 1921 varies from about $75 to $90.

STONE MOUNTAIN

This 1925 commemorative was supposed to mark the start of work on a gigantic memorial to the Confederacy. Sculptor Gutzon Borglum was carving statues of Generals Robert E. Lee and Thomas "Stonewall" Jackson and C.S.A. President Jefferson Davis on Stone Mountain, in Georgia. He also designed the coin, sending in the design three times before it was approved, on October 10, 1924.

The obverse has conjoined mounted portraits of Lee and Jackson, facing left. Around the top are four stars each at left and right of IN GOD WE TRUST and five more stars below. Under the horses' heads, at lower left, is STONE MOUNTAIN, with the date below that.

On the reverse is an eagle standing with wings spread on a mountain crag. Around top and side rims is UNITED STATES OF AMERICA and at bottom is HALF DOLLAR. Above the denomination is LIBERTY. At left, just below center, is MEMORIAL TO THE VALOR OF THE SOLDIER OF THE SOUTH.

Borglum spent a good deal of time working on the coin—in fact he neglected the monument itself! The first coins were minted January 21, 1925—"Stonewall" Jackson's birthday—and the Confederate Monumental Association fired Borglum on Feb-

FIG. 56–3. Stone Mountain commemorative half-dollar, 1925, obverse.

ruary 26. Borglum destroyed the memorial plans, fled the state and later was arrested. The great memorial wasn't finished until 1970.

This coin costs about $15 Extremely Fine and $23 to $35 Uncirculated.

FOUR COINS FOR PANAMA-PACIFIC

The event was the Panama Canal's opening, in 1914, and the U.S. issued four commemoratives for San Francisco's 1915 Panama-Pacific Exposition. All were struck at the San Francisco mint and three of them are gold.

The mint hired Charles Keck, Robert Aitken, and Evelyn Longman to do the gold and Paul Manship to design the silver half-dollar. But Treasury Secretary William Malburn wanted mint designers to produce all the coins. Eventually, Barber designed the half-dollar and the obverse of the quarter-eagle, with Morgan doing the $2.50 coin's reverse.

The half-dollar obverse shows a standing figure of Columbia, spirit of the nation; behind her stands a cherub holding a cornucopia. In the background are the Golden Gate and a setting sun. The date and S mint mark are at bottom. Around the rim is PANAMA-PACIFIC EXPOSITION. Columbia is scattering blossoms symbolizing the West's natural resources. On the reverse is a fairly lifelike eagle with outspread wings, perching on a U.S. shield. Below are branches of oak and olive. IN GOD WE TRUST is above, UNITED STATES OF AMERICA is around top and side rims, and HALF DOLLAR is at the bottom. The coin was sold for $1.

This coin costs $325 to $425 Uncirculated.

Charles Keck's gold dollar shows the head of a typical Canal laborer extending to the rim. The date is at bottom and UNITED STATES OF AMERICA is along the left rim in two lines. The rather crowded reverse has ONE DOLLAR in a circle formed by two dolphins, and PANAMA-PACIFIC EXPOSITION, SAN FRANCISCO around the rim. This is slightly smaller than Type 3 gold dollars, but the weight is the same; planchets are a bit thicker than those of regular-issue gold dollars.

The coin was sold for $2 in 1915, but it was less than a favorite. In fact, *The Numismatist* that August called it "an abomination." Today this "abomination" brings about $400 from collectors.

On the obverse of the quarter-eagle is Columbia riding a hippocampus, a mythical sea beast with horse's head and forequarters and a fish's tail. One hand holds the animal's mane, the other grasps a caduceus. PANAMA-PACIFIC EXPOSITION is around the upper rim and the date is at bottom. The reverse shows a realistic eagle perching facing left with wings spread, on a fasces. UNITED STATES OF AMERICA is around top and side rims and 2½ DOL. is at bottom. The mint mark is at right of the date.

This coin's issue price was $4, which many people thought too high. It costs about $1,800 or more today, Uncirculated.

And the fourth coin? It's more than just another commemorative. In fact, it's more than just another *gold* commemorative! It's the only $50 coin ever issued by the U.S.

Robert Aitken's design usually is described as showing Minerva, facing left and wearing a helmet; she's often listed as the Greek goddess of wisdom. But the fact is that "Minerva" is a Roman name. The goddess shown on these coins is Athena, patroness of defensive warfare, goddess of wisdom, patroness and namesake of the city of Athens and—by extension, since she's on so many coins—goddess of numismatics and patroness of coin collectors!

IN GOD WE TRUST is above her, and the date is below in Roman numerals (MCMXV). Outside a beaded circle are UNITED STATES OF AMERICA around top and sides and FIFTY DOLLARS at bottom.

FIG. 56–4. Fifty dollars, 1915–S, reverse. This is the largest size, and highest denomination, coin ever issued by the U.S. A planned regular-issue $50 gold piece never went beyond the pattern stage.

On the reverse is an owl, symbolic of wisdom, seen in a three-quarter view. This bird, sacred to Athena, perches on a branch of western pine. E PLURIBUS UNUM is at right. The rim inscription, again outside a beaded circle, is PANAMA-PACIFIC EXPOSITION at top and sides and SAN FRANCISCO at bottom, The edge is reeded.

Two types were issued—round and octagonal. The design was reduced slightly to fit evenly on an eight-sided planchet about the same size as the round one; in the corners of the octagonal coin are eight small dolphins. These coins are 1⅝ inches in diameter—the largest of *all* U.S. coins.

A special hydraulic medal press was taken from Philadelphia all the way to San Francisco to strike the $50 coins. It was returned immediately afterward.

Prices currently are about $15,000 and up for the octagonal $50 gold piece and $18,000 or more for the round one.

CHART OF COMMEMORATIVES

Some commemoratives quickly sold out, others were dismal failures. Certain coins which failed to sell were released into circulation, others were returned to the mints for melting.

For the full picture, you must be able to find out how many of a particular coin were made, whether any were melted and, if so, how many are left for collectors now. Many books list the total number minted, and some list the number still around at publication time. Even books which admit that some coins were melted fail to agree on how many.

Figures in the chart that follows are those which, by deduction and comparison of sources, I believe are the true ones. All coins listed are half-dollars unless otherwise indicated; in cases of multiple issues for one event, the half-dollar is identified as such.

Some gold commemoratives were melted in the 1930's and 1940's. Thus their true "remainder" figures are lower than those in the chart.

CHART OF ALL UNITED STATES COMMEMORATIVE COINS

Subject	Occasion	Date	Total Mintage	Melted	Released (Remainder)
Alabama	Centennial of statehood[1]	1921 T1	6,006	—	6,006
		1921 T2	64,038	5,000	59,038
Albany, N.Y.	250th anniversary of city charter	1936	25,013[2]	7,342	17,671
American Independence half-dollar	Sesquicentennial of Declaration of Independence[3,4]	1926	1,000,528[2]	859,408	141,120
American Independence quarter-eagle	Sesquicentennial of Declaration of Independence[3]	1926	200,226	154,207	46,019
Antietam see Battle of Antietam					
Arkansas	Centennial of statehood	1935	120,166	107,154	13,012
		1935–D	5,505[2]	—	5,505
		1935–S	5,506[2]	—	5,506
		1936 T1	10,010[2]	350	9,660
		1936 T2	25,265	—	25,265
	Single-year reverse honoring Senator Joseph R. Robinson[5]	1936–D	10,010[2]	350	9,660
		1936–S	10,012[2]	350	9,662

Subject	Occasion	Date	Total Mintage	Melted	Released (Remainder)
		1937	30,770[2]	25,265	5,505
		1937-D	5,505[2]	—	5,505
		1937-S	5,506[2]	—	5,506
		1938	6,006[2]	2,850	3,156
		1938-D	6,005[2]	2,850	3,155
		1938-S	6,006[2]	2,850	3,156
		1939	2,104[2]	—	2,104
		1939-D	2,104[2]	—	2,104
		1939-S	2,105[2]	—	2,105
Battle of Antietam	75th anniversary	1937	50,028	32,000	18,028
Battle of Bennington *see* Vermont					
Battle of Gettysburg	75th anniversary	1936	50,028	23,100	26,928
Battles of Lexington and Concord	Sesquicentennial of first battles of the American Revolution	1925	162,099[2]	86	162,013
Bay Bridge	Opening of bridge between Oakland and San Francisco	1936-S	100,055[2]	28,686	71,369
Bennington *see* Vermont					
Bicentennial coins *see* Chapters on Washington quarter, Kennedy half-dollar, Eisenhower dollar					

Boone

see Daniel Boone

Booker T. Washington	Centennial of birth			
	1946	1,000,546[2]	—	1,000,546
	1946–D	200,113[2]	—	200,113
	1946–S	500,279[2]	—	500,279
	1947	100,017[2]	—	100,017
	1947–D	100,017[2]	—	100,017
	1947–S	100,017[2]	—	100,017
	1948	20,005[2]	12,000	8,005
	1948–D	20,005[2]	12,000	8,005
	1948–S	20,005[2]	12,000	8,005
	1949	12,004[2]	6,000	6,004
	1949–D	12,004[2]	6,000	6,004
	1949–S	12,004[2]	6,000	6,004
	1950	12,004[2]	6,000	6,004
	1950–D	12,004[2]	6,000	6,004
	1950–S	512,091[2]	—	512,091
	1951	510,082[2]	—	510,082
	1951–D	12,004[2]	5,000	7,004
	1951–S	12,004[2]	5,000	7,004
Bridgeport, Conn.	Centennial of incorporation			
	1936	25,015[2]	—	25,015

California-Pacific

see San Diego-
California

Subject	Occasion	Date	Total Mintage	Melted	Released (Remainder)
California Diamond Jubilee	75th anniversary of statehood[3]	1925–S	150,200[2]	63,606	86,594
Captain Cook see Hawaii					
Cincinnati Musical Center	50th anniversary of both city as center of music and the Cincinnati Musical Center itself	1936 1936–D 1936–S	5,005 5,005 5,006	— — —	5,005 5,005 5,006
Cleveland, Ohio	Centennial of city's founding[3,6]	1936	50,030	—	50,030
Columbia, S.C.	Centennial of city's founding[3]	1936 1936–D 1936–S	9,007[2] 8,009[2] 8,007[2]	— — —	9,007 8,009 8,007
Columbian quarter-dollar	400th anniversary of Columbus's voyage; memorialization of Isabella I of Spain[3,7]	1893	40,023[2]	15,809	24,214
Columbian half-dollar[8]	400th anniversary of Columbus's voyage[3]	1892 1893	950,000[2] 4,052,105	— 2,501,700	950,000 1,550,405
Connecticut	300th anniversary of colony's founding	1935	25,018[2]	—	25,018
Daniel Boone	Bicentennial of birth	1934 1935 T1[9] 1935 T2 1935–D T1	10,007[2] 10,010[2] 10,008[2] 5,005	— — — —	10,007 10,010 10,008 5,005

	Date			
	1935-D T2	2,003	—	2,003
	1935-S T1	5,005[2]	—	5,005
	1935-S T2	2,004[2]	—	2,004
	1936	12,012[2]	—	12,012
	1936-D	5,005[2]	—	5,005
	1936-S	5,006[2]	—	5,006
	1937	15,010[2]	5,200	9,810
	1937-D	7,506[2]	5,000	2,506
	1937-S	5,006[2]	3,000	2,506
	1938	5,005[2]	2,905	2,100
	1938-D	5,005[2]	2,905	2,100
	1938-S	5,006[2]	2,906	2,100
Delaware	Tercentenary of landing of Swedish immigrants at Delaware[10]	1936	25,015[2]	4,022	20,993
Elgin, Ill.	Centennial of founding	1936	25,015[2]	5,000	20,015
Fort Vancouver (Vancouver, Wash.)	Centennial of building of fort	1925	50,028	35,034	14,994
Gettysburg see Battle of Gettysburg					
Grant half-dollar	Centennial of birth	1922 T1[12]	5,000	750	4,250
		1922 T2	95,061	27,650	67,411
Grant gold dollar	Centennial of birth	1922 T1	5,016	—	5,016
		1922 T2	5,000	—	5,000

Subject	Occasion	Date	Total Mintage	Melted	Released (Remainder)
Great Lakes see Cleveland					
Hawaii	Sesquicentennial of rediscovery by Captain Cook	1928	9,958[13]	—	9,958
Hudson, N.Y.	Sesquicentennial of founding	1935	10,008[2]	—	10,008
Huguenot-Walloon	Tercentenary of founding of New Netherlands	1924	142,080	—	142,080
Illinois	Centennial of statehood[14]	1918	100,058[2]	—	100,058
Iowa	Centennial of statehood	1946	100,057[2]	—	100,057
Isabella see Columbian quarter-dollar[15]					
Lafayette dollar[15]	Raising of Lafayette Monument in Paris	1900	50,026[2]	14,000	36,026
Lewis & Clark gold dollar	Centennial of their exploration[3]	1904	25,028[2]	15,003	10,025
		1905	35,041[2]	25,000	10,041
Lexington-Concord see Battles of Lexington and Concord					

FIG. 56–5. Booker T. Washington commemorative half-dollar, 1946, obverse. As with a few other coins, national identification and value appear on what has become accepted as the obverse.

FIG. 56–6. One cent, 1909 V.D.B., obverse. The first U.S. cent with a true commemorative function, this year's coin also was the first of the new regular-issue cent series.

FIG. 56–7. Silver dollar, 1921, obverse. A commemorative and a new regular issue.

Norfolk, Va.	Bicentennial of establishment of the Borough and Tercentenary of original Land Grant[3]	1936	25,013	8,077	16,936
Old Spanish Trail	400th anniversary of Cabeza de Vaca's exploration	1935	10,008[2]	—	10,008
Oregon Trail	Memorialization of the Pioneers	1926	48,030	75	47,955
		1926-S	100,055	17,000	83,055
		1928[22]	50,028[2]	44,000	6,028
		1933-D[23]	5,250[2]	242	5,008
		1934-D	7,006[2]	—	7,006
		1936	10,006[2]	—	10,006
		1936-S	5,006[2]	—	5,006
		1937-D	12,008[2]	—	12,008
		1938	6,006[2]	—	6,006
		1938-D	6,005[2]	—	6,005
		1938-S	6,006[2]	—	6,006
		1939	3,004[2]	—	3,004
		1939-D	3,004[2]	—	3,004
		1939-S	3,005[2]	—	3,005
Panama-Pacific half-dollar[8,24,25]	Opening of the Panama Canal[3]	1915-S	60,030	32,866	27,164
Panama-Pacific gold dollar[8,24]	Opening of the Panama Canal[3]	1915-S	25,034[2]	10,034	15,000

Subject	Occasion	Date	Total Mintage	Melted	Released (Remainder)
Panama-Pacific quarter-eagle[8,24]	Opening of the Panama Canal[3]	1915–S	10,017	3,268	6,749
Panama-Pacific $50[8,24,25]	Opening of the Panama Canal[3]	1915–ST1[26]	1,510	1,027	483
		1915–ST2	1,509	864	645
Peace dollar[8,16]	Signing of treaties ending World War I	1921[27]	1,006,473[2]	—	1,006,473
Philadelphia *see* American Independence quarter-eagle					
Pilgrim[8]	Tercentenary of landing at Plymouth Rock	1920	200,112	48,000	152,112
		1921	100,053[2]	80,000	20,053
Providence *see* Rhode Island					
Rhode Island	Tercentenary of colony's founding[28]	1936	20,013[2]	—	20,013
		1936–D	15,010	—	15,010
		1936–S	15,011	—	15,011
Roanoke Island, N.C.	35th anniversary of both founding of Lost Colony and birth of Virginia Dare[3]	1937	50,030	21,000	29,030
Robinson-Arkansas *see* Arkansas 1936 T2					

San Diego-California[3]	California-Pacific Exposition	1935–S	250,132[2]	180,000	70,132
		1936–D	180,092[2]	150,000	30,092
San Francisco-Oakland Bay Bridge *see* Bay Bridge					
Sesquicentennial of American Independence *see* American Independence					
Spanish Trail *see* Old Spanish Trail					
Stone Mountain[8]	Creation of the Stone Mountain CSA Memorial	1925	2,314,709[2]	1,000,000	1,314,709
Texas	Centennial of Independence	1934	205,113[2]	143,763	61,350
		1935	10,008[2]	14	9,994
		1935–D	10,007[2]	—	10,007
		1935–S	10,008[2]	—	10,008
		1936	10,008[2]	1,097	8,911
		1936–D	10,007[2]	968	9,039
		1936–S	10,008[2]	944	9,064
		1937	8,005[2]	1,434	6,571
		1937–D	8,006[2]	1,391	6,605
		1937–S	8,007[2]	1,370	6,637
		1938	5,005[2]	1,225	3,780

Subject	Occasion	Date	Total Mintage	Melted	Released (Remainder)
Vancouver *see* Fort Vancouver					
Vermont	Sesquicentennial of both Independence and Battle of Bennington	1927	40,034[2]	11,892	28,142
		1938–D	5,005[2]	1,230	3,775
		1938–S	5,006[2]	1,190	3,816
Washington, Booker T. *see* Booker T. Washington					
Washington quarter[8,16]	Bicentennial of birth	1932	5,404,000[2]	—	5,404,000
		1932–D	436,800[2]	—	436,800
		1932–S	408,000[2]	—	408,000
Washington-Carver	Memorialization of both Booker T. Washington and George Washington Carver	1951	110,018[2]	—	110,018
		1951–D	10,004[2]	—	10,004
		1951–S	10,004[2]	—	10,004
		1952	2,006,292[2]	—	2,006,292
		1952–D	8,006[2]	—	8,006
		1952–S	8,006[2]	—	8,006
		1953	8,003[2]	—	8,003
		1953–D	8,003[2]	—	8,003
		1953–S	108,020[2]	—	108,020
		1954	12,006[2]	—	12,006
		1954–D	12,006[2]	—	12,006
		1954–S	122,024[2]	—	122,024

Wisconsin	Centennial of establishment as a Territory	1936	25,015[2]	—	25,015
York County, Maine	Tercentenary of colony's founding	1936	25,015[2]	—	25,015

Notes to Chart

[1] Centennial year was 1920. First U.S. coin to show living person, Governor T. E. Kilby. Type 1 has 2 × 2 in field (22nd state), Type 2 has plain field.

[2] Official mint figure, unchallenged.

[3] Also issued in connection with an exposition held at time of issue.

[4] Only U.S. coin with portrait of living President, Calvin Coolidge.

[5] The coins were struck in 1937.

[6] Despite the date, 25,015 coins were struck in 1936 and an equal number in 1937. I know of no way to identify the 1936 (37) coin.

[7] First quarter-dollar commemorative and only U.S. coin showing a foreign monarch. Although England's King George III is on some "Colonial coins," those are tokens and not coins issued by authority of the U.S.

[8] Also see the full story of this coin, in the text of this or another chapter.

[9] Type 1 coins are the same as the 1934 issue, with date at obverse bottom; Type 2's have, in addition, the date 1934 above PIONEER YEAR at right of the figures of Boone and Chief Black Fish.

[10] Listed with 1937 mintage in official records, in spite of date. The event was observed in Sweden as well as in this country; the Swedish commemorative is a silver 2-kronor piece dated 1938, the actual anniversary year.

[11] Coins were struck at San Francisco but without the mint mark.

[12] Type 1 coins have a star in the field; Type 2's have plain field.

[13] In addition to these coins, 50 Proofs were struck.

[14] First commemorative for a statehood centennial.

[15] Our first commemorative dollar.

16 Since these coins became, or already were, regular issues, only the dates listed here can be considerd to have a commemorative function.

17 Type 1 coins have VDB at reverse bottom; Type 2's don't. I subtracted Proofs from these totals; for Proof collectors, totals were: 1909 T1, 420; 1909 T2, 2,198; 1959, 1,149,291.

18 First gold commemorative. The Louisiana Purchase Exposition was held at St. Louis in 1904. Type 1 coins have head of Jefferson, President at the time of the Purchase; Type 2's have McKinley, who authorized the exposition. 75,080 were struck in 1902, and 175,178 in 1903. I know of no way to identify these by actual year of minting.

19 This was meant for the May 10, 1920, celebration at Portland. When the coins arrived too late, they were sold afterward by the State Treasurer.

20 This usually is called our only full-face portrait coin. It isn't really a full-face portrait, but it's close.

21 The exposition was held at Sedalia in August 1921. Type 1 has the number 24, with a star between the numerals, in the field at left; Type 2 has plain field. Missouri was the 24th state. Type 2 coins were sold first.

22 The 1928 coins were held for 5 years and released in 1933.

23 First commemorative coin struck at Denver.

24 First commemorative coin struck at San Francisco.

25 First commemorative (other than 1909 Lincoln cent) with the motto IN GOD WE TRUST.

26 Type 1 coins are round; Type 2's are octagonal.

27 Released in 1922. Surrender of Germany was November 11, 1918, but the treaty was signed August 25, 1921, at Berlin.

28 The coin was issued to observe the founding of the city of Providence, too, but there's absolutely nothing on it memorializing this.

57

Private Gold—Filling the Need

Individuals and business firms issued coins that
circulated in both East and West until
official issues and prohibitive laws ended
this colorful phase of our numismatic history.

THE GOLDEN MIDGETS

When gold was found in California and the "forty-niners" flocked
westward, they found that you *could* pick a fortune out of the
streams. They also found that almost every storekeeper kept a
scale on his counter to weigh gold dust and nuggets. By about
1850 there probably was more gold in the form of nuggets and
dust in use than normal coinage. If the coin shortage was bad in
the East, then in this land of would-be millionaires it was des-
perate!

For some time it was the custom for the wealthiest members of
the upper class to sprinkle gold dust in alcoholic drinks; some
wanted to show off, others believed gold would relieve their
arthritis.

But there was one metal handy for use in coins. And there were
men on the scene who knew how to make dies and presses. So
from about 1852–82, in addition to higher denomination private
coinage, various local firms and individuals produced coins in
denominations of 25¢, 50c, and $1—in gold.

These tiny coins range from half the size of a modern cent to
nearly as big as a dime. The main shapes are round and octagonal.
Most obverses show a Liberty, Indian, or Washington head. The
reverse usually has an eagle or else the value in a wreath. As for
style, these small pieces ("coinlets"?) vary from gross examples of
poor workmanship to artistic, fine-lined creations.

FIG. 57–1. Liberty heads are on many privately issued low-denomination California gold pieces. This is the obverse of the octagonal 1853–N dollar. I don't know whose mint used that mark, but coin collectors who specialize in this type of item probably can recognize it.

FIG. 57–2. Half-dollar, 1864, privately issued in California. This tiny gold coin seems even littler when placed beside an ordinary No. 1 paper clip.

Minting of small gold pieces ended in 1882, but the tiny private issues already had become part of our coin lore. Today the quarter and half-dollar, Fine, cost about $60 to $90, the octagonal dollar $100 or so. The much rarer round dollar will set you back $500 or so in Fine, $700 in Very Fine, and up to $1,000 or even more for choice, Proof-like coins.

Many coin dealers have one or more of these items, and the small gold appears frequently in auction catalogs.

But beware of modern "California gold tokens" and fantasy pieces made in imitation of the coins. Some imitations have a fraction on the reverse. Genuine low-denomination California gold coins have "cents," "dollar," or some abbreviation of "dollar" on the reverse.

GOLD OF THE SAINTS

In 1847 the Saints arrived at their promised land. When I identify that land as the Valley of the Great Salt Lake, you'll know quickly that I'm speaking not of biblical saints but of the "Mormons," members of the Church of Jesus Christ of Latter-Day Saints.

Soon their community grew too large and complex for a barter-based economy, but coins were scarce. Some of the people, who had gone even farther west, returned to the home community late in 1848 with gold dust they had accumulated in California; for a while this gold, in bags and pouches, circulated as money. Finally, Brigham Young ordered a mint established.

The Salt Lake City mint was in a small adobe building, and Brigham Young himself is supposed to have kept careful watch over its operations. The "territorial gold" coins made here are unusual because they have religious mottoes and emblems stronger than "In God We Trust" and 15 years before it, because the Mormon alphabet and language appear on one of the coins, and because in 1849 this mint produced the first $20 gold coins issued on the North American continent.*

Coinage of eagles began in December, 1848, but ended the same month because of a lack of crucibles in which to melt the coinage alloy. One of the 46 pieces made that month had an estimated value of $20,000 in 1974. Minting operations were resumed the following September, with the mint producing quarter-eagles, half-eagles, and double-eagles. Curiously, the coins made in both 1848 and 1849 are dated 1849.

Most obverses show the Eye of Providence with a bishop's mitre (hat) above. The rim inscription is HOLINESS TO THE LORD. Reverses have clasped hands, symbolizing strength in unity and the church members' proven ability to survive through teamwork. Around the rim is G.S.L.C.P.G. (Great Salt Lake City Pure Gold) plus the value. The date is below the clasped hands; edges are plain. I must note that the coins are *not*, however, pure gold.

In 1850 a new half-eagle design appeared with a more stylized eye and mitre but more realistic clasped hands.

A newer and more interesting half-eagle was struck ten years later. One report states that James M. Barlow stopped at Salt Lake City en route to California, at Brigham Young's request, and engraved the new dies. Another story credits the coin to

---

* I purposely didn't say "in the U.S.," because this area was *not* part of the U.S., and didn't even become a Territory until 1850. Its correct name at the minting period was "Deseret."

Albert Kuner. The $5 piece of 1860 features a reclining lion on the obverse, with the date at bottom. The rim inscription still is "Holiness to the Lord," but on *this* coin it's in the Mormon alphabet and language, the almost-Greek appearing tongue of the fabled Golden Plates that Mormons believe an angel revealed to church founder Joseph Smith!

On the reverse is a lifelike eagle facing its right and holding an olive branch in its right talon and arrows in its left. We've seen many U.S. coin eagles with a U.S. shield on the eagle's chest, but this eagle wears a *beehive*. How come? The bee often serves as a symbol of industry; in addition, "Deseret," the original name of what's now Utah, means "honey bee" in the Mormon language.

Somewhat strangely, the reverse inscription is in *English:* DESERET ASSAY OFFICE, PURE GOLD, 5D.

All Mormon gold is rare. Prices range from $500 or so up to the tens of thousands of dollars. An 1849 $10 coin brought $32,000 in a 1973 auction.

AND THE OTHERS?

There are quite a few other private gold issues, but it's impossible to go into them in the space available. You'll find several in the list of mints. The Red Book has plenty of detailed information on some other issues.

FIG. 57–3. Eagle, 1849–Salt Lake City, obverse. Part of the Lilly Collection, now in the National Collection, Smithsonian Institution.

FIG. 57–4. Double-eagle, 1849–Salt Lake City. This was the first gold $20 coin issued in America.

58

Proof, Unc, and SMS

There are coins that rank above the
ones we find in circulation.

UNC SETS

As we've seen, the highest condition a regular-issue coin can be in
is Uncirculated (Unc). For many years you could buy sets of
Uncirculated coins directly from the Treasury Department. These
contained the "pick of the lot" of regular-issue coinage.

Because of the coin shortage these sets were temporarily discontinued after 1964, but the Treasury again supplied them starting in 1968, raising the price slightly that year to $2.50.

Selection and packaging of 1968 Unc sets involved so many
missing coins, sets with wrong coins, damage by packing and
sealing machinery, and so forth that Treasury officials promised
to replace defective sets returned by collectors.

The price was increased to $3.50 beginning in 1971; in 1973 it
became $6. Sets include all denominations, one cent to one dollar,
from Philadelphia; the same from Denver; and a cent or dime,
depending on the date, from San Francisco.

Orders usually are opened in the summer, with announcements
in all hobby publications and coin columns.

SMS

Late in 1964 the Treasury announced that Proof Sets would be
discontinued because of the coin shortage, and "those of our
presses that are suitable will be converted to run at higher speeds
and will be used for the production of coins for general circulation usage."

Later came word that the San Francisco Assay Office (the renamed mint) would strike "Special Mint Sets" for numismatists. All of these SMS were struck at San Francisco but none has the S mint mark, since the sets were made only in years when mint marks were omitted from U.S. coins.

All SMS coins dated 1965 were struck in 1966, in addition to those dated 1966. Those dated 1967 were struck in 1967.

The sets brought joy to some, anger to others. They were better than Unc, said the mint, but not up to Proof quality.

In *COINage* magazine, Lee Martin charged that the Treasury had defaulted on its promise and had selected coins from regular strikes for the sets. However, the ANA's Dictionary of Numismatic Terms endorses SMS as "produced under special conditions." Numismatist Ray Young praised the sets in *Coins Magazine* as generally well-struck, with excellent luster, and showing evidence of polished dies and careful striking.

The $4 SMS were scorned by some collectors, and I've seen sets advertised at $3.50 by dealers; but most of us welcomed SMS as an intermediate stage between no Proofs at all and the Treasury's November 1967 announcement of the return of the Proofs.

THE NUMISMATIC ELITE

How far back do Proof coins go? There weren't any, as we know them today, in the early years of minting; however, there were "Specimen" coins minted from polished regular-issue dies and polished blanks, and many numismatists consider these equivalent to, and deserving of the title of, Proof coins.

Individual Proof coins were available to collectors at a small charge over face value, beginning in 1858, from the Philadelphia mint. Branch mint Proofs are very few. Collectors began assembling Proof sets, and clearly considered these as single items rather than as groups of separate coins. Proof coin sales ended after 1915, possibly because of World War I and possibly because mint authorities thought regular-issue coins' high quality made Proofs unnecessary.

Sales were resumed in 1936, and continued through 1942, with coins still sold individually. World War II stopped this practice again, and this break lasted through 1949.

On May 10, 1950, President Harry Truman signed the bill authorizing Proof sets; the first ones were placed on sale July 17, at $2.10 per set. Single Proof coins no longer were available. This series of Proofs lasted through 1964. Their popularity grew slowly over the years; the 1953 set was the first whose mintage exceeded 100,000.

Proof coins have been struck at San Francisco since 1968. The 1968 coins form the first such *set*, though not the first such coins, from a branch mint. The 1968–S Proofs are the first Proof Set with a mint mark and the first series of U.S. coins with mint marks on the obverse.

The price was raised to $5, a change many of us had said we'd accept if the government would resume Proof minting.

Demand was so great for 1969–S Proofs that orders were cut off after six days. Speculators' high-volume and multiple orders probably caused the snafu. When orders were opened for 1970–S Proof Sets, the volume per order was cut from 20 to 5. This worked, and a two-month order period let every collector send in a request. Even then, so many sets were ordered that the Treasury had to reduce large-quantity orders to allow each customer at least one set.

Proof sets of 1973 included, for the first time in over half a century, a dollar coin. The sets' price was raised to $7. Sets' Proof dollars are cupronickel clad coins; 40 percent silver Proof Ike dollars are sold separately.

Orders traditionally are opened November 1 of each year for the following year's Proof Sets. As with Unc sets, opening of Proof orders is widely publicized in coin columns and numismatic publications.

Proof coins occasionally have been spent and later "rescued" from circulation by alert collectors. The spender may be a thief who stole the coins, a former collector badly in need of cash, or a family member who needed change and didn't know the coins were special (but probably learned fast!). Among such circulated Proofs are an 1864 silver dollar, an 1876 $3 gold piece, and others.

To obtain information or get added to the mailing list for order forms and announcements, write to: Bureau of the Mint, 55 Mint Street, San Francisco, California 94175.

59

Down in Dixie

> ". . . A great civil war, testing whether that nation . . . can long endure."—Lincoln's Address at Gettysburg, Pa., November 19, 1863.

In January 1861, state officials began seizing U.S. mints—they took those at Charlotte, Dahlonega, and New Orleans and turned all three over to the Confederate States of America. The Confederacy issued coins—but only two were struck in any quantity, others are in dispute and it's not settled which mints were used.

Dies for 1861 had been delivered to New Orleans, and federal officials already had made 5,000 double-eagles and 330,000 half-dollars when the mint was captured. Louisiana and C.S.A. officials reopened the mint and by that May struck an additional 12,741 $20 gold coins and 2,202,633 half-dollars. Though these are identical with earlier coins, and struck with U.S. equipment from regular U.S. dies, they *are* Confederate coins. The half-dollar costs about $9 in Fine condition, the double-eagle, about $400.

It's possible that C.S.A. authorities meant to issue—or did issue —other coins. I've seen claims that the 15 known specimens of the 1861–D gold dollar (not listed in U.S. mint records) and 1,597 1861–D half-eagles were struck by the C.S.A. At least one reference argues that an 1861–C gold dollar (not in either mint records or the Red Book) and the 6,879 1861–C half-eagles were made after the Confederacy was running the Charlotte mint.

FIG. 59–1. C.S.A., Pattern cent, 1861, obverse. The 1961 "second restrike" from defaced dies.

Unfortunately, there's no way to tell what *month* a particular coin was made, so there's no certain way to identify a coin as struck by the U.S.A. or the C.S.A., except by certain die breaks on some 1861–O half-dollars, and other similarly individual characteristics on other C.S.A. coins.

About 5,000 varieties of private tokens circulated in the Confederacy, playing the same role there as nineteenth-century tokens we examined earlier. The so-called "Confederate dime" with a portrait of C.S.A. President Jefferson Davis is one of these.

The two coins most noncollectors have heard of are actually both patterns. The C.S.A. ordered minor coins from the Philadelphia jewelry firm Bailey & Co. I don't know why this northern firm agreed, but it did, and chose engraver Robert Lovett to work on dies. Lovett had drawn a beautiful Liberty head for his own widely used 1860 storecard, and used this on the Confederate cent. Around the rim he added CONFEDERATE STATES OF AMERICA. The portrait faces left, wearing a liberty cap that rises to a tall peak. The date is at bottom. The reverse has 1 CENT in a wreath, with bales of goods at the bottom of the wreath.

Lovett made 12 cupronickel patterns. Then he realized that federal authorities might be less than happy if they learned he had worked on rebel coins. He buried the cents and dies in his basement. I don't know what he told Bailey & Co.

After the war Lovett dug up the cents. By around 1873 he was carrying one or two as pocket pieces. Inevitably he spent one by accident. The strange coin reached the hands of numismatist Capt. John W. Haseltine, who recognized the Liberty head from Lovett's storecard. He visited Lovett several times, trying to get the full story—and the coins. At last Lovett confessed all and sold Haseltine the coins and dies.

Later, Haseltine made 55 restrikes in copper, 12 in silver, and 3 or 7 in gold (references disagree); he avoided the original metal, cupronickel.

From Haseltine the C.S.A. dies eventually reached the Robert Bashlow Co. which, late in 1961, produced 20,000 "second restrikes" in bronze and over 10,000 more in platinum, silver, and goldine; these were struck by the August C. Frank Co. of Philadelphia. According to numismatist Don Taxay, these were struck *not* with Lovett's original dies but from transfer dies. The Bashlow firm presented both original and transfer dies to the Smithsonian in 1962.

Bashlow's "restrikes," at about $5 to $7 in bronze, are as close to the real thing as most of us can afford to go. The lowest catalog value for a Haseltine copper restrike is $1,500. The genuine cupronickel pattern lists at $3,000.

For the severely limited budget, a coin company made facsimile cents early in 1963 and sold them for $1. These have minor differences in the wreath detail, a slightly different lettering style, and on the reverse the fraction "$\frac{1}{100}$."

The C.S.A. struck four pattern half-dollars on an old screw press at New Orleans in April 1861. The reverse, because of the need for quick work, the lack of skilled engravers, and the presence of the usable die, is the *obverse* of the U.S. half-dollar, the Liberty Seated design. The new C.S.A. obverse shows a shield with seven vertical bars and seven stars, with a liberty cap atop the shield. Around the shield is a wreath of one sprig of sugar cane and one of cotton. CONFEDERATE STATES OF AMERICA is around the upper rim and HALF DOL. is at bottom.

Around 1879 J. W. Scott & Co. obtained the C.S.A. obverse die and one of the original patterns for $310 from Dr. B. F. Taylor, who had been chief coiner at New Orleans. This firm also got 500 half-dollars dated 1861 *from the New Orleans mint*—which might have been true C.S.A. strikes!

The coins' reverse was planed down to remove the U.S. design; then the C.S.A. die was used to make 500 "restrikes." I quote the word because it's a poor term—these were made from existing coins. They ought to be called Scott halves or facsimile C.S.A. halves. These pieces were sold for $2; the original pattern, for $1,000.

When Scott used the C.S.A. die it broke and was set in a heavy steel collar. Five hundred white metal tokens were struck immediately with this die and another reverse lettered 4 ORIGINALS STRUCK BY ORDER OF C.S.A. IN NEW ORLEANS 1861 then seven stars and REV. SAME AS U. S. (FROM ORIGINAL DIE, SCOTT). These were struck first because the softer white metal was less likely to damage the die further. The tokens were sold for 50¢.

Scott halves cost about $1,000 Uncirculated; the Scott tokens catalog at about $80 VF and $150 to $200 Uncirculated.

And the originals? One was Dr. Taylor's, sold to Scott and now owned by the American Numismatic Society. A second was given to Professor Biddle of the University of Louisiana. A third went to Dr. E. Ames of New Orleans. The fourth was presented to C.S.A. President Jefferson Davis.

Later, when Davis was a prisoner at Fortress Monroe, a Union soldier reportedly stole the pattern C.S.A. half from his trunk. This soldier is supposed to have sold the coin to a collector in Pennsylvania, who passed it on to a sister in Ohio. But efforts to trace the missing pattern failed. John J. Ford, Jr., and Eric P. Newman are collectors who own original C.S.A. patterns, but which specimens these are I don't know. Don Taxay says the Ford specimen could be the Davis piece—but who can say for certain?

60

The Newest Stars

"North to Alaska!"—title of motion
picture and popular song
"The Life of the Land is Perpetuated
in Righteousness."—motto of the
State of Hawaii

NORTH TO NUMISMATICS

Alaska was discovered by a Dane, settled by Russians, claimed by Spanish explorers, entered by French traders, inspected by British sailors, and purchased by the United States. When Secretary of State William H. Seward bought it from Russia for $7,200,000 in June 1867, the new District was labeled "Seward's Folly" and "Seward's Icebox." It became a Territory in 1912 and our 49th state in 1959.

During the 1930's, after a drought ruined many farmers, the government picked 67 families each from Michigan, Minnesota, and Wisconsin. In the spring of 1935 it sent the settlers to Matanuska Valley, where a 120-man force from relief rolls had been clearing land and putting up temporary houses.

The government lent each family $3,000, put them on ships for Alaska and said, in effect, "Here's land. Settle on it." The first settlers arrived at Palmer, near Anchorage, in May 1935 and each received 40 acres.

Resettling was up to the Alaska Rural Rehabilitation Corporation. This government agency operated supplies stores in the valley, and to make it easier to give settlers credit, issued tokens in 1935, in denominations of 1¢, 5¢, 10¢, 25¢, 50¢, and $1 in aluminum and $5 and $10 in brass.

Both sides are the same. In the center is the numeral of value;

around the bottom is ARRC and around the top is GOOD FOR plus the spelled out denomination and IN TRADE. Each token is the size of the regular-issue U.S. coin of its denomination, but the cent is octagonal.

The highest mintage (cents, nickels, and dimes) was only 5,000; quarter mintage was 3,000; there were 2,500 each half-dollars and dollars; and 1,000 each $5 and $10 pieces. About 250 Uncirculated sets were made up for collectors, plus another 100 sets of cent, nickel, and dime only. The tokens cost about $15 and up, depending on denomination and condition.

These were meant for spending only at ARRC stores, but the tokens, which became known as "bingles," were handy for small change. Local merchants and saloon keepers soon accepted them.

Actually the bingles were used for only a few months in late 1935 and early 1936; after this the settlers switched to regular coins. On February 10, 1937, the tokens were demonetized.

Some Alaskan merchants have issued private tokens at various times; these tokens, too, have become known by the "bingle" nickname. Some issuers had more than one token—Reindeer Commercial Co., of Gambell, had denominations up to $10.

ALOHA, AUPUNI HAWAII

Probably very few of those who enjoy the CBS television adventure series "Hawaii Five-O" know that Hawaii once had its own coinage.

Hawaii was an independent kingdom in 1847, when its first coin was issued. This copper piece, the size of our large cent, has a facing portrait of King Kamehameha III on the obverse, with KA MOI around the top and the date below the bust. The reverse has HAPA HANERI in a wreath, and the coin is sometimes called "the Hapa Haneri Cent." AUPUNI HAWAII ("Kingdom of Hawaii") is around the rim. Mintage was 100,000.

Modern reproductions, marked "Souvenir Alii of Hawaii" in tiny letters at reverse bottom, are sold today to tourists.

Tradesmen's tokens were issued at various times, and foreign coins also circulated.

In 1883 King Kalakaua I had $1 million worth of coins struck at the San Francisco mint. These coins match U.S. issues in weight and fineness. Proofs were struck at Philadelphia before the dies were sent to San Francisco. Mintages were 250,000 for the dime; 500,000 each for the silver dollar and the quarter; and 700,000 for the half-dollar. Many of these coins were later melted.

All four obverses show a right-facing portrait, with the date at bottom and KALAKAUA I, KING OF HAWAII around the top and side rims. As on U.S. coins of that time, higher denominations have a common reverse. It shows the royal Hawaiian coat-of-arms, with a numeral or fraction of value directly below, plus the value spelled out at the bottom rim. The rest of the rim has UA MAU KE EA O KA AINA I KA PONO, which later became the state motto. The dime's reverse, instead of a fraction, has a crowned ONE DIME in a wreath. All the coins have reeded edges.

Hawaii granted U. S. coins legal tender status in 1884 and repealed the 1880 law providing for its own national coinage.

The islands became a Territory in 1900. On August 21, 1959, Hawaii became our 50th state.

Part Six

Mints, Designs, and Other Coin Lore

61

Mints and Mint Marks

Let's take a numismatic tour.

The use of mint marks dates back several centuries. Sometimes a one-mint nation uses a mint mark, but often it doesn't. Our Philadelphia mint, for many years our only one, didn't use a mint mark at first. In fact, its P is on more foreign coins than U.S. ones! But before going into Philadelphia's operations, let's take a numismatic tour of the country.

SWEET CHARLOTTE

The branch mint at Charlotte, N.C., was established by the Act of March 3, 1835. It was built in 1836–37 and John H. Wheeler was appointed the first superintendent.

Today Charlotte is the county seat of Mecklenburg County and a medical, financial, textile, and economic center for both Carolinas. Back when it was a gold center, the mint was set up to handle gold near the Carolina mines instead of sending metal all the way to Philadelphia. A second purpose was to discourage the private issues of gold coinage.

Operations began in 1838 with 17,179 half-eagles and 7,880 quarter-eagles bearing the C mint mark. Only gold was struck here—dollars, quarter-eagles, and half-eagles.

Top mintage coin is the 1847 half-eagle, with 84,151 made. Rarest is the 1855–C quarter-eagle, with 3,677. Although four gold dollars are listed in official records for 1854, I can't imagine their being anything other than trial pieces.

The mint burned down on July 27, 1844. It was rebuilt during the next two years and reopened in October 1846. During the Civil War, the Confederacy captured the mint late in April 1861. The C.S.A. used this mint as a hospital and/or an administration building. In 1868 Congress passed a law reducing the mint's status to that of an Assay Office.

All Bureau of the Mint operations ended after June 1913. The building was dismantled in 1935, moved, and soon rebuilt on a new site as the Mint Museum of Art.

THE FIRST D

Most of us, seeing a coin mint-marked D, think of Denver, which was actually the second mint to use this letter. But being first with D is only one reason why the Dahlonega, Ga., branch mint is unusual. Another reason is that it's one of the two mints which struck only gold. And finally, it's at the site of the nation's first major gold rush.

Dahlonega is about 60 miles northeast of Atlanta. Back in 1828, gold mines opened up, and when their continuing flow proved them solid producers, the government ordered a branch mint built. The mint opened in 1838 and took as its mint mark the city's initial, D. Joseph J. Singleton was the superintendent.

From 1849, the gold dollar's first year of issue, through 1861, Dahlonega made these little coins. Quarter-eagles were struck 1839–57 and again in 1859. Dahlonega made $3 gold coins only in 1854. Its first half-eagles were struck April 17, 1838; they were the first coins struck here.

Rarest of these is the 1856–D quarter-eagle, with 874 struck. Top-mintage coin, with 98,452, is the 1843–D half-eagle.

Enthusiasm for this branch mint took a heavy blow when gold was found in California. The new gold rush stole the glamor from Georgia's mines.

Perhaps even with this the mint might have kept operating, but the Civil War closed it to the U.S., and the D mint mark for the Dahlonega mint disappeared.

The mint whose letter was O was established by the Act of March 3, 1835. The city of New Orleans used to be a lot smaller, and at one of its corners stood Fort St. Charles, whose site, at 420 Esplanade Avenue, was deeded to the government May 11, 1835. Construction of the mint began that September. Martin Gordon was appointed to the post of Mint Superintendent in December 1836; construction was finished in 1838, and operations began that year.

During the Civil War this mint served as a C.S.A. Army headquarters. It was reopened as a U.S. Mint February 20, 1879, and continued operating through 1909.

Minting was by hand until a steam press was brought to the mint in 1845.

New Orleans struck silver and gold, ranging from trimes to double-eagles. Other denominations struck here include half-dimes, dimes, quarter- and half-dollars, silver dollars, gold dollars, quarter-eagles, $3 pieces, half-eagles, and eagles.

Top mintage for this facility is the 13,320,000 of the 1901–O silver dollar. Since the 1838–O half-dollar (20 struck) and 1841–O half-eagle (50 struck, two known today) probably were trial issues, I think it's safe to give low-mintage honors to the 1856 double-eagle, with 2,250 minted.

After minting operations ended, the building served variously as a junkyard, veterans bureau, and Public Health Service station. In 1932 it was converted to a federal prison (there still are more than 30 cells). Later it was a Coast Guard receiving station. In 1946 the Coast Guard made it a supply depot, but later nearly abandoned it, providing bare-minimum maintenance.

Pleas to save the mint and restore its former glory have appeared in the New Orleans *Times-Picayune* and in *Coin World*. In 1966 the government turned this mint over to Louisiana on condition that the state maintain it and guarantee preservation as a historic landmark. The Louisiana State Museum hopes to make it a museum that "will highlight the periods in which it played an important role in the history of the City of New Orleans, the State of Louisiana and the United States of America."

THE "BIG D" OF NUMISMATICS

The Denver branch mint was established by the Act of April 21, 1862, which resulted in the purchase of Clark, Gruber & Co.'s two-story brick building housing a private mint, for $25,000. But operations beginning in September 1863 included only such non-coinage work as assaying. A new site was purchased in 1896, and construction was begun in 1897. The mint moved out of the old Clark, Gruber & Co. plant and into the new building in 1904.

Denver struck its first coins in 1906, and since then has minted coins every year. It produced the first D cents in 1911 and three years later gave collectors the famed 1914–D. Minting of nickel 5¢ coins began in 1912, but the rarest date didn't appear until 1950. No minor coins were made here in 1921 or 1923.

In silver Denver minted dimes, quarters, half-dollars, and dollars. Its best-known rarities are the 1916–D WHL dime and 1932–D Washington quarter.

Denver also made $2.50, $5, $10, and $20 gold coins. The highest mintage in gold is the 3,423,560 of the 1909 half-eagle; the lowest figure is that of the 1911–D eagle, with only 30,100 struck.

Today the mint is a major showplace for collector and noncollector alike. There are daily free tours through the building, located at W. Colfax Avenue and Cherokee Street.

Current operations include minting of cents, nickels, dimes, quarters, half-dollars, and dollars.

CARSON CITY

The Carson City branch mint, our only one with a two-letter mint mark, was established by the Act of March 3, 1863. Ground was broken July 18, 1866, and machinery began arriving November 22, 1868. The first superintendent, appointed by President Ulysses S. Grant, was Abraham Curry, founder of Carson City.

Operating dates were 1870–93 only. The lowest denomination struck here was the dime, while the highest was the $20.

Carson City also produced two coins Denver missed—20¢ pieces and Trade Dollars. Its only complete break in coinage was 1886–88, after operations were ordered suspended in March 1885. Probably the outstanding rarity is the 1876–CC 20¢ piece, with a 10,000 mintage and only about a dozen pieces known now.

Minting of Trade Dollars, halves, quarters, and dimes was halted after 1878. Silver dollars were made 1870–73; then came a break while Trade Dollars were struck 1874–78. Silver dollar coining was resumed in 1878.

The rarest gold piece is the 1879 eagle, with only 1,762 minted. Top figure is the 208,000 of the 1891 half-eagle.

The mint ceased coinage operations after June 1, 1893. It was a U.S. Assay Office until June 30, 1933, when it was closed due to scandals involving below-standard alloys and counterfeit silver dollars.

In 1938 the government declared this mint surplus and tried to sell it. Cooperative officials finally assigned a value of $5,000 and citizens led by Judge Clark Guild bought the old structure. Judge Guild evidently was the individual most responsible for leading the battle for this mint's survival.

Since 1941 the old mint has housed the Nevada State Museum. Part of the museum's exhibit is the first of the three coin presses used here. This press is more than a museum piece—during the 1964–66 coin shortage, it was taken to Denver and put back into service.

SAN FRANCISCO'S MINT

In 1850, fluctuating gold dust values, erratic prices, and multiple sorts of coins in use combined to force establishment of the San Francisco Assay Office. Then the Act of July 3, 1852, ordered a mint opened here, and the Assay Office closed on December 14 of the following year.

The Director of the Mint said in his January 27, 1854, report that the mint probably would be "ready to receive deposits and commence operations about the 1st of March next." However, there were delays, and it was April 3, 1854, before the mint began accepting deposits. That first year it produced over $4 million in gold dollars, quarter-eagles, half-eagles, eagles, and double-eagles. Starting in 1855 the S mint mark appeared on quarters, half-dollars, and $3 gold coins.

Other coins made here include cents, nickels, half-dimes, dimes, 20¢ pieces, silver dollars, and Trade Dollars.

The first mint was a three-story, 60-square-foot brick building on Commercial Street. Director of the Mint James Ross Snowden, after inspecting it, reported, "It is almost impossible to conceive how so much work can be well done.... The entrance to the business office is up a steep pair of stairs and through a dark hall rendered unwholesome by the fumes of acids, and uncomfortable by the noise of machinery and the heat of the engine."

About 1864, agitation began for a new mint. It was built 1870–73, and the government moved in during the summer of 1874. At the time, this was "one of the best appointed Mints in the world," says the Treasury. This was the building which survived the April 18, 1906, earthquake. Afterward, since the quake and resultant fires put every bank in the city out of commission, this was the sole operating financial institution.

The mint moved again, in the summer of 1937, into what the Treasury calls "an imposing marble edifice" which "housed the most modern facilities of the day, and new equipment to replace worn and obsolete machinery." The government stayed in the older building until 1968.

For the sake of economy, minting operations were discontinued at the new mint in March 1955. Only cents and dimes were struck that year. Equipment was taken out, and most of the building, after remodeling, was occupied by other agencies. The mint kept a small area to receive gold and silver deposits and carry on assay operations: once more there was a San Francisco Assay Office, now at Market Street and Duboce Avenue.

But in the summer of 1964, equipment was moved back in, and San Francisco again became involved in coining money. Today, more and more coins for circulation are being struck here. Perhaps there someday will be a San Francisco Mint in full operation once more.

As for the *old* mint, its survival was in doubt after the government left. Collectors were jubilant when the building was restored to the Bureau of the Mint in April 1972.

THE UNITED STATES MINT

On March 3, 1791, Congress passed a resolution "That a mint ſhall be eſtabliſhed under ſuch regulations as ſhall be directed by law" and "That the Preſident of the United States be . . . authorized to cauſe to be engaged, ſuch principal artiſts as ſhall be neceſſary to carry the preceeding [sic] reſolution into effect, and to ſtipulate the terms and conditions of their ſervice, and alſo to cauſe to be procured ſuch apparatus as ſhall be requiſite for the ſame purpoſe."

On July 18, 1792, the government bought a lot at what's now 7th and Filbert Streets from a surgeon barber and his wife, Mr. and Mrs. Frederick Wailer. The next day workers began tearing down the old distillery on the site and preparing to build the new mint. Construction was completed on September 7. There were two brick buildings with a frame mill-house between them.

There also was a wooden stable. A coining press was bought for $47.44 and a pair of oxen for $60; the oxen later were replaced by horses, which apparently were better workers.

On the night of January 11, 1816, somebody apparently left a barrel of hot ashes next to the mill-house. During the night the wind rose. Around midnight the barrel began to smolder. By two in the morning, sparks were flying into the wooden building. The fire was put out—but not before much damage was done. Determined workers rebuilt the mill-house, this time of brick. They added new rolling machinery, and when the Mint Director's annual report went in, January 1, 1817, most of the work was done. This is why so few coins were struck in 1816; probably most coins with this date were made in the early part of that fiscal year, between July 1 and December 31, 1815.

A steam engine was added to the new equipment on June 24, 1816. It drove rolling and drawing machines and a planchet cutter.

The first mint later was sold to private owners, and was demolished after a fire.

Mint No. 2, at what's now Chestnut and Juniper Streets, was on land bought April 30, 1829, from one Ann Poyntell and a Mr. and Mrs. R. A. Caldeleugh. Construction started in July and the mint was occupied in January 1833.

This was the mint where in 1836 the steam press invented by Uhlhorn and modified by Thonnelier was installed by the Philadelphia firm of Merrick, Agneu & Tyler. The new machinery could strike the amazing total of *one hundred coins every minute*!

This press was remodeled in 1858 by David Gilbert, but it was sold as surplus equipment when mint equipment was updated in 1875. After going on display the following year at the Centennial Exposition, and later being exhibited at other such events, it ended up in 1927 at the Franklin Institute. The museum renovated the press, converted it to electric power and put it on display, where it remains today, still striking 15¢ medals whose numismatic significance is priceless.

Also at this mint lived Peter. He came from the skies and made the U.S. mint his home, a great white-headed eagle whom mint workers named Peter. He would fly around Philadelphia each day and always return to the mint by closing time.

"The Mint Bird" was insatiably curious about things in the place that *worked*. One day he perched on a flywheel to watch a test strike of some new dies. A workman started the press, but Peter failed to notice, and the flywheel jerked and flung him to the floor. Mint personnel gave him their best care, but he died.

They hired a taxidermist, who repaired his broken wing and stuffed him in a standing position with the great wings spread wide. He remained on guard at his adopted home, and is said to have been the model for several coins.

The third mint was authorized in 1891 and completed in June 1901. It stands at 17th and Spring Garden Streets, and the construction cost was just over $2,000,000. The National Collection of coins was housed here until it moved to the Smithsonian in 1923. This mint operated through two World Wars and a growing coin shortage. Gradually its facilities were more and more overtaxed. Its final year of operation was 1970, and the mint was declared surplus property that November. In January 1971 it was donated to Philadelphia Community College.

On September 17, 1965, ground was broken for a fourth mint building. The cornerstone was set September 18, 1968, and full operations began in 1970. The fourth mint is a three-and-a-half-story structure bounded by 4th, 5th, Arch, and Race Streets. It cost $39,000,000.

Here ingots are sent through a rolling mill, emerging as foot-wide strips in proper coin blank thickness. Blanks are punched out, annealed and cleaned in a weak sulphuric acid solution. An upsetting machine gives them raised rims. Then they go to the presses.

Blanks are scooped into a hopper; they slide down a chute and are positioned by a tongue of metal over the reverse die. The obverse comes down and the panchet becomes a coin.

Finished coins are ejected into a collection hopper. They're inspected, then released into a collecting bin. At the counting room they get another inspection; then they're run through a counting machine, bagged, and weighed.

From there they go to Federal Reserve banks, which supply local banks in their areas. And from local banks they go into circulation—to smooth the workings of commerce, play a role in everyone's daily life, and join our coin collections.

THE PHANTOM MINTS

In 1883 John Dye wrote, "On the fourth day of July, 1864, a bill was passed and approved for the establishment of a Mint at Dalles City, in Oregon, for the coining of gold and silver money." What happened? Certainly there's no mint at The Dalles today!

This jumping-off point for men headed to the gold fields suffered in the 1860's from some of the same problems that had harried San Franciscans in the 1850's. Congress actually did establish a mint—but local problems, intra-city politics, and pressure from San Francisco kept stalling matters. By June 1870 only the ground floor was built, and so little was left of the former flood of gold that Congress dropped the whole idea.

The unfinished Dallas Mint was turned over to Oregon, which

sold it in 1889 to private interests. It has since then been a boiler house for a milling firm, a warehouse, and a moving and storage headquarters.

Since the physical mint itself never was completed, the true total of U.S. mints remains seven instead of eight.

Another city where a mint almost was established is New York. There's no mint branch here, but there *is* an Assay Office. Bills to establish a branch mint at New York were introduced as early as 1849. One actually passed the House (on March 3, 1849). However, the bill failed to pass the Senate, purely on a technicality. Another bill must have been in process in 1860, for in that year the Director of the Mint sent a communication to the Treasury Secretary about the "proposed branch mint at New York."

In 1875 there was a flood of publications showing why a mint should be built in each particular candidate city. The Chicago Board of Trade published a committee report showing why this was the best site; the Cincinnati Chamber of Commerce held proceedings on the matter; the St. Louis Merchants Exchange published its own report on "the proposed mint." And the Kansas City, Mo., Board of Trade provided some "reasons why Kansas City, Mo., should be selected as the site for the U.S. Branch Mint." Around 1899, the Tacoma, Wash., Board of Trade presented its case for a Tacoma branch. And other cities before and after that time have done the same.

The new fourth Philadelphia mint has probably settled matters for the next several years. By the time we do need another mint, maybe it will be possible to install new equipment at San Francisco.

62

Danger—Counterfeits!

"Counterfeiting is an offense never committed by accident, nor by ignorance, nor in the heat of passion, nor in extremity of poverty. It is a . . . sneaking offense."—Robert H. Jackson, once Assistant General Counsel, Treasury Department, later Associate Justice of the U.S. Supreme Court.

DANGER—COUNTERFEITS!

Ever since Colonial times, counterfeiters have preyed on citizens, undermined our currency, and done their best to damage this nation. I rate few criminals lower.

To counter their threat, the U.S. Secret Service was established in 1865. However, counterfeiting continued. In 1878, F. W. Helmick stated that "the large amount of counterfeit Twenty-five and Fifty cent pieces that have been in circulation for the past twenty years have been a constant annoyance to the business public. . . ."

Counterfeiting still is going on. *Coin World* reported that late in November 1969 Secret Service agents captured five men and a cache of over $4 million in fake $20 bills in Sacramento, Calif.

Since an alert and informed public is the best anticounterfeiting weapon, the Secret Service has prepared a booklet of helpful information. *Know Your Money* is available for 40¢ from the Superintendent of Documents, Government Printing Office, Washington, D.C. 20402; ask for *Know Your Money* and you'll probably get it, but it would help to mention the code number (1972–0–722–716) and/or stock number (4806–0002).

You can test a suspect silver coin by scratching or cutting the surface and pouring on it a few drops of test solution that you can buy at any drugstore for a few cents. The solution is made of: ten grams silver nitrate, one cubic centimeter nitric acid, 30 cubic centimeters water. It will not harm genuine silver coins. If a coin is counterfeit, this solution should blacken it. But there are quicker ways to check suspect coins.

Since you can't use these tests in front of someone who gave you a possible counterfeit, excuse yourself and go into another room. Then

—*Compare the coin* with another you know is genuine. Are designs, lettering, and numbers the same?

—*Feel the coin.* Many counterfeits have an oily or greasy feeling.

—*Check the reeding.* On genuine coins it's straight and perfectly regular. Counterfeits' reeding often is uneven and, appropriately, crooked.

If the passer sees you testing a coin and it *is* counterfeit, he won't wait around for test results! But here's one test you can use in his presence: Drop the coin.

If it's genuine, it should ring clearly. A false coin usually sounds dull. This test works with clad coins, as well as silver—their "clunk" is just as distinctive as silver's ring, so it can be used to check suspect items.

But whatever the sound, *don't react!* To carry off this test you *must* behave as if you simply had dropped a coin. If you do this correctly, you'll increase the passer's confidence. If you can't even hold onto a coin, he'll reason, you're not likely to be able to tell it's a fake.

What if you *do* seem to have a counterfeit?

Hang on to it! If the passer wants it back, do your best to switch coins without his being aware of it, and give him a different coin.

Delay him if you can—you'll be right back, you have to check something, phone a sick relative, put the cat out—anything.

Call the police. Tell them you think you've been given a counterfeit coin, the person who gave it to you is still there, and would they please send an officer over quickly! Keep calm and keep your voice low.

Make mental notes on the passer. If he leaves before police

arrive, your memory will be important. Is he tall or short, thin or fat? Does he repeat any gesture or phrase? What is his voice like? What is he wearing? What shape is his face? If he gets into a car, write down as much of the license number and description of the vehicle as you can.

But be sure you don't even let the passer suspect that you're watching him. Don't think about being clever—just remember that there are certain things you have to get done. The more confident the passer is that he (or she) fooled you, the more chance there is of a return visit.

If the passer does leave before you can phone the authorities, dial "O" and ask the operator for the number of the nearest U.S. Secret Service Field Office. If the passer is already off the premises, you might as well go directly to the Secret Service instead of to local police.

When police and/or Secret Service agents arrive, you'll have to hand over the counterfeit. Because you lose the value of counterfeits you turn in, some people don't call the authorities at all—instead, the victim himself gives the bad coin or bill to someone else. This makes it harder to catch the counterfeiter.

There is *no* penalty for having a counterfeit coin or bill in your possession when law enforcement agents arrive, since they're on the scene because you called them in the first place. But it *is* illegal to become a passer yourself and victimize someone instead of notifying the Secret Service. It *is* illegal to own a coin or bill that you *have reason to believe is counterfeit*.

Counterfeits can give the Secret Service valuable clues. Like artists, many counterfeiters have individual styles. If agents know a certain man is "working" a city or neighborhood, this can help them capture him.

So every counterfeit you turn in is an investment in law enforcement, better money, and a safer country. And that's no loss —it's a gain.

BEWARE THE COIN FAKERS

Coins have attracted some unsavory characters. Counterfeiters victimize everyone, but one low breed of subhuman crook specializes in preying on coin collectors. This is the coin faker, who alters common coins to make them seem to be rare ones.

Someone might offer what at first looks like a 1914–D cent, at a suspiciously low price. But the coin actually is a 1944–D whose first 4 has been ground down to resemble a 1. Look for extra space between the 9 and the 1, space left when the 4 was ground away. Also check Lincoln's shoulder—the designer's VDB is *not* on genuine 1914–D cents.

Some fakers make molds from genuine coins, then cast their own copies. This is the source of most "genuine" 1943 bronze cents. Cast coins usually have tiny pits from bubbles in the molten metal; they also often lack sharp detail.

Years when one mint issued a few of a particular coin, while other mints made many more, offer the best opportunities to fakers, especially when Philadelphia produced the rare coin. All that's needed is a branch mint coin plus equipment to grind off the mint mark. This works in reverse, too. A coin faker can solder a D onto a 1916 Philadelphia dime to create a fake rarity. You can detect this sort of fake, but it often takes a good magnifying glass. Look for discoloration around the mint mark, bits of extra metal or other telltale signs of alteration.

What can you do to fight fakers?

First, deal only with established and reputable dealers, collectors and auctioneers. *Second,* if someone offers you what appears to be a rare coin at a suspiciously low price, say you're not in the market right now. Then walk away. *Third,* if a faker (or a counterfeiter) has approached you, follow the steps I've listed in the counterfeiting section. Give Secret Service agents all the help you can in locating the crook and putting him out of business.

It is a federal offense to fraudulently alter any U.S. coin.

The man who cuts out coin designs and makes pins for ladies to wear is within the law—there's no fraud involved. But the man who changes a coin to make it seem to be another coin *is* breaking the law—and belongs in a cell!

63

The Name's the Thing

Names *on* our coins and names *of*
our coins.

INITIALS AND NAMES

Are your initials JS, AW, M or JBL? If so, you can find them on a
U.S. coin.

Many of our coins have shown designers' initials at one time or
another. The first regular-issue one to do so was the 1849 gold
dollar. Outstanding examples of initials and names which caused
strong reaction are on the Lincoln cent, Buffalo nickel, and Gobrecht dollar.

On some Continental Dollar patterns there's EG FECIT (Made
by EG) in a circle around the sundial. Nobody's proved for certain who EG was.

The first Indian Head cents (1859) had no initial. Then in 1864
an L (for Longacre) was added to the war bonnet; it was put on
late in the year, making 1864 L a rare and expensive variety.

Victor D. Brenner's initials were removed from Lincoln cents of
1909 because people thought they were too large. In 1918 they
were restored, but were made smaller than before. On the reverse
of 1959 and later, Frank Gasparro's small FG is next to the lower
right of the Memorial's steps.

There's an incuse F below the last digit of the date on Buffalo
nickels, for Fraser. But Felix Schlag's initials were off the Jefferson nickel until 1966.

Charles E. Barber's incuse B is at the base of Liberty's neck on
dimes, quarters, and halves that he designed. WHL dimes have
an AW monogram above and at right of the date. And John R.
Sinnock's JS is below the portrait on FDR dimes.

Liberty Standing quarters have an incuse M above and to the right of the date, for MacNeil. The Washington quarter carries John Flanagan's JF on the portrait's cutoff line. Most designers' initials are incuse, but the JF is raised.

In addition to the WHL dime, Weinman designed the Liberty Walking half-dollar. His AW monogram is on the reverse, at right of the base the eagle stands on. John R. Sinnock's JRS is on the truncation of the bust on Franklin halves.

Gilroy Roberts's stylized GR monogram is at the truncation of the bust on Kennedy half-dollars. Like Sinnock, Roberts suffered from a legend about his initials: many people were fooled into thinking the stylized monogram was a hammer and sickle, the emblem of the USSR! Frank Gasparro, who designed the half-dollar's reverse, put a plain FG between the eagle's tail feathers and the talon holding the arrows.

Other countries have issued coins with designers' or engravers' full names (Greece, France, Italy, Monaco), but the U.S. has restricted this practice to commemoratives, where it was accepted, and to one silver dollar, where it wasn't. This was the 1836 Gobrecht dollar, with C. GOBRECHT F. on the base line. And, as we've seen, this was the only year his name appeared; it was removed for the 1839 issue.

An incuse M is on both obverse and reverse of the Morgan silver dollar; it's at the base of the neck on obverse and on the left ribbon loop at the bottom of the wreath on reverse. Anthony de Francisci, designer of the Peace dollar, has an AF monogram on the obverse, just below the portrait.

The L on the portrait's truncation on gold dollars, the JBL on $3 gold pieces, and the same initials on double-eagles all belong to James B. Longacre.

Bela L. Pratt's BLP is above the date on his quarter- and half-eagles.

And Augustus Saint-Gaudens put his ASG monogram below the date on his beautiful gold double-eagle.

Many private gold coins, including low-denomination California gold, have initials and names. Some Templeton Reid coins have T. REID, others have the full name. Moffat & Co. put its full name on ingots and coins; and U.S. Assayer Augustus Humbert stamped his name and title on the *edge* of some 1851 $50 pieces.

COIN NICKNAMES

It adds color to language, gives history a clue to what we think—and confuses some of our noncollecting friends. What is it? The giving of nicknames to coins.

"Copper" for cent is from the fact that cents always have been pure copper or mostly copper. In *Tom Sawyer* there's a scene in which Tom says that for two cents he'd fight another boy and beat him, and the other holds out "two broad coppers."

Nickels once were "fish scales," and dimes have been called "short bits" because they're less than 12½ cents, "skinnies," and "thin ones."

The quarter has been called a "bird" from the eagle on the reverse; a "cute" and "dos reales," Spanish slang for "two bits."

"Bit" once was both underworld slang for money in general and common slang for the Spanish real. A fourth of the eight-real coin was two reales, or bits, so a fourth of our dollar became "two bits."

The appearance, weight, and size of silver dollars earned them such names as "banger," "shiner," and "wagon wheel." They're sometimes also called "cartwheels," but the British penny and twopence of 1797 have a prior claim to this nickname.

Our word "buck" for the dollar apparently came from the buckhorn handle on so many frontiersmen's knives. In card games the men often used a knife as a marker to show who the dealer was. Since in some games the dealer has an advantage, a clear marker could avoid the use of buckhorn-handled knives for more deadly purposes. I don't know exactly how the word's usage evolved, but it could have been related to the widespread use of barter on the frontier. If knives were assigned the value of $1 for the purpose of convenience, then "buck" for "dollar" might well linger after buckhorn-handled knives were replaced by "bucks" of paper, silver, and gold.

The officials names for our gold coins, except the $1 and $3, are quarter-eagle, half-eagle, eagle, and double-eagle—however, all of these show a value in *dollars*, not eagles. If you call an eagle a "ten-dollar gold piece," *then* you're using a nickname!

64

The Sign of the Dollar

Legend, lore, and fact
about our silver dollar, its insigne, its
name, and its amazing history.

$

A continuing controversy is the question of the origin of $, the dollar sign.

One popular belief, best expressed in Ayn Rand's novel *Atlas Shrugged*, is that $ comes from the combined initials of the United States. The suggestion adds to that book's ample numismatic flavor, but $ and similar symbols were used with varying meanings for centuries before the founding of this country. Hundreds of years ago, in fact, $ held our modern comma's job of separating groups of digits in large numbers. (Most Europeans use a period for this purpose today.)

A suggestion closer to the truth is that $ with the meaning of "dollars" came from /8/, an old Spanish peso symbol. Similar is the idea that $ resulted from joining the 8 for the value in reales with the Pillars of Hercules which appear on some eight-real coins. And a related idea is based on our forming of some plural abbreviations by doubling the singular: if p. for "page" becomes pp. for "pages," couldn't P for "peso" become PP for "pesos" and then grow into $? After all, various forms of $ were popular as cattle brands in the Old West, where many cattlemen were in contact with Mexicans and Mexican pesos.

But for the true explanation of our dollar sign we must go to the second unabridged *Webster's New International Dictionary* and to Dr. Florian Cajori in the August 1929 issue of *The Numismatist*.

One abbreviation for pesos was Pˢ. For some reason—most probably to make the symbol easier to write—the small s gradually was moved closer to the P, moved *over* it and then moved downward. The resulting P̩-like figure evolved into $—not the $ which already existed, but *our* $.

Dr. Cajori cited a number of late-eighteenth-century documents, among them a letter dated September 12, 1778, in which several forms of $ appear—*all of them clearly relating to U.S. dollars and all of them clearly intermediate forms of Pˢ and $.*

But if the symbol's evolution is known, that doesn't yet explain the word or the coin. For the full story we have to go far back into history.

THE MINES OF ST. JOACHIM'S VALLEY

The story of the coin we call a "dollar" began in the first century B.C. with a childless shepherd and his wife, who dwelt in that ancient city called Jerusalem. Each of them had a vision that they would have a daughter. They soon did, and named her Mary.

She also had a child—and named him Jesus.

Centuries later, in Bohemia, a valley was named for that shepherd—St. Joachim's Valley, or the *Joachimsthal*. Today it's the Jachymov, in modern Czechoslovakia.

As the Austrian Empire thrived and grew, Austria became more and more important. With imperial growth came growth in trade, and an increasing need for coins. A gold coin called a florin, or gulden, had been current in Europe since the thirteenth century, and by the end of the fifteenth century it was vital that there be some sort of silver equivalent for it. Prototype silver coins in large size were struck around 1475 in the Tyrolean Alps, but there was no large supply of the metal.

Then, at precisely the right moment for trade, Austria, and numismatics, rich silver deposits were discovered in 1516 in the Joachimsthal. The local ruler, Count Stephen Schlick (or Schlitz), appropriated the silver and within two years began issuing the needed large silver coins. These became extremely popular, and took on a name derived from their point of origin: "Joachimsthaler groshcen"—the big coin from the Joachimsthal.

Passing time generally shortens names. The coin's name followed this custom: "groschen" was dropped and the coin became simply "Joachimsthaler," then changed to "thaler," and finally became "daler," "dollar," and other modern forms of the word.

Those first talers show a portrait of St. Joachim; later ones usually show local rulers. Since most came from somewhere in Austrian territory, the reverse usually shows the two-headed imperial eagle from the royal coat-of-arms.

The last direct male heir of the House of Hapsburg was, at one point, Charles VI. His daughter married Francis Stephen, Duke of Lorraine, in 1736. Before Charles died, in 1740, he named his daughter heiress to the empire.

EMPRESS MARIA THERESA

Maria Theresa is remembered by many for her wisdom, beauty, and loyalty to the House of Hapsburg. *We* remember her as one of history's great numismatists. Her popularity with royalty and commoner alike brought constant gifts in the form of additions to her coin collection, and many of these still are displayed in a fine arts museum in Vienna.

Maria Theresa died in 1780, and her son Joseph II issued the first Maria Theresa talers that year. On the coin's obverse is a portrait of the empress facing right (compare this with early Draped Bust coins by Reich!). Around the rim is R. IMP. HU. BO. REG. M. THERESIA. D. G. (Maria Theresa, by the Grace of God Empress of the Holy Roman Empire, Queen of Hungary and Bohemia). A small SF at the lower rim is for Tobias Schol, mintmaster, and Joseph Faby, warden, of the Gunzburg mint in 1780; it's considered a Gunsburg mint mark.

The edge is lettered IUSTITIA ET CLEMENTIA (Justice and Mercy), with tiny floral designs separating the words.

On the reverse is the crowned two-headed imperial eagle. The rim has ARCHID. AVST. DUX. BURG. CO. TYR. plus the date 1780 and

FIG. 64-1. Maria Theresa taler, 1780, Proof restrike, obverse.

FIG. 64-2. Maria Theresa taler, 1780, Proof restrike, reverse.

an X. Probably the best translation is "Archduchess of Austria, Ruler of Burgundy, Countess of the Tyrol." The X is a Cross of St. Andrew, showing that the coin's weight and fineness conformed to a 1752 international agreement (weight of 26.0668 grams, fineness of .833).

So the Maria Theresa taler went out from Austria and soon became one of the major trade coins of the Middle East, northeastern Africa, and Mediterranean area. It was so popular that for over a century there were areas where people *refused any other coin* because they considered all other coinage debased!

Vienna kept minting the coins. Then mints at Paris, Rome, Brussels, and London began making talers. There was a long and complicated international legal battle and the other countries dropped out of the taler business one by one. When London quit in 1962, after making at least 24 million of the coins since 1936, Austria was supposed to have regained its traditional monopoly; some years later I learned that the USSR had continued making the talers.

But throughout the nearly two centuries of its life, this coin has kept one startling characteristic: *all* Maria Theresa talers, *including those being minted as you read these words*, are dated 1780.

To those who considered these coins the only "real" money, even a change in the date indicated debasement.

The beautiful Maria Theresa taler is one of the very few foreign coins that rates a place in U.S. coin collections. So many Proof restrikes have been made that the price is in the $2.35 to $3.50 range.

But it's still some distance between the Maria Theresa taler and our dollar.

"PIECES OF EIGHT! PIECES OF EIGHT!"

Remember Cap'n Flint, the parrot in *Treasure Island*? Her favorite words were "Pieces of eight! pieces of eight!"

In the sixteenth and seventeenth centuries, small areas of non-Spanish territory in the Americas were trading with the Orient and finding that they needed coins. With no mints of their own, they used Spanish coins pouring from Mexico's mints, especially the big silver "piece of eight." Circulating around the world, this coin took additional names—piastre, peso, and Spanish Milled Dollar are the most familiar. It was called a "piece of eight" because it's a *piece*—that is, a coin—of the value of *eight* reales.

Early pieces of eight were based on a standard one-ounce weight of nearly pure silver. They showed a crowned shield on the obverse and coat-of-arms on the reverse. Those minted in Spanish America have an obverse showing two crowned globes of the world between crowned pillars; from 1772 on they have a royal portrait obverse and crowned Spanish arms plus two elegant pillars decorated with banners on the reverse. The inscription on Spanish ones is HISPANIARUM REX (King of the Spains—meaning all Spanish territory), but that of coins minted in America is HISPANIARUM ET IND REX (King of the Spains and the Indies).

Pieces of eight from South American and Mexican mints circulated in the U.S., along with other foreign coins, for many years. In March 1835, E. J. Forstall & Co., of New Orleans, La., advertised "Spanish Dollars" for sale, in *The Courier*. The Spanish coins were legal tender until 1857, and when they were called in, there were more than 2 million in circulation!

Like the Maria Theresa taler, the piece of eight is a coin with a legitimate place in a U.S. coin collection. You can add one to your collection for as little as $5 or $6 or as much as $100, or even more, depending on date, mint, condition, and rarity. It's certainly worth the average price of $10 to $30 to own one of these fascinating coins; they appear often in auction catalogs, giving you a chance to obtain one for even less.

The "Spanish Milled Dollar" helped influence those who set up our monetary system toward "dollar" rather than "unit." But this was a direct influence, and a link that could have been bypassed in the chain of cause and effect. For our large silver coin would have been a dollar even if those who established the U.S. monetary system had never seen a piece of eight.

By 1792, many nations were issuing their own large silver coins, and because of the widespread influence of those early talers, the later coins' names all were derivations of "Joachimsthaler." The word "dollar" was part of the language, and if it hadn't come to our coin via the piece of eight, it would have reached us from another coin. For we could hardly have escaped the influences that acted over more than a quarter of a millennium—of the kings "of All the Spains," Joseph II of Austria, Empress Maria Theresa, and the great silver deposits in the Joachimsthal, the mines of St. Joachim's Valley.

FIG. 64–3. Mexico, 8 reales, 1838–Zs. When the Zacatecas mint struck this coin, pieces of eight still were legal tender in the U.S.

65

Interview with Miss Liberty

*If you could daydream yourself an interview
with anyone, would you choose Gobrecht? Longacre?
Saint-Gaudens? I chose the most important
"numismatic figure" of all.*

Puffing lazily at my pipe, I was admiring the figure on my 1859–O silver dollar. *If you could only talk,* I thought.

With a whisk and rustle of long skirts, Miss Liberty stood up and stepped from the coin! The air shimmered around the tiny figure. Suddenly she was standing next to me, full size.

"You might offer me a chair," she said calmly as I grabbed at my falling pipe.

"Please do sit down," I managed. "You really *can* walk and speak?"

"Of course. And it was quite easy to read your thoughts after so many years of practice."

"Er, just how many years—"

"One does not ask a lady's age. Your proper concern is my background."

"Sorry. No offense meant, Miss Liberty." I reached down and switched on the tape recorder I use for interviews.

"No offense taken," she said, smoothing a fold in her gown. "But my name is not really 'Miss Liberty,' at least, not always. You see, I have lived many times before, with many names. I once was a goddess. In fact—"

"A goddess!? You mean on Roman coins?"

"Not only there," she said. "I am a goddess *today*, in one sense, for all free men love and honor my spirit. And you yourself have called me the goddess of numismatics."

She settled into her well-known "Liberty Seated" pose in my

"visitor's chair," but looking forward, as I asked, "How far back do you go on U.S. coins?"

"Almost to the very beginning. President Washington was a good friend of mine, as was Mr. Jefferson. We did not always agree, but we *did* agree that a living President's portrait has no place on the coins of this nation."

"But the Red Book has four pages of Washington coins."

"Yes, but they are not United States coins. They were minted and issued privately, and Mr. Yeoman takes careful note of the fact. They never caught the public's fancy, although they did suggest good ideas that were used later."

"You mean designs that appeared on regular-issue coins?"

"Yes, of course. Compare the reverse of the 1783 'Unity States' cent with that of the early large cents. Look at 1792 half-dollars with the eagle reverse and then examine later coins of this value. You will see the relationship."

"Were you on the first U.S. coin ever issued?"

"No. The First ones were the Fugio cents, those copper coins with the sundial and the links of chain. But I was on the first coins of 1792. Those are small cents with a center plug of silver, very large cents, half-dismes, and dismes. The portraits are not at all flattering. My hair is stringy and looks horrible. But I remained on most United States coins until the current Presidential series began."

"What about foreign coins? Have you been on many of them?"

"Very many. To me no land is truly foreign. But some are very nationalistic and many are unaware of my identity and heritage. That is why so many coin catalogs call me a 'spirit of the Republic' or a similar name.

"Take Argentina, for instance. From 1881 on, many Argentine coins, even some of the modern ones, resemble early United States Liberty Head coins. And France—modern French coins picture me as a sower and the spirit of La Belle France. And the Aluminum coins of such French Union members as Cameroon, Saint Pierre and Miquelon, and others—all those show a 'bust of the republic.'"

"You've seen a lot of countries, haven't you?"

"Quite a few. Of course, not *every* nation has me on its coins. Not every one has pictured me in the past. But many have shown me at one time or another. In fact," she went on, smoothing her long hair, "I have been all over the world in gold, silver, copper, and many other metals. Designers of coins have portrayed me as a young girl, a young lady, an old woman, and an angel, sitting, standing, walking, and running. You surely are familiar with the Helvetian Confederation?"

"Just enough to know that Confoederatio Helvetica means a coin from Switzerland," I said. "I suppose the so-called 'peasant girl' portrait on the gold 20 francs is you?"

"Naturally. The Swiss cantons—Appenzell or Soleure, for instance—used to issue their own coins. They formed a confederation in 1850 and since then I have been on most of their coins. They call me 'Helvetia.'"

"Isn't there supposed to be some connection between you and Britannia?"

"Yes, I have been Britannia since even before 1660, when King Charles II put me on the British halfpenny and farthing."

"But Frances Stewart posed for the first Britannia portraits," I objected, remembering *Forever Amber* and coin books.

"Naturally. I am, essentially, a spirit, and I prefer to work through living persons of the time. That is why Frances Stewart posed for Britannia, and why Anna Williams modeled for my portrait on the Morgan dollar. You know the story of that coin—who do you think made Professor Eakins remember Anna Williams at precisely the right moment to speak of her to George Morgan? Why do you think Teresa Cafarelli was inspired so deeply by the Statue of Liberty? One need not always be physically present in order to influence the course of events. Besides," she added almost dreamily, "I did pose for the *first* Britannia portrait—but not as Britannia. That was a long time ago."

"Some countries call you by one name and some by another," I mused. "How many names have you had, Miss Liberty?"

She smiled. "How many nations' coins have shown my portrait? It amounts to much the same question. Certainly hundreds. Perhaps thousands." She shrugged.

"Do you have a favorite name?"

"That depends on the time. My favorite name is the one which means freedom and justice to the most people. 'Miss Liberty' suits me fine right now."

"You were on ancient Roman coins, weren't you?" She nodded. "What did the Romans call you?"

"Sometimes 'Roma,' spirit of the city of Rome, sometimes 'Libertas,' which is the same as 'Miss Liberty.' "

"They issued the first Liberty Seated, or Britannia, coins, didn't they?"

"Yes and no." She smoothed out a crease in her gown. "You are thinking of coins issued by the emperors Hadrian and Antoninus Pius. They wanted the people of Rome to know about their successful military expeditions in Britain, so they put the spirit of that land on some Roman coins. Those *were* the first Brittania coins. But the Romans took the idea of that portrait from the first real Liberty Seated coin.

"This was issued by a Macedonian Greek named Lysimachus. He was one of Alexander the Great's personal guards. Later he was governor of Thrace. His was the *first* Liberty Seated coin. And I posed for it in person."

"But Lysimachus used a portrait of Athena," I protested. "So how—?"

"Remember I said I have lived before? And that 'Miss Liberty' is not my only name? I am patroness not only of Liberty, *but also of the defensive warfare which protects liberty.*"

She shimmered against the air and pipe smoke. For a moment I could see right through her to the paneled wall. Her quiet voice seemed to echo from far off. "I was a *real* goddess in ancient Greece, more than two thousand years ago, and my name then was ... *Athena.*"

She faded from sight. An instant later she reappeared on the silver dollar on my desk. She sat down, smoothed her hair, and arranged her gown. Then she picked up the pole and liberty cap with her left hand, steadied the U.S. shield with her right, and turned around to look back over her shoulder. Then she was still. She has not moved or spoken again.

So I transcribed the interview. But when I went to play the tape a second time, it was totally blank and silent. It makes no difference: nobody could believe such "evidence."

Yet I keep the memory of an interview with a goddess, and the sure knowledge that Liberty is alive and aware and eternal.

TABLE OF MINTS

The private mints listed here are only a fraction of those known; I'm listing these few to give you a rough idea of the different locations and coins.

GROUP I: OFFICIAL "COLONIAL" MINTS

Location	Mint Mark or Equivalent	Operating Dates	Coins Struck
CONNECTICUT			
Morris Cove	none	1785–1788	Connecticut cents
New Haven	none	1787	Fugio cents
Westville	none	1785–1788	Connecticut cents
MASSACHUSETTS			
Iron Works	none	1652–1682	NE and tree coins
–?–	none	1787–1789	Mass. ½¢ and 1¢
NEW JERSEY			
Elizabethtown	none	1787–1788	New Jersey cents
Morristown	none	1786–1788	New Jersey cents
VERMONT			
Rupert[1]	none	1785–1788	Fugio cents

GROUP II: UNOFFICIAL "COLONIAL" MINTS

Location	Mint Mark or Equivalent	Operating Dates	Operator	Coins Struck
CONNECTICUT				
Granby	none	1737–1739	John Higley	3 pence
MARYLAND				
Annapolis	none	1783	I. Chalmers	3, 6 pence shilling
Baltimore	BALTIMORE TOWN	1790	Standish Barry	3 pence
NEW YORK				
New York	none	1787	Ephraim Brasher	doubloon ½ doubloon

GROUP III: OFFICIAL U.S. MINTS

Location	Mint Mark	Operating Dates	Regular-issue Coins Minted
CALIFORNIA			
San Francisco[2]	S[3]	1854–	Cents
			Half-dimes
			Nickels
			Dimes
			20¢
			Quarter-dollars
			Half-dollars
			Silver dollars
			Trade dollars
			Gold dollars
			Quarter-eagles
			$3
			Half-eagles
			Eagles
			Double-eagles

Location	Mint Mark	Operating Dates	Regular-issue Coins Minted
COLORADO			
Denver[2]	D[3]	1906–	Cents
			Nickels
			Dimes
			Quarter-dollars
			Half-dollars
			Silver dollars
			Quarter-eagles
			Half-eagles
			Eagles
			Double-eagles
GEORGIA			
Dahlonega[1]	D	1838–1861	Gold dollars
			Quarter-eagles
			Half-eagles
LOUISIANA			
New Orleans[1,2]	O	1838–1861 and 1879–1909	Trimes
			Half-dimes
			Dimes
			Quarter-dollars
			Half-dollars
			Silver dollars
			Gold dollars
			Quarter-eagles
			$3
			Half-eagles
			Eagles
			Double-eagles
NEVADA			
Carson City	CC	1870–1893	Dimes
			20¢
			Quarter-dollars
			Half-dollars
			Silver dollars
			Trade Dollars
			Half-eagles
			Eagles
			Double-eagles

Location	Mint Mark	Operating Dates	Regular-issue Coins Minted
NORTH CAROLINA			
Charlotte[1]	C	1838–1861	Gold dollars Quarter-eagles Half-eagles
PENNSYLVANIA			
Philadelphia[2]	P[3,4]	1792–	Half-cents Cents (large and small) 2¢ Trimes 3¢ (cupronickel) Half-dimes Nickels Dimes 20¢ Quarter-dollars Half-dollars Silver dollars Trade Dollars Gold dollars Quarter-eagles $3 Half-eagles Eagles Double-eagles

GROUP IV: UNOFFICIAL (PRIVATE) U.S. MINTS

Location	Mint Mark or Equivalent[5]	Operating Dates	Items Minted	Operator(s)
CALIFORNIA				
Benicia City	SAN FRAN-CISCO	1849	$5	Norris, Grieg & Norris
Sacramento	CAL.[3]	1849 and/ or 1850	$5	J. S. Ormsby & Co.
San Francisco	SAN FRAN-CISCO	1849–1850	$5	Norris, Grieg & Norris

Location	Mint Mark or Equiva- lent[5]	Operating Dates	Items Minted	Operator(s)
San Fran- cisco	SAN FRAN- CISCO[3]	1849–1853	ingots $5 $10 $20 $50	Moffat & Co., 1849–52; U.S. Assay Office, including A. Humbert and Curtis, Perry & Ward, 1852– 1853
San Fran- cisco	none	1850–1851	$5 $10	Theodore Dubosq & Co.
San Fran- cisco	SAN FRAN- CISCO[3]	1850–51	$5 $10 $20	George C. Baldwin & Co.
San Fran- cisco	SAN FRAN- CISCO CALI- FORNIA[3]	1852–1855	$5 $10 $20 $50	Wass, Molitor & Co.
San Fran- cisco	SAN FRAN- CISCO CALI- FORNIA	1854–1855	$20 $50	Kellogg & Co.
Stockton	STOCKTON	1850	$5	Norris, Grieg & Norris
COLORADO				
Denver	DENVER	1859–1861	$2.50 $5 $10	Clark, Gruber & Co.; sold to U.S. gov- ernment 1862
Georgia Gulch	none	1861	$2.50 $5 $10	J. J. Conway & Co., doing business as The Conway Mint
CONNECTICUT				
Water- bury[2,6]	none that I know of	1827–1919	medals tokens 1¢ 5¢	Scoville Mfg. Co.

Location	Mint Mark or Equiva- lent[5]	Operating Dates	Items Minted	Operator(s)
GEORGIA				
Lumpkin County	none	1830	$2.50 $10	Templeton Reid
NORTH CAROLINA				
Ruther- fordton	RUTHERF[3] and RUTHER- FORD[3]	1830–1852	$1 $2.50 $5	Christopher and August Bechtler
OREGON				
Oregon City	T. O. and O. T.[7]	1849	$5 $10	Oregon Ex- change Co.
PENNSYLVANIA				
Franklin Center[2]		1965–	medals	General Nu- mismatics Corp.; later changed to The Franklin Mint, Inc.
UTAH[8]				
Salt Lake City	none	1849–60	$2.50 $5 $10 $20	Church of Jesus Christ of Latter-Day Saints

GROUP V: INDEPENDENT NATIONAL MINTS

Location	Mint Mark	Operating Dates	Coins Minted	Operating Authority
GEORGIA				
Dahlonega	D	1861	$1 gold[9] $5 gold[9]	Confederate States of America
LOUISIANA				
New Orleans	O	1861	Half-dollars[10] Double-eagles Patterns	same
NORTH CAROLINA				
Charlotte	C	1861	$1 gold (?) $5 gold[9]	same
VERMONT				
Rupert	none	1785–1788	Vermont 1¢	Republic of Vermont

Notes to Appendix A

[1] See also Group V.

[2] Also struck foreign coins.

[3] Not used on all items produced. U.S. mints don't always use a mint mark on foreign coins. They omitted mint marks from U.S. coins dated 1965, 1966 and 1967.

[4] Used on U.S. coins only on 5¢ pieces of 1942–45.

[5] In the case of many private issues the mint operator's company or family name is on the coin; this might be considered equivalent to a mint mark. However, I'm restricting the listing here to mint marks showing location.

[6] This mint is credited with making some planchets for U.S. cents and nickels in 1888–1906.

[7] The initials stand for Oregon Territory; the T. O. is an engraver's error.

[8] I've called it by the modern name here, but the settlers named it "Deseret." This technically was the correct name for it during the 1847–50 period; not until September 1850 did it become the Territory of Utah.

[9] Possibly a C.S.A. issue; I've listed the "possibles" here for the sake of completeness.

[10] State officials made 1,240,000 halves for Louisiana before they turned the mint over to the C.S.A. which struck another 962,633 halves. However, state officials were acting as agents of the Confederacy in seizing the mint, and Louisianians who'd use the coins were C.S.A. citizens.

COMPLETE STAR-LINE
AND MARGINALS LIST

A dash means that no date in that particular design has qualified for this edition's list. Regular-issue coins are listed first, separated by a semicolon from Proofs. All dates following the word "Proof" are Proof coins.

Denomination	Design	STAR-LINE	Marginals
HALF-CENT	Early	——	——
	Draped Bust	1806	1803, 1804
	Classic Head	1826	1832, 1833, 1834, 1835
	Braided Hair	1850, 1854	1851, 1853
ONE CENT *(Large)*	Early	1795 LE, 1796	1793 Chain
	Draped Bust	1803, 1805, 1807	1798

Denomi- nation	Design	STAR-LINE	Marginals
	Classic Head	——	——
	Coronet	1824, 1827, 1829	1819, 1825
	Braided Hair	1854, 1855	1845, 1846, 1848, 1850, 1851
ONE CENT (*Small*)	Flying Eagle	——	——
	Indian Head	1870, 1908; Proof 1881, 1882, 1889, 1895, 1908	1880, 1883, 1884, 1889, 1895, 1896, 1909; Proof 1869, 1870, 1871, 1880, 1884, 1890, 1891, 1892
	Lincoln	1911–D; Proof 1911	1909 VDB, 1930–S, 1931–D, 1931–S, 1933–D; Proof 1909
TWO CENTS	single type	——	1868, 1869
THREE CENTS	Silver (trime)	1860, 1862; Proof 1862	1859; Proof 1867, 1868, 1869
	Nickel	1883, 1889	1884
HALF- DIME	Flowing Hair	——	——
	Draped Bust	——	——
	Capped Bust	——	——
	Liberty Seated	1843, 1847, 1848, 1849, 1852, 1861, 1870; Proof 1862	1841, 1858, 1863, 1865, 1865–S, 1869, 1872, 1873; Proof 1868, 1869
FIVE CENTS (*Cupro- nickel*)	Shield	1881, 1882; Proof 1882	1870, 1872; Proof 1879
	Liberty Head	Proof 1907, 1908	1894, 1900, 1901, 1904, 1908; Proof 1887, 1902, 1905

Denomi- nation	Design	STAR-LINE	Marginals
	Buffalo	1934, 1937–D, 1937–S	1913–S T1, 1914–S, 1929–D, 1930–S, 1931–S
	Jefferson	——	1938–D, 1946–S, 1958; Proof 1942, 1953
DIME	Early (Draped Bust)	1800	1802, 1805, 1807
	Capped Bust	1814, 1828, 1836, 1837	1829, 1834, 1835
	Liberty Seated	1863, 1864, 1865, 1866, 1867, 1879, 1881, 1885; Proof 1862, 1890	1846, 1847, 1849, 1857–O, 1858, 1860, 1872, 1873, 1877–S 1886, 1886–S, 1888, 1891–S; Proof 1877
	Barber	1903–S, 1906–D, 1908–O, 1910–D, 1910–S, 1912–S; Proof 1907, 1909	1897–O, 1908–S, 1911–S; Proof 1904, 1905, 1906, 1910, 1911, 1912
	WHL	1935–D, 1937–D, 1939–S	1916–S, 1928–S, 1929–D, 1929–S, 1930, 1931–D, 1934–D, 1937–S, 1938, 1938–D, 1940–D, 1940–S, 1944–S, 1945–D, 1945–S; Proof 1939
	Roosevelt	Proof 1959	1947–S, 1949–D, 1955; Proof 1957, 1960
TWENTY CENTS	single type	——	——
QUARTER DOLLAR	Draped Bust	——	——
	Capped Bust	1828	1833, 1834

Denomi- nation	Design	STAR-LINE	Marginals
	Liberty Seated	1857–O, 1863, 1865, 1871, 1890; Proof 1873–NA, 1875, 1878	1858–O, 1859, 1872, 1875, 1876–CC, 1877–CC, 1880, 1881, 1884, 1885, 1886, 1887, 1888, 1888–S, 1889, 1891; Proof 1863, 1879
	Barber	1894, 1906, 1910–D, 1911, 1913, 1914–D	1893–S, 1896, 1906–D, 1907–S, 1913, 1915, 1915–D; Proof 1908, 1910, 1911
	Liberty Standing	1917–D T1, 1923	1929–D, 1930–S
	Washington	1944–S, 1949–D 1959, 1960	1932–S, 1938–S, 1939–S, 1940–S, 1943–D, 1944–D, 1945–D, 1946–S, 1947, 1948–D, 1956–D, 1958; Proof 1951, 1960
HALF- DOLLAR	Flowing Hair	——	——
	Draped Bust	——	——
	Capped Bust	1811, 1817, 1828	1810, 1913, 1814, 1821, 1825
	Liberty Seated	1856–O, 1859–O 1860–O, 1861, 1861–O, 1862, 1871, 1878	1842, 1843–O, 1844–O, 1849, 1849–O, 1863, 1865, 1867–S, 1868–S, 1871–S; Proof 1866
	Barber	1908, 1911, 1915–D	1905, 1905–O, 1910, 1911–S, 1912–S, 1913–D; Proof 1914
	Walking Liberty	1934–D, 1938–D, 1939–S, 1945–S, 1946–D, 1946–S	1916–S, 1929–D, 1935–D, 1937–S, 1939; Proof 1939
	Franklin	1959–D, 1960, 1960–D, 1961–D	1948–D, 1954, 1956, 1957, 1957–D, 1958, 1959; Proof 1954
	Kennedy	——	——
DOLLAR (Silver)	Flowing Hair	——	——

Denomi- nation	Design	STAR-LINE	Marginals
	Draped Bust	1802	1800, 1801
	Liberty Seated	1867	1849, 1863, 1864, 1865
	Morgan	1893; Proof 1884	1878–CC, 1891–S, 1892, 1892–O, 1897–O, 1898–O, 1903, 1904; Proof 1887, 1888, 1889, 1890, 1891, 1900, 1904
	Peace	1927–D	1924, 1925, 1925–S, 1927, 1928–S, 1934–D
	Eisenhower	——	——
DOLLAR (Trade)	single type	1874–S, 1877; Proof 1875	1873, 1876
DOLLAR (Gold)	all types	1876, 1878, 1879, 1883, 1885; Proof 1873, 1874, 1877, 1878	1852–C, 1853–C, 1858–S, 1865, 1868, 1872, 1880; Proof 1862, 1870, 1871, 1872, 1879, 1881, 1882, 1883
QUARTER- EAGLE	Early	——	1805, 1806
	Capped Bust Left	——	1827, 1829
	Classic Head	——	1837, 1838, 1839
	Coronet	1877; Proof 1871, 1872, 1891	1874, 1876, 1891, 1898; Proof 1866, 1868, 1869, 1873, 1874, 1878, 1879, 1882, 1884
	Indian Head	——	1914, 1927; Proof 1909, 1913
THREE DOLLARS	single type	1860–S; Proof 1865, 1878, 1879	1871, 1879, 1880, 1884, 1886; Proof 1868, 1869, 1872, 1882, 1883, 1884
HALF- EAGLE	Early	1798	1796, 1799

Denomi-nation	Design	STAR-LINE	Marginals
	Capped Bust Left	1808, 1812, 1823	1813, 1814, 1834
	Classic Head	——	——
	Coronet First Series	——	1845–O, 1851–O, 1855, 1857–S, 1860–S
	Coronet Second Series	1883, 1883–S, 1888–S, 1903, 1905; Proof 1881, 1882, 1883, 1885	1867, 1873, 1873–S, 1874–S, 1878, 1882–CC, 1883–CC, 1890–CC, 1892–CC, 1892–S, 1893–S, 1894–O, 1894–S, 1895–S, 1896; Proof 1868, 1873, 1886, 1891
	Indian Head	1908–D, 1910–D; Proof 1909, 1913	1908, 1915, 1915–S
EAGLE	Early	——	1804
	Coronet First Series	——	1845, 1846, 1859–O
	Coronet Second Series	1878–S, 1892–O; Proof 1865	1880–CC, 1882–O, 1883–CC, 1894–S; Proof 1881, 1882, 1883, 1889, 1891, 1893, 1894, 1895
	Indian Head	1909–D	1913–S; Proof 1914
DOUBLE-EAGLE	Coronet	1889–S, 1891; Proof 1875, 1891	1868–S, 1873–S, 1874–S, 1875–S, 1876, 1879–S, 1880–S, 1881–S, 1882–S, 1890–S, 1891–S, 1894, 1894–S, 1895, 1895–S, 1896, 1897, 1899–S, 1900–S, 1906–S, 1907–S; Proof 1867
	Saint-Gaudens	1910, 1910–S, 1923–D; Proof 1914	1908–D WM, 1909–S, 1910–D, 1913–D, 1914–S, 1922; Proof 1909, 1912

Appendix C

THE COLLECTOR'S VOCABULARY

album   *see* PENNY BOARD, WINDOW ALBUM
alloy   mixture of metals
"Arabic" numerals   *see* WESTERN NUMERALS
assay   chemical test showing what's in a sample of ore, or other material
attribution   identification of a coin by country, design, inscription, denomination, date, mint mark, edge type, alloy, designer, engraver, former owners, and any other available information

bag marks   indentations on a coin or other item, caused by impact with other pieces in (usually mint) bags
bandrole   long, usually gently curved ribbon, used to provide a small area for an inscription and at the same time draw attention by setting that area off from the rest of the surface
banner   same as bandrole
B&D   (1) Brown and Dunn, the numismatists; (2) their book on condition grading
beaded circle   circular line of tiny dots, usually used to separate a design area from an inscription area
billon   cuprosilver alloy composed of over 50% copper; sometimes used for tin-silver alloy
book value   (1) the price listed for any coin in any catalog; when used in connection with U.S. coins, usually (2) the value shown in the Red Book

bourse   area of a coin show or convention where dealers conduct business

brass   alloy of copper and zinc; sometimes used for alloys of copper, zinc, and tin, in which there is more zinc than tin

bronze   alloy of copper with tin and/or zinc; formerly was usually 80 percent copper and 20 percent other metal(s); due to expense, tin has been dropped from many bronze alloys, and "bronze" has become equivalent, in general use, to what should be called brass— 95 percent copper and 5 percent zinc, an alloy the mint calls "penny bronze" and that metallurgists label "gilding metal"; the alloy of 90 percent copper and 10 percent zinc is called "commercial bronze"

bullion   metal in form of plates, ingots or bars; usually used to refer to gold and silver

catalog   (1) descriptive listing, often illustrated, published as a reference work, for instance, the Red Book; (2) descriptive listing, usually by sections devoted to different denominations, of coins for sale, published by a dealer, sometimes illustrated; (3) listing of coins divided into lots for an auction

cent   U.S. coin worth $\frac{1}{100}$ of a dollar

chiton   loose robe, usually associated with ancient Greece, sometimes worn as undergarment, sometimes double-folded to provide two layers of clothing

circulation   daily use; includes coins in people's pockets, cash registers, and elsewhere in other than numismatic channels

clad   (1) in design, means "wearing," as in "Liberty clad in a loose gown"; (2) in composition, coins with a center "slice" of one metal or alloy and outer "faces" of a different metal or alloy

clash die   a variety coin showing very faintly on one side the design, or part of the design, from the other side; one explanation is that obverse and reverse dies clashed when there was no planchet in position for striking, so that some of one die's design was transferred to the other die; however, *see also* SUCTION MARK

coin   an item of money, usually round and usually metal, used or meant for use as a medium of exchange and commerce, and usually having both the identification of the issuing authority and a statement of standard value indicated on it

collar   the part of the minting machinery which fits around the planchet's edge and holds it in position, while preventing the metal from spreading out under the pressure of the striking dies

Colonial   loosely, coins and tokens issued before 1792, including true Colonials, tokens, patterns, private and official issues, imported pieces, and such true U.S. issues as the Fugio cent

Columbia figure on certain U.S. patterns, and one or two coins, representing the spirit of the nation

composition *see* ALLOY

commem written and spoken numismatic shorthand for a commemorative coin

commemorative coin coin issued to mark a special occasion, take note of an anniversary, honor a person or persons, or take notice of a point in the history of a community or area, and with its purpose as a coin being secondary; often issued simultaneously with regular-issue coins of the same denomination

common (1) easy to find in change because of relatively high mintage; or (2) available at relatively low prices in coin stores because supply is larger than demand

condition grade of a coin, describing the amount of wear; sometimes used to mean description, in addition to grade, of individual piece's characteristics, such as scratches, weakness of strike, etc.

cupro- prefix indicating that copper forms part of the alloy

cupronickel popular coinage alloy of copper and nickel in any of various proportions; on U.S. coins, 88% copper + 12% nickel on Indian and Flying Eagle cents of 1857–64, and 75% copper + 25% nickel on others

currency (1) paper money (bills or notes); or, more loosely, (2) money in general

denomination the assigned value of a coin, such as "One Cent" or "Quarter Dollar"

die hardened piece of metal with design punched into it, which stamps this design onto a blank planchet to create a coin; for an incuse coin the design is raised on the die

die break (1) crack or break in the die itself; or (2) line of metal, caused by a die break, on a coin

dipping artificially brightening or darkening a coin by treating it with chemical solution

dup pronounced "doop," numismatic shorthand for "duplicate"

early strike one of the first coins struck by one or both dies, and which therefore has a great deal of luster and often a sharper than usual strike

error coin regular-issue or Proof with one or more characteristics not intended by the issuer, for instance, a coin struck in the wrong alloy or with an incorrect number or letter

essai, essay   a pattern ("essai" is the French form)

ex   Latin "from"; used with a name or collection to show that a coin is from a particular collection

exergue   space at the bottom of a coin, usually set off by a line; often used as location of date and/or mint mark

exonumia   all numismatic items other than coins; technically does include medals, but apparently rarely used for them

experimental piece   pattern-class item struck in a metal different from the one in which the coin would be issued, or as a test of the metal

fasces   bundle of rods tied together, usually around an axe whose blade projects clear of the rods; symbol of power of certain ancient Roman officers; on coins, symbolizes governmental authority

fido   formerly popular term for off-center, clipped, and other "freak" error coins; growth of variety collecting and wider use of more specific terms is making this term obsolete

field   (1) area around main design of a coin, generally plain but sometimes used as location of date, mint mark, or brief inscription; (2) (rare) entire surface of a coin

filled die   (1) die on which part of the design or a letter or number is partly or completely filled with foreign material (such as dirt or grease) and which therefore is unable to strike a perfect coin; however, usually used to mean (2) a coin which lacks part or all of one or more letters or numbers or items of design, or shows them weakly, as a result of being struck by a filled die

filler   coin in Fair or worse condition that's included in a collection only to fill a space for that particular item

fineness   proportion of precious metal in a coin, usually expressed in thousandths; most U.S. silver and gold coins have a fineness of 900 parts in a thousand, written as .900; also can be expressed as percentage: 90% silver or 90% gold

flan   planchet

fractional currency   paper money in denominations of less than one dollar

grade   coin condition

grain   unit of weight equal to .064799 gram and to 1/480 ounce

gram   unit of metric weight, equal to 15.432 grains

hair line   line indicating hair, on the head of a portrait

hairline   extremely thin die break; usually used with "die break"

half-wreath   (1) one side of a wreath; (2) a wreath extending only about half the height of the design or inscription it encloses

heads   obverse of a coin

heraldic eagle   the U.S. emblem, arranged according to (though sometimes in violation of!) the rules of heraldry; may have in beak a banner lettered E PLURIBUS UNUM, head facing to right (the eagle's right) to show courage, its right talon holding olive branch to show preference of nation for peace, left talon with 13 arrows for original states and ability to defend self in case of attack, U.S. shield on chest

high relief   design or portion of it extending far up from coin's basic surface

hub   master die which has design raised and is used not for making coins but for making the working dies which strike coins

incuse   cut in instead of being raised; only such U.S. regular-issues are the Bigelow-Pratt half- and quarter-eagles

inert   chemically inactive, tending not to form compounds with other materials; thus, safe for coin holders

ingot   lump of metal, usually shaped like a small brick

inscription   lettering on a coin or medal, other than date and mint mark

inverted   referring to eagle's wings, held close to the body and with tips pointed downward

key   a scarce or rare date

kraft paper   heavy brown paper such as that used for bags and wrapping

laureate   portrait type in which the head is shown wearing a laurel wreath

legend   same as INSCRIPTION and often used interchangeably with it, though some collectors prefer to limit one or the other to the words around the rim and sometimes to one side or the other

liberty cap   modern version of the cap given to a slave along with his freedom in ancient Phrygia; later adopted by free Romans to set themselves off from the bare-headed slaves, by French revolutionists to distinguish themselves from monarchists, and by various other groups

liberty pole   pole or spear with a liberty cap resting atop it

luster   the "shine" of a coin, often called "mint luster"

medal   an item, usually round and of metal, struck or cast to honor or commemorate a person, place, or event, and not intended for use as a medium of exchange; may be with or without date and identification of an issuing authority

medalet   small medal

medallion   (1) a medal larger than about three inches across; or (2) a small oval area on a coin, used to frame a feature of the design

milled coin   coin produced by minting machinery rather than by one or more blows of a hammer

millimeter   unit of metric length equal to $\frac{1}{1000}$ of a meter and to .03937 of an inch

milling   the raised rim on the obverse or reverse of a coin, which both protects the design and permits stacking; the term should never be used to mean reeding

mint   (1) a place where coins are made, the building used for coining operations; (2) machinery which makes coins

mint mark   letter (s) or symbol (s) or any combination of them, added to a coin's design to show where the coin was made

monogram   on U.S. coins, decorative combination of two or more initials to indicate the designer or engraver

motto   brief expression of national sentiment; IN GOD WE TRUST and E PLURIBUS UNUM ("One [Nation] Out of Many [States]") are the two which appear on regular-issue U.S. coins

mule   combination on a single item of an obverse and reverse not intended to be used together

NA   "no arrows" variety

National Collection   the coins and other numismatic items held by the Smithsonian Institution

National Medal   medal authorized by Congress and usually struck at an official U.S. Mint

NM   "no motto" variety; not made; none minted

note   a piece of paper currency

numismatics   (pronounced noo-mihs-MAA-tix) the collection, study, and enjoyment of coins, tokens, medals, paper currency, and similar and related items

numismatist   (pronounced noo-MIHS-muh-tist) someone involved in a phase of numismatics

obv   numismatic shorthand for OBVERSE

obverse   the collector's term for the "heads" side of a coin; in the case of U.S. coins, the side with a Presidential or Liberty portrait; by legal implication, the side other than the one with national identification and denomination

oddity   a variety coin

off-metal piece   coin struck in a metal other than that intended for the regular-issue coin, either by error or as part of the testing procedure; in the former case, it's a variety; in the latter, it's a pattern-class item

orig   original, as opposed to a restrike or processed coin

overdate   (1) date having one or more numerals punched over different ones; (2) coin with an overdate

overstrike   coin or other item struck on an already minted piece

pattern   trial or test piece minted as part of the planning process, or to see how a proposed design would look on a coin or in a certain size or metal

PDS   a set of coins consisting of one each from Philadelphia, Denver, and San Francisco; usually used in dealers' ads to save space

penny board   simple coin album consisting of cardboard pages with holes punched into the cardboard, and a sheet of paper covering the holes on one side to prevent coins' falling out; often has two or three pages which fold over one another; given this name because it originated with collectors of U.S. cents

Phrygian cap   liberty cap

pileus   liberty cap

planchet   the coin blank before being stamped with a design, as long as it remains a blank disc

pocket piece   coin carried for sentimental or other reasons and not meant by the owner to be spent

private gold   gold coin issued by an individual or company rather than by the government or with governmental authority; often called "territorial" gold because much of it came from areas which were Territories rather than states, or were still so regarded by most people ("wild territory")

private issue   any piece issued without governmental authority

processed   dipped

Proof   coin struck on polished or specially cleaned planchets with specially polished dies, at low speed and high pressure, which has sharp and perfect detail, unusually bright surface, and high "wire rim"; also including sandblast or matte Proofs, which lack the high luster; Proofs are struck for numismatists and as presentation pieces, and never intended for circulation; term is used and listed as a coin condition, but technically is a special class of coin

rag-picker   a collector of paper currency
rare   (1) hard to obtain, usually expensive coin; (2) my working definition is a coin with a mintage of 3 million or less
rays   lines representing light or importance, such as those around a sun or around or above the eagle on certain coins
real   Spanish coin worth ⅛ peso
realistic   design which faithfully reproduces something from the world of life
recut   re-engraved to correct an error or allow longer use of a die, and therefore showing more than one outline
Red Book   (1) *A Guide Book of United States Coins*; (2) when used with "description" or "price," means that description or price as it appears in the Red Book
reducing machine   the pantograph device invented by Janvier, which reduces coin or medal designs to the required size and engraves them on a die
reeded   usually used with "edge"; an edge protected by ridges extending straight across the coin's thickness
reeding   the ridges on a reeded edge
regular-issue   (1) an adjective, usually with "coin" to mean a coin released, or meant for release, into circulation (however, I exclude from this the $20 of 1933); (2) a noun, meaning a regular-issue coin, usually without the hyphen; (3) also can mean the mintage from a particular mint or in a particular year
replica   a facsimile; a privately or officially issued piece in imitation of a numismatic item, but not intended to defraud; often has minor differences from the original in order to prevent deception
restrike   coin struck in a year later than the date it carries
rev   numismatic shorthand for "reverse"
reverse   (1) the "tails" side of a coin; (2) on U.S. coins, by legal definition, the side with the national identification and the denomination
"reverse of"   (1) a coin with the obverse of one year but the reverse of an earlier or later date; (2) a pattern with the reverse as it later appeared on regular-issue coins
rim   the raised line around a coin's obverse or reverse edge, which protects the design and allows stacking; *see* MILLING
Roman numerals   system of letters used as numbers, as in ancient Rome; equivalents are: I = 1, V = 5, X = 10, L = 50, C = 100, D = 500, M = 1,000

rust   oxide formed by air's oxygen and the metal in a coin; usually used in reference to copper and bronze coins

scarce   too few to be considered common but too many to be called rare; there's no precise limit

screw press   minting device which gets power through the turning of a large screw gear which brings dies together slowly but with great pressure

scroll   a banner with ornate and usually curled-up ends

semi-key   a coin that's hard to get, but not really rare; a scarce coin

series   coins which share at least one common characteristic, for example, all coins of a single nation ("U.S. series"), all coins with a single design ("Barber series," "Liberty Seated series"), all coins of a single denomination ("the U.S. half-eagle series"), all coins of a single denomination and design ("the Jefferson nickel series")

Spadone   (1) variety expert Frank G. Spadone; (2) his reference work, *Major Variety and Oddity Guide of United States Coins*

specialization   the collecting of a single nation, metal, design, subject, date, denomination, mint, or other type of coin (or other numismatic item) with a distinguishing characteristic

strike   (1) the coming together of coinage or medal dies with a planchet between them; the creation of a coin from a blank planchet; (2) the sharpness of design on a coin, as influenced by the pressure of the dies, as in "a good strike" or "a weak strike"

stylized   in numismatic art, a representation of some object from the real world in a manner in which the artist's talent, impressions, and artistic style play a major role, rather than a strict or literal representation

suction mark   marks caused when dies pull away from a newly struck coin—the tremendous suction pulls an impression of the design from one side through to the other; suction marks are raised, while true clashed die marks are incuse.

tails   reverse side

tarnish   same as rust, but usually in reference to silver and gold coins

token   (1) privately issued piece meant to serve a commercial or advertising purpose; (2) a token specifically meant to pay for transportation, a transit token

truncation   bottom of a portrait, where it's cut off at the base of the neck or start of the trunk; I prefer "cutoff line"

type coin   any coin representing a series, such as any half-cent to represent all half-cents, a 1953 quarter-dollar to represent .900 fine silver coins, a Saint-Gaudens $20 gold piece to represent coins showing full-length figures of Liberty, and so forth

type set set of type coins in which all appropriate types are represented; for instance, a twentieth-century type set of cents would include a 1900-or-later Indian cent, a Lincoln cent from 1909–58, a 1943 steel cent, and a 1959-or-later Lincoln to show the Memorial reverse; it also could include branch mint coins, a 1944 shell-case copper cent and varieties

Unc (pronounced Uhnk) written and spoken numismatic shorthand for "Uncirculated"

Uncirculated never placed in circulation; a coin, token or medal in the state of wear in which it left the mint; top grade for regular-issue coins

uniface numismatic item with a design on only one side

value (1) the worth or desirability of a numismatic item in the mind of a collector; (2) after "book" or "catalog," the price of the numismatic item as shown in either a specified catalog or in coin catalogs in general; (3) the price of a coin

V&O Guide short term for Spadone's book

variety coin or other numismatic item different in some way from others of the same denomination, date, and mint; if the difference is major and intentional, the variety may be a sub-type of a design; if the difference is accidental, the variety might be called a mint error

vecture transit token

vecturist collector of transit tokens

WA "with arrows" variety

Washington piece any of the tokens, patterns, and medals showing George Washington and issued privately here and in England 1783–95.

Western numerals the numbers we use, 1, 2, 3, and so forth, which are so far removed from their Arabic ancestors that there's very little resemblance

white metal alloy containing mostly lead and tin, in several different combinations, and sometimes including one or more other metals; usually a soft alloy; should *not* be used to refer to the cupronickel cents of 1857–64

whiz to polish or otherwise treat a coin in order to make it appear less worn

whizzer a coin or other item that has been whizzed; also (rarely), a person who whizzes a coin

window album   coin album formed of heavy cardboard pages with holes into which collectors can insert coins, and with transparent plastic slides over the holes to allow coin insertion and removal and the viewing of both obverse and reverse of all coins in the album; usually with pages inside a common cover rather than with pages folding over one another

wire edge   extremely thin and high rim, often found on Proofs, caused by a strike with tremendous pressure

WM   "with motto" variety

working die   the die actually used for striking coins

Yeoman   (1) author and numismatist Richard S. Yeoman; (2) the Red Book; (3) with "price" or "description," that price or description as expressed in the Red Book (or in one of the Yeoman foreign catalogs)

BIBLIOGRAPHY

This listing of source material is strictly a selection—since somewhere between 350 and 500 sources were consulted, it is simplest to provide a representative sample.

Books and Pamphlets

Adams, Edgar Holmes, and William H. Woodin. *United States Pattern, Trial and Experimental Pieces*. New York: The American Numismatic Society, 1913.

Adams, James T., Editor-in-Chief. *Album of American History*. New York: Charles Scribner's Sons, 1944.

Battelle Memorial Institute. *Final Report on a Study of Alloys Suitable for Use as United States Coinage*. Columbus, Ohio: Battelle Memorial Institute, 1965.

Bleyer, Willard G. *Main Currents in the History of American Journalism*. Boston: Houghton Mifflin Co., 1927.

Brown, Frances Williams. *Coins Have Tales to Tell*. Philadelphia: J. B. Lippincott Co., 1966.

Brown, Martin R., and John W. Dunn. *A Guide to the Grading of United States Coins*. Racine, Wisconsin: Whitman Publishing Co., 1964 4th ed.

———. 1969, 5th ed.

Carothers, Neil. *Fractional Money*. New York: Augustus M. Kelley, 1967, reprint edition.

Chamberlain, C. C., and Fred Reinfeld. *Coin Dictionary and Guide.* New York: Barnes & Noble, Inc., 1961.

Clain-Stefanelli, Vladimir. *History of the National Numismatic Collections.* Washington, D.C.: U.S. Government Printing Office, 1968.

The Congressional Globe. 30th Congress, 2nd Session. Washington, D.C.: Blair and Rives, 1849, pp. 1, 187–88, 366, 389, 560, 566–68, 579, 666–67, 681, 694.

Dickeson, Montroville W. *The American Numismatical Manual.* Philadelphia: J. B. Lippincott & Co., 1859.

Dye, John S. *Dye's Coin Encyclopedia.* Philadelphia: Bradley & Co., 1883.

Hobson, Burton. *What You Should Know About Coins & Coin Collecting.* Greenwich, Conn.: Fawcett Publications, Inc., 1965.

Helmick, F. W. *Helmick's New Illustrated Counterfeit Detector.* Cincinnati: F. W. Helmick, 1878.

Jacobs, Saul. *Collecting Coins.* New York: Grosset & Dunlap, 1968.

Jones, Edgar R. *Those Were the Good Old Days.* New York: Simon & Schuster, 1959.

Judd, J. Hewitt, M.D. *United States Pattern, Experimental and Trial Pieces,* 3rd ed. Racine, Wisconsin: Whitman Publishing Co., 1965.

Kuhn, Ferdinand. *The Story of the Secret Service.* New York: Random House, 1957.

Lindheim, Leon. *Facts & Fictions About Coins.* New York, Cleveland: The World Publishing Co., 1967.

Mehl, B. Max. *The Commemorative Coins of the United States.* Fort Worth: B. M. Mehl, 1937.

Mosher, Stuart. *United States Commemorative Coins,* 2nd ed. New York: Wayte Raymond, 1946.

Reed, Mort. *Cowles Complete Encyclopedia of U.S. Coins.* New York: Cowles Book Company, Inc., 1969.

Reinfeld, Fred. *A Treasury of American Coins.* Garden City, New York: Hanover House, 1961.

Riddell, John L. *A Monograph of the Silver Dollar, Good and Bad.* New Orleans: E. Shepard of Cincinnati, 1845.

Sandage, C. H., and Vernon Fryburger. *Advertising Theory and Practice,* 7th ed. Homewood, Ill.: Richard D. Irwin, Inc., 1967.

Spadone, Frank G. *Major Variety and Oddity Guide of United States Coins,* 2nd ed. East Orange, N.J.: The Author, 1963.

———. *Major Variety-Oddity Guide of United States Coins,* 4th ed. Iola, Wisconsin: Krause Publications, Inc., 1967.

Taxay, Don. *Counterfeit, Mis-Struck and Unofficial U.S. Coins.* New York: Arco Publishing Co., 1963.

U.S. Treasury Department, Director of the Mint. *Domestic and Foreign Coins Manufactured by Mints of The United States, 1792–1965.* Washington, D.C.: U.S. Government Printing Office, 1966.

Yeoman, Richard S. *A Guide Book of United States Coins, 1949,* 2nd ed. Racine, Wisconsin: Whitman Publishing Co., 1948.

————. *1959,* 12th ed., 1958.

————. *1969,* 22nd ed., 1968.

————. *1970,* 23rd ed., 1969.

Articles

Adams, Edgar H. "Beautiful Coin Types by a Calico Designer." *The Numismatist,* January 1909. Reprinted in *Selections From The Numismatist,* vol. 1, p. 289. Racine, Wisconsin: Whitman Publishing Co., 1960.

Boyd, F. C. C. "Engravers of the U.S. Mint in Philadelphia." *The Numismatist,* July 1940. In *Selections,* p. 259.

Bradfield, Elston G. "Double Eagle and Gold Dollar in the 1849 Congress." *The Numismatist,* April 1949. In *Selections,* p. 216.

Breen, Walter H. "How Coinage Became Mechanized." *The Numismatist,* March 1951. In *Selections,* p. 269.

————. "The Secret History of the Gobrecht Coinages, 1836–1840." *The Coin Collector's Journal,* Sept.-Oct., Nov.-Dec., 1954.

Cajori, J. "Origin of the Dollar Mark." *The Numismatist,* August 1929. In *Selections,* p. 80.

Coin World. "Latest Ike Dollar Reports Says [*sic*] 20 Million Proofs, No Apollo II," March 25, 1970, pp. 1, 3.

Culver, Lillard W. "The Sesquicentennial of the Quarter Dollar." *The Numismatist,* March 1946. In *Selections,* p. 159.

Dale, Elwin L., Jr. "U.S. Has 'Grab Bags' for Coin Collectors." *The New York Times,* March 21, 1964.

Duffield, F. G. "The New Dime." *The Numismatist,* December 1916. In *Selections,* p. 154.

Dumonte, Andre. "There's Art and History in Oldtime Pattern Coins." *Coins Magazine,* June 1965, p. 12.

Dunn, John W. "Mistakes Can Be Fun." *COINage,* January 1969, p. 35.

Glaser, Lynn. "Collecting Large Cents." *Coins Magazine,* January 1963, p. 41.

Gould, Maurice M. "A.R.R.C. Bingles of Alaska." *The N.A.S.C. Quarterly,* 1st Quarter 1968.

————. "Historic Half Cents." *COINage,* January 1969, p. 28.

Hammer, Ted R. "The Twenty Cent Piece." *The Numismatist*, February 1947. In *Selections*, p. 157.

———. "The Romance of Money," *Coin World*, Dec. 1969, p. 35.

Hering, Henry. "History of the $10 and $20 Gold Coins of 1907 Issue." *The Numismatist*, August 1949. In *Selections*, p. 212.

Kosoff, A. "A Brief History of the Double Eagle." *The Numismatist*, April 1949. In *Selections*, p. 220.

Martin, Lee. "When the Cents Went to War." *COINage*, June 1969, p. 44.

Mishler, Clifford. "The Goddess of Liberty." *Coins Magazine*, August 1969, p. 28.

Moss, Joseph. "Peace Dollars." *The Numismatist*, July 1942. In *Selections*, p. 132.

Nexsen, John A. "The Dollar of 1804." *American Journal of Numismatics*, April 1891. Reprinted in *The Numismatist*, July 1937. In *Selections*, p. 119.

Norse, Marguerite. "The Girl on the Quarter." Newspaper article, reprinted in *The Numismatist*, May 1917. In *Selections*, p. 167.

Numismatic News. "Legislation Seeks Stone Mtn. Medal," March 3, 1970, p. 1.

Pfalser, I. F. "The Old Steam Press." *COINage*, November 1969, p. 36.

Reagan, Lewis M. "Sesquicentennial of the Silver Dollar." *The Numismatist*, April 1944. In *Selections*, p. 113.

Rony, George. "The Fugio Cent." *COINage*, February 1969, p. 50.

———. "Messages on Coins." *COINage*, November 1968, p. 47.

———. "The Saga of the Silver Dollar." *COINage*, March 1970, p. 32.

Ryker, Lois. "Whose Nickel's Worth?" *Coins Magazine*, January 1963, p. 46.

Sipe, Arthur. "Franklin Institute Celebrates Debut of the Benjamin Franklin Half-Dollar." *The Numismatist*, June 1948. In *Selections*, p. 169.

Slabaugh, Arlie. "The Private Coin Makers." *COINage*, July 1969, p. 32.

"To Marry a Goddess." *New York Mail and Express*. Reprinted in *The Numismatist*, May 1896. In *Selections*, p. 131.

Yeoman, Richard S. "The 1848 Quarter Eagle with CAL." *The Numismatist*, July 1953. In *Selections*, p. 193.

———. "The U.S. Eagle and Half-Eagle." *The Numismatist*, March 1945. In *Selections*, p. 221.

Zerbe, Farran. "U.S. Pattern Coins." *The Numismatist*, March 1938. In *Selections*, p. 277.

Index